Biking

by Tyler Benedict

A Wiley Brand

Biking For Dummies®

Published by: **John Wiley & Sons, Inc.,** 111 River Street, Hoboken, NJ 07030-5774, www.wiley.com

Copyright © 2024 by John Wiley & Sons, Inc., Hoboken, New Jersey

For general information on our other products and services, please contact our Customer Care Department within the U.S. at 877-762-2974, outside the U.S. at 317-572-3993, or fax 317-572-4002. For technical support, please visit https://hub.wiley.com/community/support/dummies.

Wiley publishes in a variety of print and electronic formats and by print-on-demand. Some material included with standard print versions of this book may not be included in e-books or in print-on-demand. If this book refers to media such as a CD or DVD that is not included in the version you purchased, you may download this material at http://booksupport.wiley.com. For more information about Wiley products, visit www.wiley.com.

Library of Congress Control Number: 2024934525

ISBN 978-1-394-21871-4 (pbk); ISBN 978-1-394-21873-8 (ebk); ISBN 978-1-394-28172-1 (epdf)

SKY10072717_041524

Contents at a Glance

Introduction 1

Part 1: Starting Off on the Right Wheel 5

CHAPTER 1: Almost Everything You Need to Know about Bicycles 7

CHAPTER 2: Sizing Up the Right Bike and Fit 15

CHAPTER 3: Cockpit, Part 1: Handlebars, Grips, and Headsets 31

CHAPTER 4: Cockpit, Part 2: Stems, Seatposts, and Saddles 47

CHAPTER 5: Brakes, Wheels, and Tires 59

CHAPTER 6: Drivetrains 93

Part 2: Buying a New Bike and Other Gear You Need 113

CHAPTER 7: Finding the Perfect Bike 115

CHAPTER 8: Purchasing Your New Set of (Two) Wheels 145

CHAPTER 9: Getting the Necessary Gear and Equipment 157

Part 3: Using and Maintaining a Bicycle 181

CHAPTER 10: Preparing for Your First Ride 183

CHAPTER 11: Riding a Bike 101 193

CHAPTER 12: Riding Safely: Following the Rules of the Road, Path, and Trail 205

CHAPTER 13: Fixing and Maintaining Your Bike 225

CHAPTER 14: Finding Good Places to Ride 263

Part 4: The Part of Tens 277

CHAPTER 15: Ten Training Tips 279

CHAPTER 16: Ten Bucket List Events 287

Index 293

Table of Contents

INTRODUCTION 1
  About This Book... 1
  Foolish Assumptions....................................... 2
  Icons Used in This Book 3
  Beyond the Book... 4
  Where to Go from Here 4

PART 1: STARTING OFF ON THE RIGHT WHEEL 5

**CHAPTER 1: Almost Everything You Need to Know
about Bicycles**.. 7
  Recognizing Where Bicycles Come From...................... 8
  Identifying the Parts of a Bicycle....................... 10
  Producing a Bike for Every Rider......................... 11
  Weighing the Benefits of Riding a Bike................... 12

CHAPTER 2: Sizing Up the Right Bike and Fit 15
  Measuring Up to a Bicycle's Angles....................... 15
  Special Considerations................................... 22
  Choosing the Proper Bike Size............................ 23
  Fitting Yourself to Your Bike............................ 26

**CHAPTER 3: Cockpit, Part 1: Handlebars, Grips,
and Headsets**... 31
  Handlebars... 32
    Drop bars 32
    Flat bars and riser bars............................... 34
    Bullhorns (and aero bars).............................. 36
    Mustache handlebars.................................... 37
    Handlebar materials.................................... 37
  Grips and Handlebar Tape................................. 39
    Grips 39
    Handlebar tape 40
  Headsets... 41
    Threaded headsets 41
    Threadless headsets 42
    Stealth routing 44

CHAPTER 4: Cockpit, Part 2: Stems, Seatposts, and Saddles 47
  Stems.. 47
    Stem angle 48
    Stem length 49

Bar clamp diameters 49
Quill stems 50
Seatposts 50
Dropper seatposts 51
Suspension seatposts 51
Seatpost diameter 52
Alternative diameters 52
Saddles 55
Saddle width 56
Saddle angle 57

CHAPTER 5: **Brakes, Wheels, and Tires** 59
Brakes: The Best Invention Ever 59
Caliper 60
Lever: Mechanical 60
Lever: Hydraulic 60
Alternative (old school) brakes 70
Wheels 71
Hubs 72
Hub widths 77
Spokes and nipples 77
Bracing angle 79
Rims 80
Wheel sizes 83
Tires (and Tubes) 84
Valve types 84
Materials and terminology 86
Rubber 86
Tread cap 87
Casing 87
Breaker 87
Bead 88
Apex 88
Treads and siping 88
Sizes and widths 89
Typical tire widths by bike type 91
Wider tires: The better choice 92

CHAPTER 6: **Drivetrains** 93
First Things First: Systems versus Components 94
Crankset 95
Crank arm material 95
The spindle 96
Crank arm length 96

Bottom Bracket 97
Chainring 100
    Narrow-wide chainrings 102
Chain 103
Cassette (or freewheel) 104
Derailleur 106
Shifter 107
Bearings 108
    It turns out that size does matter 108
Pedals 109
    Installing pedals 109
    Differentiating types of pedals .111

PART 2: BUYING A NEW BIKE AND OTHER GEAR YOU NEED 113

CHAPTER 7: **Finding the Perfect Bike** 115
Road Bikes 116
    Racing 117
    All-Road / endurance 118
    Aero 119
    Climbing 119
    Crit 119
    Track 120
    Triathlon 120
Gravel Bikes 121
    Basic gravel 122
    Racing gravel 122
    Adventure gravel 122
    Bikepacking / touring 123
Cyclocross Bikes 124
Mountain Bikes 125
    MTB wheels, suspension and geometry 125
    Cross country (XC) 127
    Downcountry / light trail 128
    Trail 128
    Enduro (EN) 129
    All mountain / freeride (AM/FR) 129
    Downhill (DH) 130
    Fat bikes 130
    Dirt jump / slopestyle 131
    Trials 131
Commuter Bikes 132

Fitness/Hybrid Bikes 132
Cruiser Bikes 133
Cargo Bikes. 133
    Standard cargo. 133
    Bakfiets cargo. 134
e-Bikes. 135
Recumbent Bikes. 136
Adaptive Bikes 136
Kids' Bikes or Balance Bikes. 137
Bikes by Frame Material 138
    Steel. 138
    Aluminum 140
    Titanium 140
    Carbon fiber 141

CHAPTER 8: **Purchasing Your New Set of (Two) Wheels** 145
Considering Your Favorite Type of Riding .145
Finding Where to Buy a Bicycle 146
    The Local Bike Shop 147
    The big-box store. 147
    The Downsides of Really Cheap Bikes .148
    An Online Store 149
    Direct-to-consumer brands 149
Knowing What You Can Expect to Spend. .150
    Breaking down cost. 150
    The benefits of bike shops 151
    Taking a chance by buying online 153
Buying a Used Bike 155
    Determining whether a used bike is right for you 155
    Knowing where to find a good used bike. 155

CHAPTER 9: **Getting the Necessary Gear and Equipment** 157
Safety for Your Head: Helmets 158
    Helmet types 158
    Helmet features. 160
    Helmet care 161
    Brain safety: A game of millimeters 161
    The vital five-star rating 162
Safety for Your Eyeballs: Sunglasses and Eye Protection 162
Safety Illumination: Lights and Reflectors .163
    Reflectors 163
    Headlights. 164
    Taillights 165
Lock It Up 165
    U-locks. 166
    Chains 166

Cables 166
Folding locks. 166
Security ratings 167
Bike lock strength 168
How to lock up your bike 168
Ah-Oogah! Horns and Bells 168
Items Made for Comfort. 169
Water bottles 169
Bottle cages 170
Bike shorts 170
Cycling gloves. 171
Maintenance Supplies. 172
Floor pump. 172
Basic repair kit 172
Chain lube. 174
What's the best way to lube my chain? 175
Cleaning kit. 175
Common Accessories 176
Commuter gear 176
Road cyclist gear 177
Gravel cyclist gear 177
Mountain bike gear 178
Cargo bike gear 179

PART 3: USING AND MAINTAINING A BICYCLE. 181

CHAPTER 10: **Preparing for Your First Ride** 183
Before Your First Ride. 183
Knowing what to do if something isn't right 184
Adjusting the saddle height 184
Adjusting the handlebars 187
Airing up the tires 190
Before Your Next Ride 192

CHAPTER 11: **Riding a Bike 101** 193
The Basics of Riding a Bike. 193
Mounting your bike 193
Getting in the saddle. 194
Balancing the bike 194
Steering the right way. 195
Pointers on pedaling. 196
Braking like your life depends on it .198
Shifting gears the right way 200
Teaching a Kid How to Ride a Bike 202
But they already have a bike with training wheels 202

But kids grow so darn fast 202
Be encouraging! 203
Let them learn at their own pace 203
But I want them to keep up with me! 203

CHAPTER 12: **Riding Safely: Following the Rules of the Road, Path, and Trail** 205
Keeping Safety in Mind 206
Following the rules of the road (and bike path) 206
Reflecting their headlights 207
Wearing your helmet the right (or wrong) way 208
Rules of the Road 211
Ride with traffic 212
Ride on the right 212
Ride no more than two abreast 213
Make passing easy 213
Signal your turns 213
Stay off busy urban roads 214
Ride predictably 214
Predict other's behaviors 214
Take your lane 215
Know your route 215
Know your surroundings 215
Resources for bicycle laws 216
Follow Etiquette for Group Rides 216
Hold your line 217
Be consistent 217
Avoid slamming on your brakes 217
Signal turns, stops, and obstacles 217
Avoid soft-pedaling 219
Respect no-drop rides 219
Rules of the Bike Path 220
Prepare for Riding in Bad Weather 221
Rules of the Trail 222
Riders yield to pedestrians and horses 222
Downhill riders yield to uphill riders 223
No riding trails after it rains! 223
Look before you leap 224

CHAPTER 13: **Fixing and Maintaining Your Bike** 225
Cleaning Your Bike 225
Cleaning the Chain 227
Good chain cleaning 228
Better chain cleaning 229
Best chain cleaning 229
Post chain cleaning 230

Lubing the chain 230
Between chain cleanings 232
Pumping Up the Tires and Checking for Wear 232
Setting up tubeless tires. 234
Buying the proper tubes. 236
Maximum tire pressures 237
Checking for tire wear. 237
Adjusting the Brakes. 238
Adjusting pad contact with cable length 238
Wait — what is pad contact spacing?. 239
Adjusting the pad contact space. 239
Adjusting the pad contact spacing 239
Adjusting rim brakes. 241
Centering road bike brakes 241
Centering mountain bike and cyclocross brakes 241
Adjusting the brake pad toe-in and rim contact point. 241
Adjusting disc brakes 242
Every time I tighten the caliper, it moves! 244
Knowing What to Do When a Ride Goes Wrong 245
Fixing a flat 245
Replacing an inner tube 245
Plugging a tubeless tire. 248
Patching a tire 250
Patching a tubeless tire 250
Using a CO_2 cartridge or a pump 251
Adjusting Gears and Shifting: Mechanical Derailleurs. 251
Front derailleurs 251
Rear derailleurs 252
Where shifting gets tricky. 253
The bike is shifting, but it's not happy about it 253
Repairing and Replacing a Chain. 254
What to Do If You Wreck 256
Minor tumbles 256
Major tumbles 256
If you hit someone. 256
If someone hits you. 257
Taking photos for documentation 257
If you're too injured to take stock of the situation 258
Help others, too. 258
Get back in the saddle 258
Repairing, Replacing, and Retiring Old Bikes and Parts. 258
When to repair or replace a part. 259
When to replace your bike. 260
What to do with your old bike and parts .261

CHAPTER 14: **Finding Good Places to Ride** 263

There's an App for That 263

Locating Local Hotspots 265

Scouting out safe roads and routes .265

Hitting the trails 266

Riding with the Family. 266

Setting a compatible pace and distance 267

Riding with kids on the bike. 267

Riding alongside your kids 268

Joining a Cycling Club 268

Taking a Biking-Focused Vacation. .269

Transporting Your Bike 270

On the car. 270

On a plane 274

Shipping it 276

PART 4: THE PART OF TENS. 277

CHAPTER 15: **Ten Training Tips** 279

On-the-Bike Workouts 280

Base miles. 280

Off-the-Bike Workouts 282

Deadlifts 282

Single-leg step-ups 282

Single-leg deadlifts 283

Core 283

Hip flexor exercises. 284

It's all about overload 284

Don't forget to recover!. 284

CHAPTER 16: **Ten Bucket List Events**. 287

RAGBRAI 287

Five Boro Bike Tour 288

Levi's GranFondo 288

Multi-Day Bicycle Tours 288

Belgian Waffle Ride 289

Grinduro 289

24 Hours of Old Pueblo 290

Sea Otter Classic 290

Breck Epic. 290

Great Divide Mountain Bike Route .291

But what about 291

INDEX. 293

Introduction

"*Don't buy upgrades, ride up grades.*"

—EDDY MERCKX, LEGENDARY PRO CYCLIST

I thought writing this book would be fun, but I had no idea just how much I would enjoy it — or how much work it would be!

I started geeking out on bikes, their components, and their tech long before writing about them. I've obsessed over the specs and details that might make my own bike better, tweaked and upgraded my setup, and modified stock parts to suit my needs (or to shave off a few grams).

What I've realized is that none of those efforts compares to training harder. My bike got lighter, but my friends who consistently put in the work got faster and better at riding. We all had nice bikes, but I wasn't putting in the required level of work.

That's why I quote Merckx at the top of this introduction. As you'll see, having a good-quality bike is important, but beyond that, the key to enjoying the bike is to just get out there and ride — whether your goal is fitness, green transportation, exploration, or racing trophies.

About This Book

My goal in writing *Biking For Dummies* is to help you find the best bike for you, get you riding it quickly and safely, bring you up to speed on the latest cycling trends, tech, and terms — and share my passion for cycling.

The point of writing any *For Dummies* title is to explain subjects so that beginners can understand and learn from them. But I challenged myself to do that and to write content that even my nerdiest bike friends would enjoy reading, too.

The result was an enormous first draft! We ended up cutting more than 100 pages during editing. Unfortunately, that included three full chapters on e-bikes, plus deep dives on mountain bike suspension, tips for evaluating used bikes, a guide to working with your local bike shop, and a lot more. Visit Dummies.com/go/bikingfd for content that didn't make it into the book.

At times, I may sound overly harsh when talking about the cheapest bikes. I totally understand that budgets vary wildly, but hear me out. My first mountain bike was from a Target department store, and it wasn't a good one. I've worked on many low-cost bikes over the years (because my friends didn't listen and bought their kids a department store bike anyway), and I can tell you that the frustration from dealing with poorly functioning drivetrains, inaccurate shifting, and plastic parts that break easily leads to overall lower enjoyment that isn't worth saving a few bucks. A bike is no good if it doesn't work properly and you have little interest in riding it.

Sometimes, increasing your budget by as little as $100 gets you a bike that works much better, lasts longer, and makes you happier. That said, I'm stoked to see *anyone* riding a bike, so there's no bike shaming here. I just want to help you find the best bike possible, so I dive deep into what makes one bike or part better than another.

This book replaces *Bicycling For Dummies,* and a lot has changed since that one was last updated in 2011! Electronic drivetrains have become the norm, disc brakes are on every type of bike, and e-bikes are taking over urban landscapes!

For better or worse, more and more bikes need batteries, but their shifting and performance have never been better. You can also find a wide variety of apps for planning, mapping, and tracking your rides, and even for customizing your bike's performance! Technology is here to stay, but as you'll see, it's (mostly) not that complicated and truly does improve many aspects of cycling. Fortunately, you can still get a simple "analog" bike and just go ride, too.

Some of the bike terminology I mention may be new to you. To make things easy to digest, I italicize new terms and follow them up with simple-to-understand explanations.

If you run across a word or phrase you don't immediately understand, rest assured that I explain it at the appropriate spot. I also provide sidebars to explain big-picture concepts that add perspective, on both cycling culture and technology trends.

Foolish Assumptions

The most foolish assumption I made as I wrote *Biking For Dummies* was that you'd know where I was coming from — as a cycling enthusiast. Writing this book made me rethink how to explain topics to a noncyclist audience, and that led to my rewriting entire sections and spending more time explaining basic concepts earlier in the book to bring you along for the ride at a beginner-friendly pace. This approach assumes that one or more of the following statements are true about you, the reader:

>> You believe that a bike is a bike is a bike. They're all the same, right?

>> You've been given this book by a friend who thinks you'd enjoy riding a bike.

>> You have one or more friends who love riding and want you to join them.

>> You rode bikes as a kid but you are intimidated by starting again later in life.

>> Your kids or grandkids are all about biking and you want to join them.

>> You're ready to ditch the car and ride a bicycle to commute to work, school, and the store.

>> You want to buy a higher-performance bike and start riding for fitness or to train for an event but don't know what to look for, what type to buy, or how much to spend.

>> You borrowed a friend's bike and enjoyed riding it and want to learn more before investing in a new bike of your own.

>> You want a reference for cycling terms and technology and basic tips on maintaining and repairing your own bike.

Regardless of how you ended up here, I wrote this book to share my love for the sport and the bicycle itself. It has changed my life and provided incredible opportunities to explore the world, reach deeper into various wooded areas and communities, and see things not possible from a car or on two feet. And, I'm fitter and faster at 50 than I've ever been! I hope you read this book and are inspired to use your bike to improve your own health and expand your horizons!

Icons Used in This Book

To break topics into bite-size chunks and therefore make this book easier to read, I've added a few icons in the margins to help call attention to important ideas, tips and tricks of the trade, and even more detail on specific topics.

REMEMBER

This icon is meant to help jog your memory about important aspects. Of course, I don't give you quizzes on this stuff, but this info might help you when talking to your local bike shop or repair personnel, for example.

TECHNICAL STUFF

When I'm about to delve a little deeper into a particular subject, I slap this icon on the text. You don't have to take the deep dives with me, but they may be helpful on your journey toward greater understanding of the world of bikes.

TIP

The Tip icon points to insider knowledge and other info I've learned about throughout my journey in the biking world. The tips may save you time, money, or headaches!

WARNING

The Warning icon points out common pitfalls that people often fall into with regard to biking, or common misconceptions about a particular topic.

Beyond the Book

To view this book's Cheat Sheet, go to www.dummies.com and search for *Biking For Dummies Cheat Sheet* for a handy reference guide that addresses common questions about bikes and biking.

Where to Go from Here

Where you start reading is up to you. If you're brand-new to the world of bikes, just turn the page and start with Chapter 1, which is a fun overview of biking! If you've been around bikes for a while, browse the table of contents and pick a chapter that interests you.

If you're figuring out which type of bike to buy, I suggest reading Chapter 2 and then Chapters 7 through 9, in order. If you're technically inclined and want to understand what makes some bike parts better than others, reading Chapters 3 through 6 will get you up to speed (heh!) on the latest drivetrain, brake, and component technology. And once you're into it, check out Chapters 15 and 16 for training tips and details about some of the most fun bike trips, rides, and events on the planet!

1

Starting Off on the Right Wheel

IN THIS PART . . .

Discovering the origins of the bicycle.

Determining the right size bike for you.

Exploring the basic components of a bicycle.

Chapter 1

Almost Everything You Need to Know about Bicycles

The bicycle is mankind's most efficient machine: gloriously simple, and simply glorious in its ability to move us around quickly and easily. Harnessing just two wheels and a little leg (or battery) power lets us roll around town faster and easier than walking and sometimes helping us transport goods, perform services, and even transport friends and family.

Riding a bike means freedom and independence. It provides transportation to school and work — or increasing opportunities for education and income. But that's not all: Cycling is fun! It provides exercise and a chance to take in some fresh air. It allows people to see more of an area to explore than walking, and we can experience it better than driving.

In this chapter, I explain the basics of this remarkably simple machine, which has stood the test of time (with a few innovations along the way). Granted, there is a lot of the technology that goes into modern racing bikes and long-travel full-suspension mountain bikes, but they are all based on easy-to-understand principles and mechanics. Let's take a quick look at how the modern bicycle came to be and how it works.

Recognizing Where Bicycles Come From

In about 1818, Baron Karl von Drais invented the Velocipede, more commonly referred to as the "running machine" or "hobby horse" (shown in Figure 1-1), which wasn't much more than two wheels attached to either end of a plank of wood to sit on. Riders scooted along on them by kicking the ground like Fred Flintstone, much the way kids use Balance Bikes to learn how to ride today. (Training wheels are no longer recommended; I explain why in Chapter 7.)

FIGURE 1-1:
The hobby horse.

Credit: alexrow / Adobe stock

Numerous iterations of the Velocipede were made throughout the 1800s, leading to "the Boneshaker" in the late 1860s (see Figure 1-2), which got its name from the extremely uncomfortable experience while riding it. (Ouch!) The boneshaker added a crankset and pedals directly to the front wheel. This meant you could pedal it, which was deemed more elegant than running atop the bike. But steering it got a little tricky — you had to turn the wheel that your feet were pedaling! Plus, speeds were limited by the size of the front wheel. These major design hiccups eventually led to the penny-farthing bike.

In the 1870s, the penny-farthing (so named because the wheels varied in size, much like the two British coins) was also known as the "high-wheel bicycle." It introduced a much larger front wheel (see Figure 1-3). That meant riders could go faster, but, unfortunately, it put them 4 to 5 feet off the ground! Not only did this make mounting (and dismounting!) the bike a bit tricky, but falling off a bike that high could seriously hurt someone!

The "safety bicycle" (see Figure 1-4) followed in the 1880s. So called because it has a much safer design than the penny-farthing, it incorporates the classic iteration of a double triangle design — a front triangle and a rear triangle, connected by the seat tube. Not only does this place the riders in a lower, more comfortable position, but the crankset is also finally detached from the wheel. Instead, a chain connected a chainring at the pedals to a cog on the rear wheel.

FIGURE 1-4:
The safety
bicycle.

Credit: Oleksandr Babich / Adobe stock

This allowed more freedom of steering, different gear ratios, and a wider range of sizes and designs to fit a wider range of riders. As you'll see, there are a *lot* of variations on this model now available, but they're all based on the original safety bicycle concept.

Identifying the Parts of a Bicycle

Most people are familiar with the basic parts of a bicycle from when we were kids. And everyone likely has a general idea of how bicycles work, from the time we first rolled (wobbled, likely) on our own with a parent (or two) running along behind — just in case — to those days when we learned just how important brakes were as that tree closed in frighteningly fast!

With few exceptions, the bicycle still consists of just two wheels, a frame, a saddle, a handlebar, and a human-powered, pedal-driven *drivetrain*, or the pedals and gears that convert power into motion.

Take a moment to familiarize yourself with the main parts (shown in Figure 1-5) of a basic bicycle. I'll show specific examples of various styles of bikes and go into much more detail in Chapters 2 through 6.

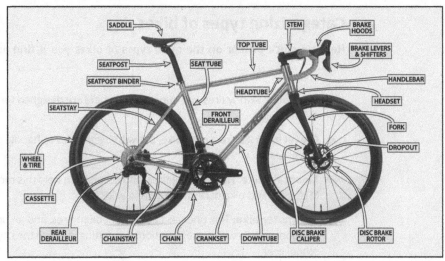

FIGURE 1-5:
The basic
components of a
modern bicycle.

Tyler Benedict

If you read this book, you'll become more familiar with other parts of the bike so that you can make informed decisions about which bike is right for you. Or, let's say you need to get something repaired and you want to meet your repair person at eye level ("You know — the crank thingy?"), this book will provide you with all the tools to know your bike inside and out.

Producing a Bike for Every Rider

It's a great time to be a cyclist, but it may also be a confusing time to be a newbie. Nowadays, there's literally a bike for every purpose.

Not to confuse you right away, but in road riding there are race bikes, endurance bikes, criterium (or crit) bikes, climbing bikes, and aero bikes. Some bikes blend features from multiple categories to become solid all-rounders, but you can always find something for any niche — or custom build one to meet your specific needs.

Mountain bikes have cross-country (XC), downcountry (more trail-capable cross-country bikes), trail, all-mountain, enduro, freeride, and downhill. And for gravel, there are race, adventure, and bikepacking models. Cargo bikes have front loaders, rear loaders, and family haulers.

Whew! That was a lot, but don't worry. In Chapter 7, I explain every variant and help you narrow it down to the best bike for the type of riding you will do.

Categorizing types of bikes

Here's a quick primer on the main types of bikes you'll find and where they're used.

>> **Road bike:** Skinny tires and curved handlebars are designed for going fast on roads.

>> **Gravel bike:** It's like a road bike, but with bigger tires to handle dirt and gravel roads.

>> **Mountain bike:** Flat bars, big tires, and suspension help this model tackle MTB trails and bike parks from mild to wild.

>> **Commuter bike:** This one has flat bars, medium tires, and an upright seating position, usually with storage options for getting through the city with work or school gear.

>> **Fitness/hybrid:** This upright bike with skinnier tires blends road bike speed with commuter bike comfort.

>> **Cargo bike:** Usually an e-bike, this one has mounting points for baskets, trays, bags, shelves, and other ways to transport gear and people.

>> **e-bike:** A bicycle with an electric motor to assist your pedaling, this one comes in all varieties, though you still have to pedal. Otherwise, it's a moped.

I can name more, including kids' bikes and specialty models for special use cases. Again, I'll explain all of them in great detail in Chapter 7. And I'll share tips on where and how to buy a new (or used) bike in Chapter 8.

Weighing the Benefits of Riding a Bike

From getting in shape to saving money to exploring new areas, the benefits of riding a bike go way beyond the obvious. This section details a few of my favorite reasons for cycling.

Taking a look at the physical health benefits

Exercise in any form is beneficial. Our human bodies are meant to move, but modern life has diminished the need for movement (or, sadly, effort).

Riding a bike is obviously exercise, but it provides so many different ways to push your body and improve its physical state. In Chapter 15, I provide tips on training to prepare for biking adventures and explore ways to get the full benefit of seeing the world on two wheels.

WARNING

Now's a good time to remind you to check with your doctor before starting any exercise program. Cycling is an enjoyable, low-impact form of exercise that you can ease into, but (and especially if you're starting from pure couch potato status) it's a good idea to see your doctor first for a basic checkup to make sure you have no underlying health issues.

Examining the mental health benefits

Studies have shown that physical exercise boosts blood flow to the brain, which can help you learn and concentrate better.

Dr. Peter Attia, a well-known longevity practitioner and the author of *Outlive*, says all the research he's seen (which is *a lot*) shows that regular, daily, and varied exercise is one of the most powerful ways to slow cognitive decline and boost overall vitality, too.

That's huge. Imagine boosting your performance at work or school by riding there instead of driving, with the additional perk that it's probably helping you live longer with a better overall quality of life.

And there's more.

All riding requires coordination between what you're seeing and what you're doing — braking, shifting, turning, pedaling — which helps improve coordination.

Mountain biking cranks this neuromuscular coordination to 11, introducing varied terrain and obstacles like trees, rocks, roots, drops, and jumps as well as more frequent shifting and braking. Talk about a full body *and mind* workout.

If you had to pick one full-body workout, there's not much that beats mountain biking.

Saving money

Sure, you have to buy the bike, but any form of transportation (car, metro pass, ride sharing) is going to cost something. The beauty of a bicycle is that you get exercise while also saving money on gas or fares.

The savings go deeper if you consider how the long-term health benefits will likely offset doctors' bills for lifestyle-related conditions. Many of the most expensive and most common modern medical issues are caused by sedentary lifestyles (and a poor diet, but that's another book), and riding a bike frequently and with an intentional effort on improving fitness can reduce the likelihood of dealing with expensive health issues.

Some health insurance companies and employers even provide discounts for physical activity, so why not get all the other benefits of cycling while also saving money?

Chapter **2**

Sizing Up the Right Bike and Fit

Originally, I was first going to describe all the different types of bicycles that you can buy and then add this chapter. But, as the chapters came together, I realized that you should first understand how a bicycle's *geometry* — the lengths of the tubes and the angles between them — affect its handling and why it differs from bike to bike and from category to category.

You should also understand the various types of components, drivetrains, cockpits, wheels, and tires — and how they affect your bike's comfort, handling, and performance. I cover these topics in Chapters 3 through 6.

Of course, if you just want to see the bikes, skip to Chapter 7, and then come back here to learn how to determine the proper bike size and dial in a proper fit.

Measuring Up to a Bicycle's Angles

The geometry chart shown in Figure 2-1 shows a typical road bike, but the measured angles and distances are the same for every type of bike, and most brands post their geometry charts on their websites. Familiarizing yourself with what each angle and measurement means and where it is on the bike will help you understand the difference between a bike with slack angles versus one with steep angles, for example. If you need a refresher on the basic parts of a bicycle, check out the section in Chapter 1 about recognizing the parts of a bicycle.

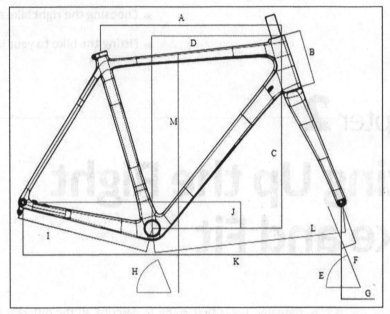

FIGURE 2-1:
A geometry
chart for a
typical bicycle.

This list describes what all the numbers on a geometry chart mean:

Effective Top Tube (A): The horizontal distance from the center of the steering axis at the top of the head tube backward to the center of the seatpost is called the *effective* top tube (or ETT) length because it's a straight-line measurement of the distance, which is a more useful measurement than the actual top tube's length — those can be angled.

Whereas bicycles used to have fairly standard proportions and their size was often conveyed by the seat tube length (for example, a bike with a 58-centimer seat tube would be designated as a size 58 bike), nowadays most cyclists look at ETT along with reach (D) to get a good sense of whether the bike is the right size.

Head Tube Length (B): The head tube length is simply the height of the head tube. Racier road and gravel bikes will have a shorter head tube to help the rider maintain a low aero position (because the lower you are, the more aerodynamic you are, of course), and endurance bikes have taller head tubes to provide a more comfortable, upright riding position. For performance bikes, the goal is to find the head tube height so that most riders don't need to add a lot of spacers or oddly angled stems to achieve a good fit.

Mountain bikes follow a similar design philosophy but must take fork length and fork travel into account. As fork travel increases, so does the fork's height, and so longer-travel bikes tend to have very short head tubes in order to avoid a tall stack (C) and keep the rider in a low, racy riding position.

Stack (C): Stack is the vertical height from the center of the bottom bracket to the top of the head tube's center. Many bicycle fitters use stack and reach (D) as their starting points for fitting a rider to a new bike. Even though you then add a stem above the head tube, the stack gives you a general idea of how tall the front of a bike will be in relation to the bottom bracket.

Reach (D): Reach is the horizontal measurement from the center of the bottom bracket to that same point on the top of the head tube. It gives you (or your fitter) a good idea of how far you'll reach forward to meet the handlebars, and it's a more apples-to-apples comparison between bikes, because different seat angles between models make ETT a less-than-reliable comparison.

REMEMBER

The stem length & angle, handlebar width, handlebar sweep, seatpost setback, and saddle position allow you to fine-tune your position forward or backward on the bike and stretch you out or help you sit upright. So, knowing your ideal form (from a good bike fit or just test-riding a few bikes) lets you get a close-enough fit and then use the components to dial in the perfect fit.

The head angle (E), fork offset (F), and trail (G) all work together to comprise the main factor in designing a bike's overall handling. Changing one affects the others, so I've lumped them here with another graphic (see Figure 2-2) to illustrate how they combine forces to give your bike its steering personality.

Head Angle (E): The head (and seat) angles are measured as degrees from 0, where 0 is parallel with the ground and 90 degrees is perpendicular (straight up) from the ground.

Most road bikes have head angles between 71 and 73 degrees. In the grand scheme of things, this would be considered a *steep* head angle. As that number gets smaller, people in the industry like to say that it gets *slacker*.

Gravel bikes get a slightly slacker head angle, usually between 69 and 72.5 degrees, depending on the intended use. Mountain bikes range from 68 to 69 degrees for short-travel XC (cross-country) bikes all the way down to between 62 and 63 degrees for long-travel downhill bikes — and everything in between.

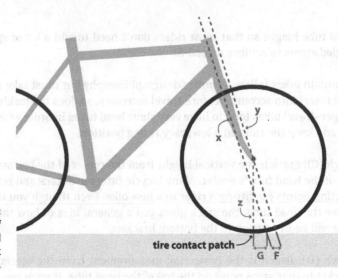

FORK OFFSET
Fork Offset (F) is the distance between the steering axis (x) and a parallel line (y) that intersects the front axle (F).

FORK TRAIL
Fork Trail (G) is the distance between a vertical line (z) drawn from the front axle to the tire's contact patch and the point where the steering axis (x) intersects the ground.

Offset (F) and Trail (G) have an inverse relationship. As Offset increases, Trail gets shorter.

tire contact patch

FIGURE 2-2: Closeup of head angle and fork offset measurements.

Generally speaking, the steeper the head angle, the sharper a bike turns but the twitchier it feels at higher speeds. Slacker head angles create a more stable ride but feel slower to turn. However, this can be fine-tuned by the fork offset, described next.

Fork Offset (F): Imagine a straight line running down the head tube and through the center of the fork's *steerer tube*, or the part of the fork that goes through the head tube, to a point on the ground (x). Now imagine a parallel line sitting slightly in front of the fork offset that intersects the fork's axle, and note where it hits the ground (y). The distance between those two lines at the ground is the fork's offset.

Most forks have 40–52mm of offset. Offset is how a bike designer tweaks the handling because it will change the trail, described next.

Trail (G): Now imagine a line intersecting the fork's axle and drawn straight down to the ground. The distance between that point (z) and (x) is the trail, and it's extremely important to overall steering stability.

Trail and fork offset have an inverse relationship. Increase offset and trail will decrease, and vice versa. Imagine how a slacker head angle will also increase the trail by pushing (x) further forward from (z), and then you can see how a designer can use fork offset to fine-tune the trail.

So, what does trail do? If you can imagine a shopping cart you might find at the local grocery store, you may able to visualize how the front wheels trail behind the little metal housing on the outside. The point where that housing connects to the cart is the steering axis. When you push a cart forward, the wheels drag behind the axis, which is how they maintain a generally straight path. (Except for that one particular grocery cart — I always get that danged wobbly cart!)

If you were to lengthen the arms that hold the wheel (essentially the cart's forks), you would create a longer trail figure, which would make the cart even more stable — perfect for standing on the back and coasting through the parking lot. Its turning radius, however, would increase and make it harder to maneuver through the aisles.

It's the same with bikes: A longer trail makes the bike more stable but increases the turning radius. This works well for longer-travel mountain bikes where you're riding down steep terrain at high speed, and their extremely slack head angles have the added bonus of pushing the front wheel farther out in front of you so that you're less likely to go OTB ("over the bars") if you hit an obstacle.

Conversely, a shorter trail gives the bike quick handling, where small inputs have more dramatic effects on steering — but it won't feel as stable and requires more vigilance from the rider. You'll often find steeper head angles and a short trail on road racing bikes where snappy handling is important, but you wouldn't want to get lazy while riding in a pack.

The rest of a bicycle's measurements combine to create safe handling, proper fit, and good biomechanics as you ride.

Seat Angle (H): Measured the same as the head angle, the seat angle determines how a bike situates your body in relation to the wheels and cockpit, or the combination of handlebar, stem, seatpost, and saddle, but most importantly, it puts your hips and knees in the proper position over the pedals for optimum biomechanics.

The goal is to position you in the sweet spot that also has your body weighting the bike just right for both climbing and descending. Some bikes prioritize comfort by placing you a little farther back (beach cruisers, for example), and others move you forward to prioritize your power output (time trial bikes, for example).

Mountain bikes sometimes show an effective seat angle that is the equivalent of the angle of a straight line drawn from the center of the bottom bracket upward to an *average* seat height. That's because a lot of full-suspension mountain bikes (Figure 2-3 shows a good example) don't place the seat tube in the same place as on a traditional bike. The reason is that aspects such as suspension linkages and shocks need to be in specific places to achieve the desired *kinematics*, or suspension performance and rear wheel travel, so the seat tube has to work around those parameters.

FIGURE 2-3:
A mountain bike with a weird seat tube angle.

This makes it trickier to achieve the correct fit on certain models because some bikes have an actual seat tube angle that's extremely slack, so taller riders may have a saddle that ends a lot higher than average — and thus farther back. The opposite happens for very short riders. You can remedy this primarily by adjusting the saddle's position, but if you're on the extreme upper or lower end of fitting a particular frame size, just note that it may be an issue unless you size up or down on the bike itself.

Chainstay Length (I): The chainstay length is a horizontal line from the center of the bottom bracket to the center of the rear axle. You might see it labeled as the *effective* CS length because, much like the top tube, a straight horizontal measurement is what you need to know. Some bikes will show an *actual* measurement, which is the actual length of that tube and usually longer than the *effective* measurement because the axle almost always sits higher than the bottom bracket (see the later section "Special Considerations"), so there's a slope to it.

A shorter chainstay length tucks the rear wheel under you for a snappier feel when you pedal. It helps you maintain traction on steep climbs; however, on mountain bikes, where terrain can be quite steep and sometimes loose, you have to balance between maintaining traction and keeping enough weight on the front wheel to maintain steering control.

A longer chainstay feels more stable and usually more comfortable, too, but just like a long trail, it slows down handling because it increases the overall wheelbase (K). Just like big vans or trucks, a long wheelbase (see its entry later in this list) creates a larger turning radius on bikes, too. The extra stability is helpful for *loaded touring*, or riding for multiple days while carrying your clothes and other possessions with you, and bikepacking, where the extra weight on the bike can make it a bit unwieldy — though performance racing bikes want as short a chainstay as possible.

Bottom Bracket Drop (J): This is the vertical distance measured from the center of the rear axle to the center of the bottom bracket (BB). A higher number means the bottom bracket is sitting further below the axle. This creates a feeling of being "in" the bike, as opposed to a higher bottom bracket, making you feel like you're "on" the bike.

Road bikes typically have more bottom bracket drop because they're less concerned with having to clear obstacles. Gravel bikes are riding on rougher terrain, but may have similar bottom bracket drop figures as road bikes because their tires are bigger (and thus taller), which effectively puts the *BB height* higher than on an equivalent road bike.

That distinction, *BB drop* versus *BB height*, is important. The *BB height* is the distance from the ground to the center of the bottom bracket. In other words, it's how much ground clearance you have. Though this concept is important for comparing bikes, it has little to do with how a bike fits, which is why most geometry charts show bottom bracket drop.

The ground clearance isn't just for your bicycle's frame — it's also for your pedals because those are reaching closer to the ground on every pedal stroke. You may begin to notice a theme of interaction between all the parts of the bike here, depending on how long the crank arms are. (I'll explain why those vary, later in this chapter.) Ideally, you might be able to get away with more bottom bracket drop on smaller frames when using shorter crank arms, which helps shorter riders fit their bikes better. But, honestly, I'm starting to delve into the nuances of bike fit, which you don't need to worry about if you're just getting started. (Forgive me for geeking out for a sec!)

Wheelbase (K): The wheelbase is the horizontal distance between the front and rear axles. This is mainly shown so that you can compare one bike to another, and the main thing you need to know is that a shorter wheelbase helps the bike steer more quickly but also feel a bit less stable; a longer wheelbase steers more slowly but feels more stable.

Front Center (L): This is the horizontal measurement from the center of the bottom bracket to the center of the front axle. Modern gravel and mountain bikes typically have a longer front center (and thus reach), but pair that with shorter stems in order to keep the rider in the same position.

The benefit of a longer front center is that it pushes the front wheel farther out in front of the rider, which helps keep that person from flying over the bars if they hit an obstacle (like a log, rock, curb, or pothole), and improves steering control on steep descents.

Designers have to balance these benefits with a rider's ability to hold their weight over the front wheel for aggressive cornering and being able to keep the front end of the bike down when seated and climbing steep terrain. If there's not enough weight on the front of the bike, you'll just end up popping a wheelie on every pedal stroke, which is less fun than it sounds like when you're grunting your way up a 15% incline!

Standover (M): This is the vertical measurement from the ground to the top of the top tube, as measured a few inches in front of the BB. Why here? Because when you throw a leg over the bike and are straddling the top tube, that's about where you'll be standing.

This measurement helps determine whether the bike fits. If the standover height is longer than your inseam, you won't be able to straddle the bike — and that's not safe. You should have at least two to three inches of gap between the top tube and your groin. Some bikes use a *sloping* top tube (it slopes downward toward the back of the bike) to increase standover, and many mountain bikes use either a dramatically sloping or bent top tube to give you as much room as possible to move the bike around underneath you as you wiggle through tight, tree-lined trails.

Special Considerations

Generally, most of a bike's measurements increase as the frame size grows, with the exception of chainstay length. Some bikes increase this length slightly on larger sizes, but usually only by a few millimeters. Most of the correction for balancing the rider's weight is done by adjusting the seat angle across the size range.

As for the angles, larger bikes sometimes have slightly steeper seat angles (H), and the goal is to keep the rider's weight properly situated on the bike.

Head angles also change along with frame sizes, but not for the obvious reason. Because bikes are designed in conjunction with a fork's length, rake, and offset to provide certain handling characteristics, that group of measurements isn't used to position the rider on the bike. That's where the reach, stack, and ETT enter the scene.

However, extremely small frame sizes often have slacker head angles and/or adjusted fork offset figures in order to keep the front wheel far enough in front of the rider's feet so that their toes don't overlap with the front wheel. This is called, fittingly, *toe overlap*, and you'll want to avoid it because you don't want to make a sharp turn and have the back of the front wheel rub the front of your shoe. That is highly unsafe and can cause you to wreck!

Choosing the Proper Bike Size

Geometry numbers are helpful for anticipating how a bike might fit and handle, but there's no substitute for just hopping on a bike to see how it fits you.

The first thing you should do is straddle the bike and make sure you can comfortably stand over it (see the Standover bullet in the earlier section "Measuring Up to a Bicycle's Angles"). If you can't, try a smaller size.

After that, you need to get two main aspects right when it comes to bike size: saddle height and effective top tube (ETT) length. Figure 2-4 shows the proper leg extension for a rider, and Figure 2-5 demonstrates proper body positioning.

KNEE SLIGHTLY BENT WHEN FOOT IS AT BOTTOM OF PEDAL STROKE*

140° to 150°

HEEL SLIGHTLY RAISED AT BOTTOM OF PEDAL STROKE

*measure angle from ankle bone to center of knee to hip bone

FIGURE 2-4: Proper leg extension.

FIGURE 2-5:
Proper body
position.

Saddle Height: This term basically just means, "Can you move the saddle to the appropriate height?" If a frame is too small, you may not be able to find a seatpost long enough to reach proper leg extension.

When you're sitting on the bike with your feet placed on the pedals, you should have a 35 degree bend in your knee at the bottom of your pedal stroke. This maximizes power output and helps split the work between your quads and glutes. (I mention quadriceps again later in this chapter).

Effective Top Tube: You might remember this term from my description of the geometry chart at the beginning of this chapter. It refers to the horizontal distance from the seatpost to the head tube. Basically, this term just means "How much room will I have for my body on the bike?"

If the ETT is too short, you'll feel cramped and your knees will probably hit the stem and handlebar. Ouch! If it's too long, you'll feel stretched out, and handling may feel sluggish. But find the sweet spot and then you can fine-tune your fit with stem, saddle, and handlebar adjustments.

If you've owned, borrowed, or test-ridden a few bikes, look up the ETT for the ones you liked and use it as a starting point.

At the simplest level, when you're seated on the bike and resting your hands on top of the handlebars, your torso and arms should form an angle between 80 and 90 degrees.

This is a good rule-of-thumb starting point for most riders to determine whether a bike fits. From here, you can make adjustments to sit more upright (for comfort) or sit lower (it's more aerodynamic, for performance riding).

If you can't test-ride bikes or you have nothing to compare to, let Table 2-1 serve as a general guide:

TABLE 2-1: ## Measurements for Bike Frame Sizes

Frame Measurement	Frame Size	RiderHeight
48	Extra Small	4'11"–5'2"
50	Small	5'1"–5'5"
52	Small/Medium	5'4"–5'7"
54	Medium	5'6"–5'10
56	Large	5'9"–6'1"
58	Large/Extra Large	6'0"–6'3"
60	Extra Large	6'2"–6'5"

In this chart, the frame measurement *usually* refers to a bike's seat tube height, which scales along with their top tube lengths, so it's mildly useful for bikes with a traditional double diamond frame. Full-suspension mountain bikes may list this number, but it's mostly useless for gauging frame size since those bikes' designs are often swoopy and curvy and have nontraditional seat tube shapes, positions, and angles because they're working around linkages and shock placement.

Before we dive into how you can fit yourself to your new bike, here's a recap of the three main questions you need to ask to find the correct bike size:

>> **Standover:** Can you easily straddle the bike?

>> **Seat Height:** Can you position the saddle high enough or low enough for proper leg extension?

>> **Top Tube Length:** Do you feel like you have enough room on the bike without being too cramped or too stretched out?

Fitting Yourself to Your Bike

Once you've found the right bike size, it's time to make some small adjustments so that it fits perfectly and puts you in the safest, most comfortable, and most efficient riding position.

A good starting position for most bikes (see the nearby sidebar "The exception to the bike fit rule") is to feel like your weight is evenly spread between your rear end and your hands. That is, you want to feel like you're supporting your weight equally on the saddle and the grips. Too much pressure on either end can lead to discomfort. And trust me: On longer rides or along rough terrain, that means extremely sore body parts!

Figure 2-6 shows all the little details that a professional bike fitter will analyze, but *you* don't need to worry about all of them when you're just getting started.

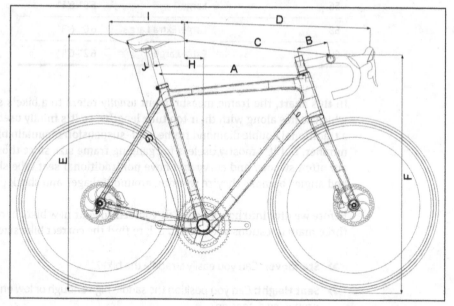

FIGURE 2-6: A professional bike fit diagram.

Courtesy of Pursuit Cycles LLC.

Here are the four easy things you can do (and parts you can swap) to create the perfect fit:

>> Saddle height (G)

>> Handlebar height (F)

» Saddle position (J)

» Stem length (B)

Saddle Height (E) is the first place to start. Set this so that you get proper leg extension, as explained a little earlier in this chapter. Too low and you'll tax your quadriceps and be unable to create nearly as much power as possible. Too high and you'll feel like you're rocking back and forth on your saddle and tiptoeing on your pedals. Either one is likely to cause knee pain, too, and just generally feel wrong.

Handlebar Height (F) comes next. Most bikes come with a few spacers under and/ or above the stem, and you can use these items to move the stem (and thus the handlebar) up or down on the steerer tube. It's all about personal preference. If you like a more upright position, which is typically more comfortable (particularly if you have poor flexibility) and gives you a more commanding view of the road ahead, move the stem higher. If you want a more aerodynamic, racy position, move it lower.

Many stems have a slight rise to them, which is usually indicated by a +/– measurement, like +/–6°. You can then (usually) flip the stem to make the angle go up or down and further adjust the handlebar height.

Saddle Position (J) is the next adjustment to make. Sliding the saddle forward or backward helps balance your weight on the bike, but its primary role is to optimize pedaling biomechanics.

THE EXCEPTION TO THE BIKE FIT RULE

Every rule has exceptions, and comfort bikes — like beach cruisers, certain hybrids, and adult trikes — are the exceptions.

On bikes where you're usually riding more slowly and in an upright position, most of your weight is on the saddle. Fortunately, most of these bikes have wider, cushier saddles to support your weight.

You still want to be able to comfortably reach your handlebars *and* maintain proper leg extension. Those rules *always* apply.

Obviously, nontraditional bikes — like recumbents, hand cycles, and adaptive bikes — don't obey these rules, either, but those are special designs that usually require special fit services, which I discuss in Chapter 7.

Most saddles have about 1 to 2 inches of fore/aft adjustment, which helps you achieve proper knee position over the pedals, as shown in Figure 2-7.

TIP

For casual riding, particularly on comfort bikes, saddle position isn't a big deal (unless you have knee pain or other physical issues that require special attention). But for road, gravel, mountain, and other performance bikes, the ideal situation is to have the bottom of your kneecap directly above the *pedal spindle*, or axle, when the crank arm is level and pointing straight forward.

That said, there's wiggle room. Every body is different, and a few millimeters fore/aft of this position works better for some riders. If you're just getting into cycling, focus on finding a comfortable riding position first, and then make small adjustments over time to position your knees over the pedals and find the position that works best for you.

If you're riding with clipless pedals, where a cleat on the bottom of your shoe clicks into the pedal, you can also fine-tune your knee position by adjusting the cleat position.

You can also adjust your saddle's angle to tilt its nose up or down. This can help you get more comfortable on it and further fine-tune your position. Go slow, small changes of just 1-2 degrees can make a big difference – go too far and it'll feel like you're sliding off, so you'll be waisting energy just staying in the saddle!

Stem Length (B) is the final piece of the puzzle. If you've adjusted all the other aspects and you're comfortable on the bike, you can skip this description. But if you feel like you're too upright or too stretched out or you have too much weight on your hands (or your behind), then swapping stems can help.

I put this topic last on the list because in order to *swap* your stem, you have to *buy* a new stem. These can range from $25 to $450 (seriously — and I already know, so you don't have to say it), so this is where building a good relationship with your local bike shop helps, as explained in Chapter 8. Any good bike shop has a box of used stems lying around, and the proprietor will probably let you borrow a couple to try out different lengths and rises before you buy one from them.

TIP

Listen to your body — for all these items, personal preference comes into play. I like my saddle pushed a little more forward because I'm able to generate more power and it feels like a good balance of comfort and performance for me. I also dislike the way stems longer than 110mm make the steering feel. So feel free to experiment until you find what works for you. It's amazing how much of a difference just 10mm can make!

These bike fit tips are just a warmup. In Chapter 10 I go over every part of your cockpit with tips for setting up brake lever and shifter position, swapping stems, adjusting handlebar angles, and a LOT more to get your bike fitting you perfectly!

SLAM THAT STEM!

If you ever see a pro's road, gravel, or XC mountain bike, chances are good that their stem is *slammed* — it's sitting directly on top of the bike's headset, with no spacers underneath it . . . sometimes not even a top cap!

Any true cyclist will tell you that this is the best aesthetic, but that doesn't mean it's right for you, me, or anyone else.

Those pros are also often riding smaller frames than their height would suggest they need (because smaller frames get them lower and more aero), so they compensate with longer stems. Sometimes, those stems also have severe negative rise to move the rider into an even lower, more aerodynamic position. This strategy works for them because they train their bodies to ride like this, putting in 20 to 30 hours per week, and they're quite flexible.

You and I, on the other hand, are probably much less flexible because we more than likely sit at a desk all day, and maybe ride a few hours per week — or less. So, the fastest overall position for you (and me) is the one that is comfortable enough for us to stay in for the duration of our ride. Likely, that's not achieved by slamming our stems. Yet.

Chapter **3**

Cockpit, Part 1: Handlebars, Grips, and Headsets

B efore I begin to describe the various types of bikes, you should know about the parts that make them whole. I'll start with the *cockpit*, which — as in a fighter jet — refers to the parts you sit in (or, in this case, sit *on*) and use to control the vehicle.

A bicycle's cockpit is composed of the handlebar, headset, stem, and seatpost, plus the contact points of the grips (or bar tape) and saddle. In this chapter, I cover the front half of the bike — the handlebar, grips, and bar tape — along with the headset, which enables the fork to turn so that you can steer. I explain what each part does and how its measurements and details affect fit, comfort, and performance.

If you just want to see the bikes, skip ahead to Chapter 7, or Chapter 8 to read about the best way to buy one, and then come back to Chapters 3, 4, and 5 for an overview of the parts that make them work.

Handlebars

Handlebars come in two basic varieties: the curvy drop bars and the straighter flat and riser bars, but you can also find other options, such as bullhorns and mustache bars.

Drop bars

Drop bars are what you typically find on road and gravel bikes (see Figure 3-1).

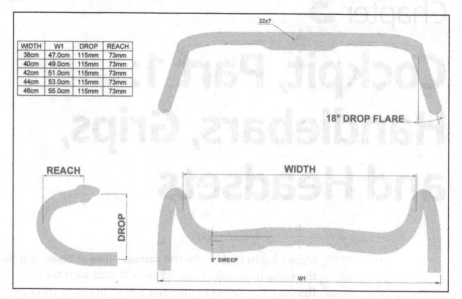

WIDTH	W1	DROP	REACH
38cm	47.0cm	115mm	73mm
40cm	49.0cm	115mm	73mm
42cm	51.0cm	115mm	73mm
44cm	53.0cm	115mm	73mm
46cm	55.0cm	115mm	73mm

FIGURE 3-1: A drop bar and its key measurements.

Courtesy of Ritchey Logi

Sometimes jokingly called curly bars, drop bars are the ones that have a C-shaped curve on each side that ends up pointing backward. They're designed to offer multiple hand positions on the top, so you can rest them on the climbs and grip them on the sprints. The *drops,* which are the parts on either side that loop downward, let you move into a more aerodynamic position, and many riders feel that they have better control on descents with their hands positioned lower, too.

Most traditional road bike bars have *straight drops:* The curved lower part is directly under the top part, and gravel bikes and some all-road bikes (see Chapter 7 for a description of bike types) use *flared bars,* where the drops start to flare outward. (See the nearby sidebar, "Flared handlebars," to see why).

Drop bars have three key measurements: width, reach, and drop, as described next.

Handlebar width

Handlebar width generally refers to the distance from edge to edge as measured on the top of the bar where it starts pointing forward. Most brands list it as measured from the center of the tube to the center of the opposite tube, so you may see it listed as "center to center" or "C-to-C." A few brands measure from the outer edges, but their method is usually listed in the specs. Some drop bars flare the lower sections outward for improved wrist clearance when riding in them. This also makes them slightly wider, which enhances control on descents and in technical terrain, which is particularly helpful for gravel bikes.

Your ideal handlebar width is usually just a bit wider than your shoulder width. You don't want your bars to be narrower than your shoulders, because it puts your hands and arms in a weird position and can strain your neck and shoulder muscles. Put simply, it's uncomfortable and feels unnatural.

Reach

Reach is the measurement from the top of the bar forward to the front of the drop, generally measured C-to-C. A longer reach gives you more area to rest your hands on, but it pushes the brake/shifter levers farther out. Most modern bars have a short-ish reach and combine with the brake hoods to provide an adequate platform for your hands.

Drop

Drop is the vertical distance from the tops to the bottom of the drops, also generally measured C-to-C. Your effective drop will vary slightly depending on how you angle the bar on your bike, but it's a good comparison metric when evaluating different options.

A short, or shallow, drop means you won't change your overall position as much when transitioning from tops to drops. Gravel bars tend to have shorter drops because riders are using them mostly on descents and they need to be able to keep their heads up to navigate the chunky terrain.

A long, or deep, drop puts you much lower and into a more aerodynamic position, but it's mostly favored by pro riders. Honestly, it's not comfortable to ride in deep drops, and it requires good hamstring and lower-back flexibility to hold that position. Most riders (myself included) prefer a shallow drop and ride mostly on the hoods and tops anyway.

Flat bars and riser bars

Flat bars are what you typically find on mountain bikes, commuters, and kids' bikes: They're "flat" in the sense that they lack curved, curly ends, like a drop bar. But they aren't actually straight, and many of them have a slight rise.

A true flat bar has a level surface, whereas a riser bar (see Figure 3-2) has anywhere from 5mm to 80mm of rise, so the ends are higher than the center section that clamps into the stem.

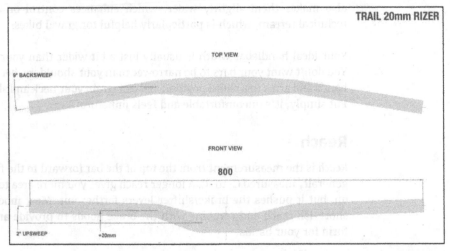

TRAIL 20mm RIZER

TOP VIEW

9° BACKSWEEP

FRONT VIEW

800

2° UPSWEEP   +20mm

FIGURE 3-2:
A flat bar with a
20mm rise.

Courtesy of Ritchey Logi

Though cross-country (XC) racers often prefer flat bars because they want a low, aggressive racing position, most other mountain bikers prefer somewhere between 15–30mm of rise. This keeps them in a slightly higher position for a more commanding view of the trail but is also helpful when dropping way back, behind the seat, on steep descents.

Commuters often like an even more upright riding position, so their bars might have a little more rise, and then comfort bikes can have 100mm rise or more.

In addition to rise, you should know three main measurements for flat and riser bars: width, backsweep, and upsweep.

Width

For casual bikes and commuters, you generally want to have the bars about 3 to 5 inches wider than shoulder width (so each hand is about 1.5 to 2.5 inches outboard from being directly *under* your shoulders and *not* 1.5 to 2.5 inches *past* your shoulders). That range is comfortable and lets you easily support your weight without straining your shoulders. It also makes it easy to handle the bike, and it's usually narrow enough to fit alongside other users in bike lanes, greenways, and other spots where you're riding with or passing other cyclists.

Mountain bikers get more specific with their bar width. The minimum width is usually dictated by your shoulders. It's the same as with road bikes: You don't want to have your bar narrower than your shoulders. XC racers usually use 720mm to 760mm. Trail and enduro riders may go from 760mm up to 800mm, and downhill and bike park riders may go up to 820mm. (See Chapter 7 for an explanation of the bike types.)

Backsweep

Only a few bars are actually straight. Most have some *backsweep*, which means they angle backward from the center section. Generally, this makes the bar more comfortable to hold, because your wrist stays in better alignment with the fore-arm, and it's why wider bars usually have more backsweep than narrower bars.

REMEMBER

If you hold your fists, palms down, straight out in front of you and then swing your arms slowly outward, you can see how the angle of your wrist changes. That's why you get more backsweep on wider bars.

For casual bikes, you typically get more backsweep (up to about 20 degrees) and even some downsweep, putting your hands and arms in a more relaxed position. This works well for these bikes because you're typically riding slower and not negotiating challenging terrain, so comfort is the priority.

For mountain bikers, backsweep typically varies from 3 to 10 degrees because handling and performance through technical terrain is the priority. (Fortunately, they have big tires and suspension to assist with comfort.) The goal is to put you in a commanding position when you're standing and hovering over the bike — typically, with elbows slightly out and arms bent to absorb bumps and maneuver the bike.

WARNING

Backsweep can become up- or downsweep, depending on how you rotate your bars in the stem. This falls under the category of personal preference, but you don't want to rotate them to the point where it becomes 100 percent up- or downsweep — or even *forward*-sweep.

Upsweep (and downsweep)

Some mountain bike handlebars add a little upsweep, and it's usually found on the wider bars for more aggressive riding. This helps mimic the natural angle of your wrists as your bars get wider, with the added benefit of making it just a little harder for your hands to slip off the sides on a big hit.

On casual bikes, where you don't need an aggressive riding position and you're typically sitting more upright, a little downsweep is more comfortable.

Bullhorns (and aero bars)

Triathletes and time trial riders use an aero handlebar setup (see Figure 3-3) that's very different from what's on traditional road bikes. It's technically two parts:

» **Base bar:** Often called a bullhorn because that's what it looks like

» **Aero bar:** Juts out from the center and has adjustable padded arm cups for riders to rest their forearms

FIGURE 3-3:
L3GION's Cory Williams rides in an aero-bar-and-base-bar combo on a time trial bike.

Courtesy of Predator Cycling.

Before electronic shifting entered the picture, most of these bikes had mechanical (cable-actuated) shifters stuck on the ends of the aero bars and brake levers on the ends of the base bar. Now, there's usually a set of wireless shifter buttons at the ends of both bars.

The effect of these parts is to put the rider in the most aerodynamic position possible, and riders spend 99 percent of their time in the aero bars. The only time they need to leave their aero tuck is when they need to brake, steer through a challenging section, or a tough climb requires them to stand out of the saddle and crank on the bars *and* pedals.

This strategy works because most time trial and triathlon courses are designed with minimal climbs or sharp turns that require braking or standing. Though they look cool (or not, depending on your point of view), they're not something you'd want to install on a normal bike for everyday riding.

Mustache handlebars

Picture the shape of a mustache curving up and then down and you can imagine what mustache handlebars look like. You usually find these on casual commuter bikes because they put the hands and arms in a neutral, relaxed position — so they have a lot of backsweep.

To achieve that high degree of backsweep, the handlebars need to jut forward from the stem first and then angle back sharply, which is what gives them their namesake. Mustache handlebars work well for city bikes, commuters, and even some mountain bikers — and usually for fun bikes with rigid or short-travel suspension forks.

Handlebar materials

Handlebars are mostly made from aluminum (aka *alloy*) or carbon fiber. You might find steel handlebars on certain niche or cheap bikes, and some fancy models use additional composite fibers, which I explain after I cover the main two materials.

Alloy handlebars

Aluminum bars are extremely common. If your bike has a metal handlebar, chances are it's an alloy of aluminum. Depending on the finish applied to them, some are shapely enough to look like they're carbon, though a gentle tap on it with your keys or wedding ring will give that telltale "ting" of metal-on-metal.

Pro: Alloy bars are much more affordable, generally ranging from $40 to $120 for good-quality ones, with upgrade-worthy bars starting usually around $55–$65. They're also tough, so riders who tend to wreck more often (such as criterium or cyclocross racers and mountain bikers) like them because they hold up to impacts and are cheaper to replace.

Con: Typically heavier than carbon fiber bars, they won't absorb vibrations as well, so more vibration (aka *road buzz* and *trail chatter*) are transferred to your hands, arms, and body, which can cause fatigue.

Carbon fiber

My preference is carbon fiber because it's lighter, has more compliance, and soaks up vibrations. The longer or rougher your rides, the more that extra comfort matters. If your bike feels a little harsh, particularly on rougher surfaces, a good carbon bar will help smooth things over.

Because carbon can be laid up in layers and with different fiber orientations, a reputable brand can add a bit of vertical compliance to soak up small bumps, too. This is usually touted as a feature, and some brands that do it well are Race Face, OneUp, and Lauf.

Pro: Lightweight and excellent ride quality with more advanced ergonomic and aerodynamic shaping possible.

Con: More expensive.

Specialty materials

Besides the carbon fiber and aluminum, you'll sometimes see other composite materials blended with carbon fiber to add strength and/or compliance, and some boutique brands make titanium and wood handlebars. Here's the deal on those:

>> **Composite:** Some brands add Kevlar or Aramid fibers to their bars, both of which add strength without adding weight and may slightly improve vibration absorption. Lauf adds S2 glass fibers to their drop bar, which can handle dramatic bends without breaking (it's used in prosthetic foot leaf springs for sprinters!), making it one of the most comfortable, compliant road/gravel handlebars on the market.

>> **Titanium:** As with titanium bike frames, the material offers a better ride quality than aluminum for about the same weight, but it's much more expensive. It's mostly used for flat bars, and boutique ones, at that, but you may find other shapes, too.

>> **Wood:** Wood has effective natural vibration damping, and certain types (cherry, maple, bamboo) are more than strong enough for use on commuter or casual bikes. You won't find this material used for complex shapes, like drop bars, or for mountain bikes, but it can be a cool way to set your city bike apart.

Grips and Handlebar Tape

Bikes with flat bars have grips, and those with drop bars are usually wrapped with handlebar tape (or bar tape, for short). These items enhance control, keep your hands from slipping off the bar, and they provide some cushioning.

Grips

Handlebar grips come in several materials and several designs (see Figure 3-4 for two examples), but one of the biggest considerations is their diameter, or thickness. Most come in various thicknesses; the general idea is that thinner ones are for smaller hands, and thicker ones are for larger hands.

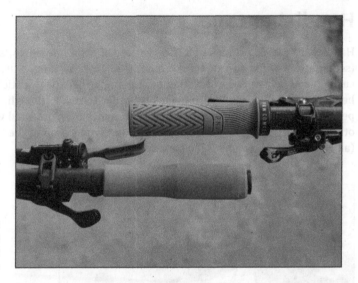

FIGURE 3-4: A lock-on grip (top) and foam grip (bottom).

Personal preference rules, however. Thicker grips usually offer more padding, but if you go too thick, you may have a hard time holding on to it firmly enough over rough terrain. Thin grips don't offer much grip, but some riders prefer the direct bar feel they provide, saying the enhanced feedback lets them feel more in tune with their bike. Most brands that offer multiple diameters have a guide to help you decide.

Most grips are made of rubber, with various patterns molded into them to provide additional grip. Those patterned textures might be ribbed, dotted, bumpy, wavy, or diamond-shaped.

Silicone foam grips, also sometimes called just foam grips, are usually the lightest weight option. They come in varying thicknesses, and some even taper from thick to thin, putting more padding on the outer edges where your palm rests, but thinner for better control under the braking fingers.

If you ride bare-handed, without gloves, skip the foam grips. If your palms get sweaty, they'll get slick and your hands could slip off them. But if you wear gloves, they work well —and can shed 40–60g from your bike!

A few brands make cork grips — most notably, Ergon. The grips look cool, and they absorb vibrations well, making them a comfortable grip. These are mostly meant for commuter, cargo, and casual bikes, not mountain bikes, because they can tear more easily if they knock into something (like a tree or a rock).

Handlebar tape

Handlebar tape also comes in a wide variety of colors, textures, and thicknesses (see Figure 3-5 for an example). Some have a gel backing, which adds a lot of cushion and helps prevent twisting or slipping. Others have a sticky backing that helps it stay in place, but also makes it harder to reuse (though, honestly, most people don't reuse their tape, because it stretches over time and wears out). And others are just plain old fabric or leather that wraps around the bar for a classic (albeit not quite cushioned) look and feel.

FIGURE 3-5:
Handlebar tape on a gravel bike.

A lot of bar tapes are made from a synthetic material or microfiber, ranging from rubbery to leathery. Some are smooth, and some have a fine texture, but the grippiness comes down to the material more than the surface.

There is no shortage to the choices for colors, and Supacaz is one of the most popular (I don't know anyone who doesn't like their bar tape), but I'd also recommend checking out Lizard Skins, Blackburn, and Wolf Tooth Components' offerings.

Plenty of videos online show you how to wrap your handlebars, and it's just about the easiest and most affordable way to make any bike look and feel new again.

Headsets

Though the stem sits between the bar and the headset, understanding how the headset works will help you understand modern stem design, so I'm skipping around a bit. The headset is the item that your fork's steerer tube spins in so that you can steer.

Headsets come in two varieties, threaded and threadless, and the latter comes in three main types, internal, external, and integrated. All of them have upper and lower bearings, which is what lets the fork spin freely, and all of them use a crown race that sits on the fork's crown and is angled so that it nests into the lower bearing.

But the rest of them vary by design and type, so let's dive in.

Threaded headsets

Threaded headsets (see Figure 3-6) set the standard for every bike until the late 1990s and early aughts. The design uses external metal cups that hold the bearings, and those cups press into the head tube.

The *threaded* part of the name refers to the way the headset connects to the fork and holds it in the bike. It's basically like a nut and bolt, where the fork is the bolt and the top of the headset is the nut that threads onto it to hold it tight. A second nut threads down on top of the first one, and the two create a lock nut of sorts that prevents the system from coming loose.

The top of the fork's steerer is threaded and the headset's upper section threads onto it. As you tighten the nut, it pulls the fork's crown race snugly into the lower bearing cup while simultaneously pushing the upper headset race into the upper bearing cup.

FIGURE 3-6:
A threaded
headset shown
with the top of
a steerer.

Threadless headsets

Threadless headsets (see Figure 3-7) are made for forks without threaded steerers, and they're the most common nowadays. Why? Because they're much easier to install, and they allow for easier adjustments to the bike fit.

FIGURE 3-7:
A threadless
headset, installed
on a bike.

A threadless steerer is a smooth round tube, and the headset simply slides over it. Then the stem slides over that, and you can put spacers under or over the stem, which makes it quick and easy to adjust stem height, or even to flip the stem to change its angle.

But riders still need a way to compress everything so that the bearings are properly seated in their races, and that's where the top cap and star nut (see Figure 3-8) enter the picture. For forks with alloy steerer tubes, a star nut is inserted into the tube. The metal prongs snag into the tube and are angled so that the star nut can't pull out. The center has a threaded nut, and a top cap screws into it.

FIGURE 3-8: A top cap, star nut, and compression plug.

Carbon fiber steerers do *not* use a star nut, because those metal prongs can damage the fibers. Instead, they use an expansion, or compression, plug, which expands to wedge itself into place.

The idea is the same for both, to put a "nut" into the steerer that the top cap can thread into. The reason these are a separate part is that most forks come supplied with a long steerer tube so that they can be cut down to the proper size to fit the bike and rider. Once the steerer tube is cut, you install the star nut or plug so that it sits about 1 centimeter below the top of the tube.

The top cap is wider than the steerer, and you need to stack spacers or your stem so that they sit 2–3 millimeters above the top of the steerer. As you tighten the top cap, it presses down on the stem and spacers, compressing everything until there's no play in the system.

Compared to threaded headsets, threadless is *much* quicker to install and easier to adjust. Once everything feels snug, you straighten the stem to align it with the front wheel (so that your cockpit is pointing you straight ahead) and tighten the stem's bolts to lock everything into place.

"WHAT IF MY HEADSET FEELS LOOSE?"

Both types of headsets can come loose over time. Sometimes, it just seems rattly and loose. At other times, it might feel like the handlebar shifts forward just slightly when braking. Either way, a loose headset is bad news because it can wear out your bearings (and possibly your fork) prematurely, and then you'll need to replace it.

You can check for looseness (or *play*) by grabbing the stem and fork leg and trying to wiggle it inside the headset. Some people pull the front brake lever so the front wheel can't move, and rock the bike back and forth with your other hand on the headset. If it's loose, you will feel it knock, but you might also feel the brake pads shifting and confuse that for headset movement. Try both and you should get a good sense of whether it's loose or if it's something else.

If you find any play, tighten things down as described in the sections "Threaded heasdets" or "Threadless headsets," using the appropriate method for whichever type of headset you have. You don't want it too tight or too loose, so don't be afraid to keep making adjustments until all the play disappears but the fork spins freely and easily inside the headset.

A too-tight system feels sluggish or "crunchy," which is the result of having too much pressure (or *preload*) on the headset bearings. If you just can't seem to get it right, have your local bike shop check it, because you might need more spacers or a new headset.

Stealth routing

A more recent variation of threadless headsets allow for stealth cable routing. These debuted around 2020 but grew popular in 2023, and they allow any or all of the cables and hoses and wires from shifters and brake levers to run through the upper headset bearing and directly into the frame and fork.

Some brands run the cables inside the bar and stem for completely stealth routing, where you don't see any of the cables or hoses (as shown in Figure 3-9). Others run those lines under the stem and then through the headset's top cap for a partial stealth setup.

Either setup typically requires a larger-diameter upper bearing, which means the bike's head tube is a little thicker, and the partial stealth setup requires holes in the headset top cap, which can be an entry point for water or dust. They look awesome, but they can sometimes make the cockpit harder to adjust and require more work to service or replace those lines, so your shop may charge more when you need work done.

FIGURE 3-9:
Stealth routing
shown (or, rather,
hidden) on a
road bike.

Now that you understand how handlebar shape, width, and design affect fit and comfort, how the right grips and bar tape give you better control, and how headsets work, it's time to look at the rest of the bicycle's command center.

For more information about handlebars, grips, and headsets, visit Dummies.com/ go/bikingfd.

TIP

IN THIS CHAPTER

» Leading the way with a good stem

» Sticking with the right seatpost

» Sitting pretty on saddle options

Chapter 4

Cockpit, Part 2: Stems, Seatposts, and Saddles

I n this chapter, I cover the part of the cockpit that includes the stem, seatpost, and saddle. You may believe that I should discuss stems with handlebars, and you might be right, but, like a seatpost, the stem connects the part of the bike you're touching (the saddle and handlebar) to the rest of the bike, so I describe it here.

Stems

Describing the *stem* is simple: It's the part that connects your handlebar to your bike. The stem clamps onto the bar and your fork's steerer so that when you turn the bar, it turns the wheel.

Mostly, I talk about a threadless stem, which refers to one that clamps directly to the fork's steerer tube. This type replaced the quill stem, which I also describe, when headsets switched from threaded to threadless (refer to Chapter 3). Regardless of which type your bike has, the following angle and length descriptions apply to both.

The main items you need to know about are angles, length, and bar clamp diameters. But first, here are a few terms that are helpful:

>> **Stem clamp:** The part that clamps to the fork's steerer tube.

>> **Bar clamp:** The part that clamps to your handlebar.

>> **Faceplate:** The part that clamps over your handlebar on the front.

>> **Top cap:** The part that threads into the star nut to compress the headset (explained later in this chapter). Usually, the top cap comes with the headset, but some stems include them if they use a proprietary shape or add features, like computer mounts.

>> **Spacers:** The small rings above and/or below the stem on the steerer tube (See Figure 4-1).

FIGURE 4-1:
A bicycle stem and spacers.

Stem angle

The angle of the stem is often expressed as a +/− number (ex. +/− 12 degrees) because you can usually flip the stem to cause either a positive or negative *rise*, where the angle is compared to 90 degrees. So, if the stem were clamped to a vertical tube, a positive rise would have the body of it angled upward, and a negative rise would angle it downward.

Many stems are about +/−6 degrees. Combine that with the ability to slide the stem up and down on the steerer tube by moving spacers under or over it and you end up with a decent range of fit adjustment.

A bike's head angle will affect the actual angle of the stem on the bike. Many road bikes have approximately 73-degree head angles, so a -6-degree stem sits at an 11-degree angle (90° – 73° = 17°; then 17° – 6° = 11°). So, if you want a nearly level stem for fit or aesthetic purposes, look for a stem with a bigger angle.

Stem length

The length of the stem is measured from the center of the stem clamp area to the center of the bar clamp area. Most road bikes come with stems ranging from 70 to 110 millimeters, with larger frame sizes usually getting longer stems than smaller bikes.

Gravel bikes are often about 10–20 millimeters shorter than road bikes, mostly because gravel bikes tend to have a longer reach measurement in order to push the front wheel farther forward so that their larger tires don't overlap with your toes.

For the same reasons, modern mountain bikes come with much shorter stems than road and gravel bikes (often, just 35–70 millimeters), and many of them have a 0° angle. In this case, you use spacers combined with any handlebar rise to adjust your fit.

There is no rule specifying a standard stem length. Rather, it's a tool for dialing in your bike fit and handling preferences. A shorter stem gives you a more direct feeling of control on rougher terrain but might feel a bit twitchy on smooth straightaways. A long stem can make the bike feel more stable, but also a bit slower to turn, and going too long can provide downright sluggish handling.

Bar clamp diameters

The bar clamp *diameter* refers to the outside diameter of the handlebar's center section, where the stem clamps onto it. It comes in four standard sizes:

>> **22.2mm:** Used on BMX bikes and some bikes with steel handlebars, particularly beach cruisers and older bicycles with quill stems.

>> **25.4mm:** Still found on kids' bikes, casual/commuter bikes, and certain cruisers and other basic bikes. It was a common standard for mountain bikes until the early 2000s, when most switched to 31.6mm, and road bikes followed shortly thereafter.

>> **31.6mm:** The current standard for most road and gravel bikes. The larger diameter allowed for stronger and lighter handlebars for higher-performance bikes. You might also find this size on certain commuter and cargo e-bikes. Some mountain bikes, particularly shorter-travel hardtails and cross-country

bikes, still use this standard because it's not as stiff as 35mm, making it a bit more comfortable when there's not as much suspension there to take the edge off.

>> **35mm:** The current standard for many mountain bikes. It's stiffer and stronger than 31.6mm, which helps, because bikes have become burlier and have much more suspension travel. Smaller riders may find that these bars can be too stiff, so if you switch to a 31.6mm bar, you need to switch your stem, too.

Quill stems

The quill stem (see Figure 4-2) was the original design. Rather than clamp to the outside, it uses an expansion wedge to tighten itself into the fork's steerer tube. If you only see one bolt on top of your stem and the stem's neck disappears into the headset, you have a quill stem.

FIGURE 4-2:
A quill stem.

Seatposts

Seatposts are the gizmos that connect your saddle to your bike. They come in several diameters and various lengths and can be straight or set back. Dropper seatposts can telescope up or down with the push of a lever, and suspension seatposts add a little "cush" to your ride.

Dropper seatposts

A *dropper* is a telescoping seatpost that lets you raise and lower the saddle on demand (see Figure 4-3). Before dropper posts entered the picture, a mountain biker would often stop at the top of a climb, loosen and lower their seatpost, bomb down the hill, and then stop and raise the seatpost again before the next climb. Dropper posts absolutely changed the game.

FIGURE 4-3:
A dropper
seatpost, fully
extended and
compressed.

Modern droppers use a handlebar-mounted remote to let you compress it using your body weight. Push the lever without sitting on your saddle and an air spring pushes it back up, and hydraulic valves let you stop it at any point in its travel. Lowering your saddle makes it easier to get further back on the bike on steep descents, or just rest your feet on the ground at a stop light.

Suspension seatposts

Suspension seatposts come in a couple of varieties. Some have a simple up-and-down telescoping design, and others mount the saddle on a pivoting lever that uses an elastomer spring to give it some squish. The best ones, like the Cane Creek Thudbuster or Redshift Shockstop, use a parallelogram design (see Figure 4-4) that better controls the motion and keeps the saddle level throughout its travel.

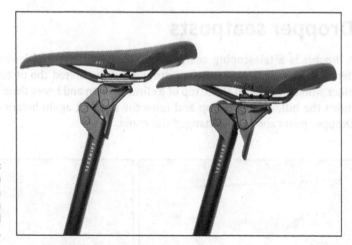

FIGURE 4-4:
A parallelogram
suspension
seatpost, shown
upright and
compressed.

These designs are usually limited to 20–35 millimeters of travel and are mainly designed to take the edge off small impacts. Cheap ones, or those found on inexpensive bikes, are what they are. Better ones can be adjustable by swapping springs or elastomers to match your body weight.

Seatpost diameter

Most modern seatposts are one of three diameters: 27.2 millimeters, 30.9 millimeters, or 31.6 millimeters. There is honestly no good reason why we have two standards that are so close together, but that's the way it is.

Many road and gravel bikes use the slimmer 27.2mm diameter because those seatposts tend to be more compliant, particularly when they're made with carbon fiber. Some are even designed with intentional flex, and some have single- or dual-leaf spring designs that can move up to 15 millimeters to absorb impact! Absent suspension and fat tires, anything that can take the edge off those bumps before they reach your bum is a good thing. Slimmer posts are also more aerodynamic and lighter.

Most mountain bikes use the larger-diameter posts because most mountain bikes now come equipped with dropper posts, and the larger diameter makes more room for their telescoping internals. Larger-diameter tubes are also stiffer and stronger, which is needed to support those moving parts.

Alternative diameters

You may also see some mountain bikes with larger 34.9mm-diameter posts, which offer an even stiffer design. With dropper posts, this makes more room for the moving parts and a more robust design, but only a few bike brands spec this size, and not every seatpost brand offers it.

And, you may find BMX and kids' bikes and, rarely, specialty road bikes with a smaller 25.4mm diameter. This smaller diameter makes sense for smaller bikes, but like the larger 34.9mm, aftermarket options may be limited.

Seatpost length

For performance bikes, most seatposts come in lengths ranging from 300–400 millimeters, and good brands usually offer more than one length for their best-selling posts.

All seatposts have (or should have, anyway) a *minimum-insertion* line marked on them: This line indicates the line at which you need to stop raising your saddle because the post needs the length below that line to be inside the seat tube, to ensure that it can support your weight.

Basically, if you can see the minimum-insertion line on your post, you should lower your saddle until it's just under the top of the bike's seat collar. If that causes your saddle to be too low (check our bike-fit guide in Chapter 10), you need a longer seatpost. Conversely, if you have barely any seatpost showing, you can get away with a shorter post to save weight.

Kids' bikes, BMX bikes, and other nonperformance bikes might have shorter or longer posts, depending on how they're set up.

Seatpost setback

Some seatposts are straight, with the saddle clamp directly inline and centered over the top of the post. Some have a *setback*, or offset, that shifts the saddle clamp behind the centerline of the post (see Figure 4-5). Offsets typically range from 10–25 millimeters.

Which one you choose is determined by how you want your bike to fit, or by what you need to make your bike fit. I like a straight post with my saddle in a more forward position, but I know riders with setback posts who slide their saddles way back. It's all up to personal preference and what works for you.

Some specialty bikes, particularly time trial and triathlon bikes, may have a forward offset or an adjustable offset. This puts the rider farther over the pedals, for a more powerful and aerodynamic pedaling position.

FIGURE 4-5:
Straight versus
offset seatposts.

Seatpost material

Cheap bikes, vintage bikes, and niche modern bikes may have a steel seatpost (some even use titanium!), but most bikes nowadays have alloy or carbon fiber posts. These can vary dramatically in quality and weight, with high-end posts weighing 30 to 50% less than cheap posts.

An aluminum alloy post is a good, reliable option, but just like an alloy frame, it transmits more vibration and impact forces to your saddle. If you're perched on a giant padded comfort saddle, that won't matter. But for performance riders with slimmer saddles, it's something to consider.

Carbon fiber posts, like frames, will damp those vibrations better than alloy. Some have intentional flex, too, which makes for a more comfortable ride without giving up any performance. And, usually, they're lighter and may even have some aerodynamic shaping.

Saddle clamp

All modern seatposts have a saddle clamp at the top. Designs may vary, but most of them have one or two bolts, and two plates that capture your saddle's rails. You can find other designs out there, but they're rare and not worth covering in detail here.

Most single-bolt designs will have the lower plate resting on a curved surface, so when you loosen that bolt, you can adjust the saddle's angle and also slide it forward and backward.

Two-bolt designs (see Figure 4-6) usually have one bolt in front of the post and one behind, and these make it easier to fine-tune the saddle's angle. You need to loosen at least one of them significantly in order to slide your saddle fore-aft, but these tend to hold the saddle more securely.

FIGURE 4-6:
A typical 2-bolt saddle clamp (left) and a side-bolt saddle clamp (right).

Sadly, many of these 2-bolt designs' front bolt points straight downward, which makes it hard to turn more than one-quarter turn at time, and some longer, bulkier hex wrenches and tools barely fit. One day, I hope, seatpost makers will figure out how to angle that front bolt for easier tool access. Until then, here's the workaround: Finger-tighten the front bolt first, turning it just a bit farther than it needs to be, so that the saddle's nose is slightly lower than where you want it to end up. Then use a tool to tighten the rear bolt more and pull the saddle back to level. Allen wrenches with a ball-end are also a big help here.

Saddles

Atop the seatpost is the saddle, and it's what you sit on. Saddles range in size from big and cushy, like on a beach cruiser, to slim and thin — sometimes with no padding at all. You find the latter on race bikes, but that doesn't mean you have to be a racer to appreciate them.

In fact, sometimes a thin saddle can be more comfortable over the long term than those thick, wide ones. That's because the saddles found on performance bikes have more anatomical shaping, have more widths and lengths to choose from and often have male- and female-specific designs.

Some saddles sit (pun intended) between these, and you often find them on hybrids, fitness bikes, and commuter e-bikes. They have 1–1.5 centimeters of padding and look similar to a performance saddle, just a bit wider and softer. Those are helpful for city bikes and times when you might be riding for 30 to 60 minutes but probably aren't wearing padded bike shorts.

The two key saddle measurements are width and length (Figure 4-7). Of them, width is the most important, but it's not as simple as you might think.

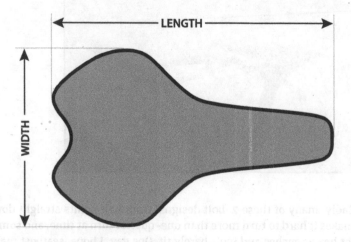

FIGURE 4-7:
Saddle width
and length.

Saddle width

Measured at the widest part of the saddle, performance saddles typically range from 137–154 millimeters. Hybrid and comfort saddles can get much wider than that.

For hybrid and comfort bikes, whatever comes supplied with your bike will probably be fine to get you started. Ride it for a while and see what you think. If you can't get comfortable on it, there are plenty of tips in this chapter to help you find a saddle you'll like better.

For performance bikes, the width is designed to match your sit bone width — in particular, the part of your ischial bone (or *pelvis*) that is resting on the saddle. Because that bone angles outward from front to back, where it rests on the saddle depends on how flexible you are and how much pelvic tilt you can achieve (see Figure 4-8).

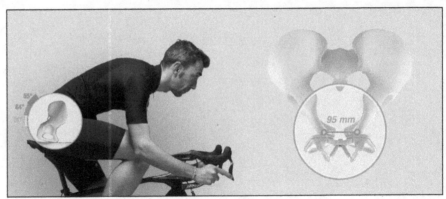

FIGURE 4-8:
Saddle width
versus sit
bone width.

Courtesy of Prologo.

Saddle angle

I recommend starting with your saddle perfectly level and then go for a ride. Pay attention to where the pressure points are and to whether you feel like you're sliding toward the front or back of the saddle as you pedal. If you're sliding forward, tilt the nose up a bit. Sliding backward? Tilt the nose down a bit. Small changes can make a big difference. Micro adjustments are your friend; think 0.5° at a time.

If you're not sliding in either direction but still have pressure points, it's time to play with your bike fit by moving the saddle forward or backward on the post and then adjusting the stem length. If you feel that your fit is dialed in and you're still getting uncomfortable pressure points, it's likely time to try a different saddle.

Cutouts and channels

Some saddles have a central cutout or relief channel that helps take pressure off the perineum and other delicate body parts. The shape may vary for men's and women's saddles, but the idea is the same. If you routinely ride in wet locations, a channel is better than an open cutout because the rain will spray off your rear tire and through the cutout, and leave a nice wet spot on your crotch. Try explaining that at the office!

That's the cockpit, from tip to tail. Anytime you plan to swap your bar, stem, saddle, or seatpost, give these last two chapters a quick check for tips on how to get the right replacement or upgrade plus tips on how to set them up.

TIP

For more information about stems, seatposts, and saddles, visit Dummies.com/go/bikingfd.

Chapter **5**

Brakes, Wheels, and Tires

After you know all about your bicycle's cockpit, it's time to look at the parts that make it roll — and stop. Your brakes are probably the most important safety feature on your bike, and when you know how to use them well, you can ride faster.

Your bike's wheels and tires are how you roll. As you're probably figuring out, modern bikes have a lot of wheel and tire options, and each is optimized for its intended use. Fortunately, you can find simple all-purpose solutions, too, but it's good to know why different sizes, diameters, widths, and treads are available so that you know when and why you may want to upgrade.

Brakes: The Best Invention Ever

Think of that last time you were headed toward an object at high speed and had to stop suddenly. That object you avoided is where you'd be without brakes.

Brake design has come a long way, from simple blocks of wood that pressed against the tire when the rider pulled a giant lever to finely tuned rim brakes with multiple linkages to amplify their power. Mountain bikes evolved from hard-to-maintain cantilever brakes (described later in this chapter) to V-brakes, which provide easy adjustments and massively improved power and modulation, or the ability to finely control braking force by feathering the lever in and out.

And then came disc brakes. Long the standard for cars and motorcycles, hydraulic disc brakes changed the game. Early disc brakes were mechanical, but by 1996, mountain bikes had full hydraulic brakes that finally provided the power, modulation, and control to help riders take their performance to the next level.

Nowadays, you'd be hard-pressed to find a new performance bike of any kind with anything but disc brakes, and most models costing more than $800 have hydraulic disc brakes.

That said, plenty of bikes still use rim brakes, and I'll explain all of the types of brakes below. Bur first, let me define the parts of the brake.

Caliper

The *caliper* is the part of the brake that does the braking. A rim brake caliper arches over the wheel and tire and squeezes the brake pads against the rim. A disc brake caliper presses the brake pads against a disc rotor that's mounted to the hub on the left (non-drive) side of the bike.

Lever: Mechanical

The *mechanical* brake lever is the gadget you squeeze to activate the caliper. The lever pulls a mechanical cable attached to the caliper, causing it to perform its stopping task. You'll find both rim and disc brakes with mechanical operation.

Lever: Hydraulic

A *hydraulic* brake lever is a bit more complicated than the mechanical version. Here's how it works, step by step:

1. The lever is attached to the master cylinder, and as you pull the lever, it pushes a plunger into the cylinder.

2. The master cylinder typically has an overflow reservoir that allows the brake fluid to expand if it heats up, but once you pull the lever, a piston moves past the port that allows overflow to fill that reservoir.

3. This action closes the system and starts to push hydraulic brake fluid through the hose toward the caliper.

4. Fluid fills the spaces behind the caliper's pistons and pushes them toward the rotor.

5. The brake pads sit in front of the piston, so as the pistons move toward the rotor, the brake pads make contact with the rotor and start slowing you down.

6. Once you release the lever, the pads and pistons retract (thanks to lip seals and a pad spring, as described a little later in this chapter), letting the rotor spin freely through the caliper again.

If you release the lever all the way, the system is once again open, and any pressure built up in the system from heat can expand into the master cylinder's reservoir. Most modern brakes work well at dissipating heat so that it doesn't cause problems, but extended descents with lots of long, sustained, hard braking can cause *brake pump*, or a feeling of reduced power and modulation.

The solution to this problem is to simply let off one brake or the other for one or two seconds. Surprisingly, that's all the time it takes for the system to cool off, reset, and balance the pressure, letting you get right back on the brakes. I recommend letting off only one at a time if you're on a steep descent and need to maintain control, and then alternate as needed. Later in this chapter, I cover other tricks that help you brake more effectively.

Rim brakes

As the name *rim brakes* suggests, the wheel's rim doubles as the braking surface — rim brakes press brake pads into a flat surface on the side of the rim. The three types worth explaining — traditional, cantilever, and linear pull — all use mechanical return springs built into the calipers to open up the brakes when you let go of the lever, but otherwise have quite different designs.

TRADITIONAL BRAKES

Picture a road bike from the 1990s and you're seeing a traditional brake caliper (see Figure 5-1). This caliper usually mounts at the top of the fork or on the seatstays (the tubes that lead from the top of the seat tube to the rear axle) and curves around the top of the wheel and tire. Most brakes attach with a single bolt in the top-center of the caliper. Some direct-mount designs had a 2-bolt mounting system that increased stiffness, but their time was short lived as manufacturers started using them just before disc brakes really took over.

Traditional calipers evolved from single-pivot designs to more complex multi-linkage designs that increased the leverage to apply far more braking power.

FIGURE 5-1:
A traditional
road bike
brake caliper.

CANTILEVER BRAKES

Cantilevers use left and right arms, each mounted directly to the fork legs, or seatstays, that are attached to each other by a piece of brake cable running through a triangular loop that was attached to the main brake cable leading to the lever (see Figure 5-2). As you pulled the brake lever, it pulled the triangle upward, and that pulled the cantilevers, which pushed the brake pads attached to them closer to the rim.

FIGURE 5-2:
Cantilever brakes.

As you can tell just from looking at it, there's a lot of power lost in those mechanics. The best cantilever brakes had arms that stuck out as wide as they could to create more leverage, but the design was inherently limited by the small amount of cable that could be pulled, coupled with the short distance they could rotate.

Cantilever brakes never had much power, and the only sport they were good for was cyclocross. Why? Because you rarely need to come to a full stop in cyclocross, and mud clearance is more important than stopping on a dime. It's a weird, wonderful sport where weak brakes turn out to be a benefit.

LINEAR PULL BRAKES (OR V-BRAKES)

Linear pull brakes (see Figure 5-3) got their name because they had two separate arms, each attached to the frame or fork independently, and the brake cable would pull in a straight (linear) line from one arm to the next. This arrangement let both arms pull in perfect unison, and because the arms were taller than cantilever brakes, they had more leverage and thus more power.

FIGURE 5-3: Linear pull brakes.

These linear pull brakes were commonly called V-brakes because of the V-shape the arms made (and because it sounds cooler than *linear pull*). These were so much stronger than cantilevers that they could cause seatstays to twist, so some riders added a U-shaped brace over the top of them to prevent frame flex. Until disc brakes took over, linear pull brakes ruled the roost for MTB. They still show up on some less-expensive bikes, but even many of those have moved on to disc brakes.

RIM BRAKE PADS

For rim brakes, the brake pads you use are typically specific to the type of rim material. Alloy rims use "normal" pads, and carbon fiber rims use specific pads that work better on a composite surface. Though wheels are covered in the next section, you should know that carbon rims generally brake normally in dry conditions, but their braking performance falls off a steep, scary cliff when they're wet — as in, they barely work. Seriously. If you ride in the rain, I advise sticking to alloy rims. Also, some rim brands make special pads specifically for their proprietary braking surfaces, so stick with those for optimum performance.

Disc brakes

Disc brakes press the brake pads into a brake rotor that's attached to the wheels' hub, and they're much more powerful than rim brakes. The brake calipers are mounted on the fork's lower left leg, and the rear brake is mounted on either the left chainstay or the seatstay.

REMEMBER

You *must* bed in your disc brakes before your first ride. (I explain this topic later in this chapter, in the section "Brake bed-in procedure," but it's absolutely critical if you want your brakes to perform well. Okay, here we go — er, stop — no, *go!*

HYDRAULIC DISC BRAKES

I explain the basics of how hydraulic disc brakes work in the prior section "Lever: Hydraulic," so let's talk now about the details so that you know how to check them and how certain features help or hurt performance.

Hydraulic disc brake pistons (see Figure 5-4) use a combination of a tiny pad return spring and lip seals to retract the pistons away from the rotor when you release the lever. Each of the caliper's pistons slides inside a lip seal, which is an angled seal made from rubber (or another, similar material) that flexes as the piston moves toward the rotor. When you let go, that seal snaps back to its original resting state and pulls the piston back with it.

FIGURE 5-4:
A 4-piston hydraulic disc brake.

The beautiful part about this design is that it lets the piston slide more and more as your brake pads wear, so it automatically compensates for pad wear and keeps your brakes working the way they should — as long as you don't mess it up. If you remove your wheel (say, to change a flat) and pull the brake lever, it can push the pads all the way in because the rotor isn't there to stop them. Effectively, this pushes the pistons too far out, and they can't automatically retract far enough to make room for you to fit the rotor back between them — which makes it hard to reinstall the wheel back on your bike!

TIP

The easy fix that usually works is to *carefully* slide a large/broad flathead screwdriver in there (or an actual pad spacer tool, ideally) and press the pads and pistons back toward the caliper. This usually resets the system and opens them up enough to slide your wheel in there — just make sure to press both sides evenly so that the next time you use your brakes, it's moving the pads evenly, too. (If that doesn't work, it's time to haul the bike in to your local bike shop and have the brakes bled and reset.)

Hydraulic disc brake calipers usually have two or four pistons, though a couple of 6-piston versions are out there. The smaller, 2-piston caliper has one piston on each side, and the larger, 4-piston caliper has two on each side. Typically, 2-piston calipers have smaller brake pads, and 4-piston models have longer brake pads, offering more surface area for rubbing against the brake rotor. More surface area equals more friction, which equals more stopping power.

MECHANICAL DISC BRAKES

Mechanical disc brake calipers, which function quite differently from hydraulic, come in two types: single-sided and dual-sided. Figure 5-5 shows a mechanical disc brake.

FIGURE 5-5:
Mechanical
disc brake.

Both types work by transferring the cable pull from the lever into the lateral motion of a brake pad. This is typically done by having the cable pull a lever on the caliper, and that lever rotates a ramped cylinder that pushes the brake pad toward the rotor as it does.

Single-sided versions only move the outer brake pad, whereas the inner pad is static inside the caliper. This ends up flexing the rotor toward the inner pad, which is fine, but it takes that much more pad movement before you achieve full power.

Dual-sided versions move both pads toward the rotor simultaneously, so you're getting more power more quickly. Neither version will compensate for pad wear on its own, but you can usually twist a dial or a barrel adjuster to move the pads inward. It's definitely a less sophisticated system, but it's still much better than rim brakes.

HYBRID DISC BRAKES

The mechanically actuated hydraulic disc brake calipers are *rad* (see Figure 5-6). If mechanical disc brakes are 50 percent awesome and hydraulic disc brakes are 100 percent awesome, hybrids get you to 80 percent. They basically use a mechanical brake lever and cable, but put a hydraulic master cylinder on the caliper. The cable pulls a small lever that drives a plunger into the master cylinder, much like it would on a hydraulic brake lever on the handlebar. It's just that there's no brake hose — it's pushing the fluid directly into the caliper.

FIGURE 5-6:
Mechanically
actuated
hydraulic disc
brake.

The upside is that you get dramatically improved braking power and modulation compared to a full mechanical setup, and it's easy to swap these in for standard mechanical calipers without having to change anything else.

The downside is that there's less fluid, so hybrid disc brakes don't have as much tolerance for heat buildup. This is why you don't usually find these on mountain bikes, though they're useful on road, gravel, and cyclocross bikes (or even commuters), as long as you're not bombing down big mountains.

The other caveat for both mechanical and hybrid disc brakes is that their absolute performance is dependent on the quality of the brake cable housing. Opt for high-quality, compressionless housing for the best performance and you'll be amazed at the quality of this upgrade simply by swapping the calipers.

TIP

The TRP HyRD and Yokozuna Ultimo are the two best hybrid brake calipers (they're both awesome), and Yokozuna's Reaction cable housing is excellent for this purpose.

BRAKE ROTORS

Braking comes down to heat management. The friction between the pads and rotor creates a lot of heat — *don't touch your rotors after a long descent!* — and the hotter they get, the more heat will transfer into the caliper, and then the fluid. If too much heat gets into the brake fluid, it can cause a loss of modulation and power, which can cause you to lose control.

One of the easiest ways to increase braking power is to increase rotor size. Larger-diameter brake rotors help in two ways:

First, they have more mass to absorb more heat, and they usually have more surface area to dissipate that heat, too. Most rotors have holes or slots to increase the surface area, so they can cool faster, and some use fins to increase it even more. Shimano's ICEtech rotors sandwich aluminum between the steel braking surfaces, which helps pull more heat toward their fins and away from the caliper.

Second, a larger-diameter rotor is like a longer lever, giving you more leverage over it. Imagine spinning a wheel and pinching the brake rotor with your fingers. Now imagine pinching it at the rim. At which spot do you think you'd have an easier time bringing it to a stop? The rim, obviously. So, increasing the rotor size has a similar effect, making it easier to modulate the braking power. Good handling is all about having good control, and being able to feather the brakes gives you the ability to finely control your speed.

This list describes typical brake rotor sizes:

» **140mm:** Good for cyclocross, where you don't need much braking power; sometimes also used for rear brakes on road and gravel bikes in less hilly areas.

» **160mm:** Commonly found on road and gravel bikes, and on some cross-country mountain bikes.

» **180mm:** Commonly found on trail mountain bikes, front and rear. XC bikes might pair a 180mm front with a 160mm rear, and bigger trail bikes might pair a 200mm front with a 180mm rear.

>> **200mm/203mm:** Commonly found on large trail and all-mountain bikes, and sometimes paired with a 220mm in the front.

>> **220mm/223mm:** The largest common rotor size, though some bigger ones are out there. You'll find these on enduro, freeride, and downhill bikes.

It's totally fine to mix rotor sizes, but always put the bigger one in the front. As in a car, most of the braking power is in the front, so it makes sense to have your most powerful brake there, too.

WARNING

As in a car (again), if you're braking too hard while trying to turn, you won't turn as well. When you need to brake through a corner, you feather the front so that the wheel can keep rolling, and brake harder on the back. If the rear locks up and skids, that's fun. If the front does it, that's a wreck.

For a given bike category, an e-bike typically runs one or two rotor sizes larger than the non-electric equivalent. That's because e-bikes are usually from 10 to 30 pounds heavier, so they need bigger brakes. Consider that most performance bikes are designed with riders from 110 to 200 pounds in mind. So, if the rider — plus any, cargo, gear, etc. — exceeds that range, sizing up your rotors can help because the more mass that you need to decelerate, the hotter the brakes will become while doing it.

WHY ARE DISC BRAKES BETTER THAN RIM BRAKES?

Technically, with rim brakes, a bicycle's wheel is like a giant brake rotor, and the larger rotor should have more power, right? So why is it that a small brake rotor outperforms a rim brake using the much larger wheel as its rotor?

Several reasons. First, disc brakes have a much more direct path of applying force to the rotor, so you're not losing any mechanical advantage to levers and hinges. That's especially true for hydraulic disc brakes, but holds up well enough for mechanical versions, too. Basically, more of the lever force goes into squeezing the rotor than it would with a rim brake squeezing the rim, so you get more power.

Second, you get more consistent, smoother power because rotors offer a more consistent braking surface. Rims can get bent, or wobble, which can create undulating braking power. Add a little rain and rims get slick. Add mud and you're basically sandpapering your rims, causing premature wear to an *expensive* component! But disc brake rotors don't care — they slough off the muck and keep right on working. They might squeal a bit, but they work.

REMEMBER

Yes, you can find 200mm and 203mm rotor sizes, and yes, it's silly that we have two sizes that are so close together — but if you're using adapters or spacers to fit either size on your bike, get the correct one for the rotor size you're using.

TECHNICAL STUFF

Most bikes are designed with an ideal (or at least a typical) rotor size in mind to minimize the use of spacers, but if you want to use a larger rotor, you need to move the caliper farther from the bike or fork leg. Check your bike's or fork's original specifications to find the minimum-and-maximum rotor size compatibility.

Lastly, brake rotors range from about 1.8mm to 2.3mm in thickness. Thicker rotors are heavier, but their increased mass helps them deal with heat better, so you often find those on larger rotor sizes.

BRAKE PAD MATERIALS

Like rim brake pads, disc brake pads come in different materials, each with their own performance attributes. The three basic types are described in this list:

>> Organic: Also called resin pads, organic brake pads use a mix of Kevlar, rubber, and silica, mostly (some brands add other ingredients, like graphene), all bound together in a resin. These tend to be the quietest pads and have good initial bite, and they don't transfer as much heat from the rotor to the caliper. That's good for short braking spurts, but their power can fade faster on longer sustained descents with constant braking. They also wear faster and are more prone to glazing.

>> Sintered: These fully metallic pads typically last the longest, particularly in foul conditions; however, they also need to "warm up" before they'll perform at their best, so they're good for hard-core braking and aggressive, drag-the-brakes-for-minutes descents. They typically handle heat well, but because they're metal, they also conduct that heat into the pads and calipers more easily. And they're the noisiest.

>> Semi-metallic: Add a little metal to an organic resin pad and you have semi-metallic. It's a good compromise between braking performance and durability, and between low noise and solid bite. If you're not sure what to get, start with semi-metallic pads and see how you like them.

BRAKE BED-IN PROCEDURE

Bedding in simply means embedding brake pad material into a new (or clean) brake rotor surface. This process coats the rotor's smooth, shiny metal surface with a thin layer of pad material, which provides much better friction with the pad. Better friction means better braking, so if you want the best possible braking, take ten minutes to do this right.

WARNING

Regardless of which type of pad you choose, it's *critical* that you bed in those brakes. This warning applies to any new bike purchase, too, especially if you bought the bike online or from a department store. Most good bike shops will do this on any bike they sell, but if you didn't support your local shop, it's on you to bed in your brakes if you want them to work well.

Here's how to do it:

1. **Find an open space where you can ride around slowly and perform frequent stops and starts.**

2. **Ride along at approximately 10 mph, gently brake until you *almost* come to a stop, and then pedal back up to about 10 mph and do it again. Repeat this process 20 times.**

   This step gently embeds pad material in the rotor without causing too much heat and glazing the surface.

3. **Now ride a little faster and brake harder, releasing the brakes just before you come to a complete stop. Do this five or ten times.**

4. **Ride around for a minute to let the rotor cool off.**

5. **Test the brakes however you like — they're now ready for maximum stopping power!**

Repeat this process anytime you get new rotors.

If you switch brake pads to a different material, you should clean or swap rotors, too, and then re-bed the brakes with the new pad material.

If you've just made an epic run and your rotors are glowing, possibly with a permanent rainbow discoloration (rad!), it might be time to check the pads. Some, especially organic pads, can glaze over from extreme heat.

TIP

Try sanding down the pads with fine-grit sandpaper until the shiny surface glaze is gone. If that doesn't restore the quiet and/or the power, try cleaning your brake rotors. I use sandpaper with a superfine grit and a light touch for a couple swipes over the braking surface, followed by wiping them down with rubbing alcohol and then re-bedding them. That usually helps, but in the worst case, it's time for new pads (with a proper rotor cleaning and re-bedding, too).

Alternative (old school) brakes

Two other types of brakes are still in use — coaster and drum — though they become more rare by the day. Both work by pressing brake shoes (located inside the rear hub) against the inside surface of the hub shell, but they're activated differently. Drum brakes have a normal brake lever, but you won't see any rim or disc brakes on the bike.

Coaster brakes (see Figure 5-7) work by trying to pedal backward. If you remember stomping back on the pedal and skidding to a glorious stop, you were using a coaster brake. Many single-speed kids' bikes still use coaster brakes, sometimes paired with a front rim brake. You can also still find these on some beach cruisers and similar bikes. If you don't see a brake lever anywhere on the handlebar, it probably has a coaster brake.

FIGURE 5-7:
A coaster brake is inside the hub and requires an arm fixed to the chainstay.

If you remember how a larger brake rotor allows for more leverage and stronger braking, you can imagine how *little* power a drum brake has by using a nonabrasive pad against the inside of a tiny hub. I like to say that drum brakes are more of a *suggestion* to stop than a *command*, but they work for low-speed applications like cruisers and comfort bikes.

Now that I've covered the controls and stopping, let's get rolling with wheels and tires!

Wheels

Your bike's wheels are made up of rims, hubs, and spokes. The *rim* is the outermost part that the tire mounts to, the *hub* is the central part that attaches to your bike, and the *spokes* are the gizmos that connect the rim to the hub. I give you a closer look at each of these parts from the center out, and then I talk about the various wheel sizes.

Hubs

The hub is the center of the wheel — the device that connects the wheel to your bike and lets the wheel spin. Figure 5-8 shows a cutaway view of a typical rear hub, which includes the freehub body and ratcheting mechanism. A front hub would be similar, but without those additional parts.

FIGURE 5-8: Cutaway cross section of a rear hub.

The following few sections describe what all the parts do.

Hub shell and flanges

The *hub shell* is the outer shell of the hub. It has the spoke flanges that the spokes pass through. Hub shells are usually made of aluminum, but some cheaper ones might be steel, and some fancy ones are composed partly or entirely of carbon fiber.

The spoke flange is the part that sticks up on either side with holes for the spokes to go through. Taller flanges are generally better for building stiff wheels (which I explain later in this chapter, in the section "Spokes and nipples"), but some hubs use shorter flanges, to save weight.

Disc brake rotor mounts

A disc brake hub has a mounting point for the brake rotor on the left side of the hub. There are two standards: Center lock and 6-bolt (see Figure 5-9). Center

Lock uses a single lock ring to secure the rotor and is quicker and easier to install, and it makes for lighter hubs (but the rotors are typically heavier than 6-bolt, so it kinda evens out).

FIGURE 5-9:
Center Lock
versus 6-bolt
mounting
interface.

If you're replacing the center lock rotor's lock ring, make sure to get the right size to fit over the thru axle. Road and gravel bikes using 12mm thru axles have smaller holes and install with a standard cassette tool. Larger, 15mm thru axles used on MTB suspension forks have a larger hole and so they have notches for a bottom-bracket installation tool instead.

WARNING

These larger lock rings for 15mm thru axles may not fit in road/gravel forks, because the taller flange can rub the inside of the fork's leg!

The 6-bolt brake mount uses a taller flange and more material to create six threaded attachment points. Six-bolt brake rotors are lighter, but the hubs are a bit heavier, and you have to tighten six T25 (Torx 25) bolts. It's more work, but the benefit is that most bike mini tools have the necessary T25 bit to tighten these, so they're more easily fixed while out riding. That said, properly tightened center lock rings are unlikely to come loose.

TIP

Ultimately, buy the hub or wheelset you want. Don't let the type of rotor attachment point be the deciding factor unless you really want or need to be able to tighten or swap rotors with a mini tool.

Freehub body

The freehub body is where the cassette mounts to the hub. There are several types to match various brands and types of cassettes, and you can check those out in Chapter 6.

Ratcheting mechanism

The freehub body is connected to the hub shell with some sort of ratcheting mechanism that lets it turn the hub when you pedal, but also let it *coast*, or spin freely, when you're not pedaling but still moving forward. There are two common types of ratcheting mechanisms: pawl and ratchet, and drive rings (star ratchets), as shown in Figure 5-10.

FIGURE 5-10: Pawl and ratchet on the left, drive ring on the right.

A pawl-and-ratchet system works by using spring-loaded directional pawls to catch into teeth on a ring. When you pedal, they catch, and when you coast, the toothed ring just rolls over their smooth side.

A drive ring works by using two toothed rings (one or both might be spring-loaded to push against each other) that engage when you pedal, but roll past each other when you coast.

Both use hardened-steel "teeth," so they'll last a long time even though you're putting a lot of torque into them and they're constantly rubbing against each other. That's also why you hear that rapid fire "click-click-click" sound when you coast!

DEGREES OF ENGAGEMENT

When you start to pedal and the cranks move a little before they engage and start turning the rear wheel, the amount of free rotation is called the *degrees of engagement*.

What's happening is that the pawls inside the hub are between teeth and need to move forward to the point where they engage, or make contact, and start turning the hub. That distance is determined by how many teeth are on the drive ring(s) and how many pawls the system has. More teeth and more pawls means less space between them, which means quicker engagement.

Some hubs use three pawls, some use six, and some have six with alternating engagement so that only two or three at a time are turning the wheel. By alternating pawl engagement, you can have larger, stronger teeth (more space between them) but still get quicker engagement.

Mountain bikers prefer quicker engagement because they're negotiating trickier terrain with small pedal movements, so any wasted pedal stroke could mean the difference between making it, or not making it, up a rooty climb. Road and gravel riders don't need it to be as quick because they're (usually) maintaining a consistent cadence, and once the hub is engaged, it stays that way until you coast.

Typical road and gravel hubs have 10 degrees to 6 degrees of engagement, mountain bike hubs have 6 degrees to 3 degrees, and some high-end hubs have 1 degree down to 0.6 degree, which is *quick!*

You can find other variations of these, but they function the same. A few boutique brands replace ratcheting systems with a roller clutch, or sprag clutch, which offers nearly instant engagement, but also tends to be a bit heavier.

Bearings

Most hubs use cartridge bearings, which contain both the bearing race and balls in a single cartridge that's pressed into place. (See Chapter 6 for a detailed description of bearings.) Some use cup-and-cone bearings, but they all do the same thing: Allow the hub shell and freehub body to spin freely on the axle.

WARNING

Some wheels found on the cheapest bikes use loose ball bearings behind a threaded end cap. These don't last long if not properly adjusted and maintained (and they aren't always easy to adjust or maintain!), are easily contaminated, and are usually impossible to repair or replace after they've worn down.

Axle/thru axle

The *axle* is the part that fastens the hub to your bike, and there are three types: bolt-on axles, quick-release (QR) axles, and thru axles (shown in Figure 5-11). Before quick-release and thru axles became popular, bikes would actually have the wheels bolted to the bike, and many still do. You'll often find bolt-on axles on kids' bikes, BMX bikes, dirt jump bikes, cargo bikes, and many of the less-expensive e-bikes.

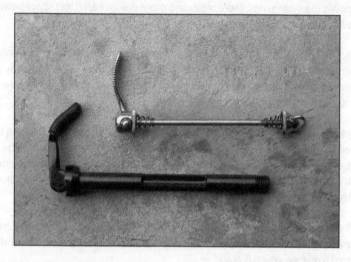

FIGURE 5-11: Quick-release skewer (top) versus thru axle.

For decades, all bikes that didn't have bolt-on axles used quick-release hubs, which have a skewer sliding through the hub that clamps onto the fork or rear dropouts. Like bolt-on hubs, quick-release hubs have the axle built into the hub – only the axle is hollow. The skewer, which inserts through the hollow axle, is only there to secure the hub inside the dropouts — it doesn't support any of the wheels' load. Many kids' bikes, cruisers, and less-expensive commuter and fitness bikes still use the quick-release, but most performance bikes have switched to thru axles.

Thru axle hubs have no built-in axle. Rather, a *thru axle* slides through the dropout and then through the hub, and then threads into the opposite dropout. The thru axle *is* the axle, and this arrangement makes the axle part of the bike *and* the hub, which is much stronger and stiffer. The bad news is that various bikes use nearly 100 combinations of lengths and thread pitches, so if you have to replace one, you have to order the right part or else it won't fit your bike. Robert Axle Project makes nothing but thru axles, so I'd start there.

Hub widths

Hubs have different widths based on the type of bike, and front hubs are usually narrower than rear hubs. Hubs with quick-release skewers are generally 100mm wide in the front and 135mm wide in the rear. Thru axle widths vary by category:

	Road	Mountain Bike			Fat Bike
		Standard	Boost	Super Boost	
Front	12x100	15x100	15x110	15x110	15x150
Rear	12x142	12x142	12x148	12x157	12x177/197

All measurements are in millimeters. The 12mm and 15mm figures denote outside axle diameter.

The standard MTB axle width is rarely used any more except on the most basic of bikes or commuter e-bikes with MTB suspension forks. Most MTBs now use Boost spacing, and some more aggressive bikes use Super Boost spacing. The main benefit of Super Boost is that the wheels can be stiffer in the rear, but some require wider chainstays on the bike, which may increase heel rub as you pedal.

A few road bikes use a road-boost standard (110mm front, 148mm rear). Though rare, these are typically on heavier e-road bikes and bikepacking bikes that are often ridden fully loaded with gear. The benefit is a stiffer, stronger wheel to handle the weight, but fewer wheel options if you want to upgrade.

You may also find the occasional fat bike or cargo bike that uses a 135mm front axle spacing. Be sure to check your bike's specs if you're swapping hubs.

Spokes and nipples

Spokes are the long, thin metal bars connecting the hub to the rim, and as with every other part of the wheel, weight matters. Most spokes are made of steel, but you can find some made from titanium. Some high-end wheels use carbon fiber spokes, and Spinergy and Berd make composite "string" spokes made of high-strength fibers that are incredibly lightweight. Both of these are built into proprietary wheelsets, but you can modify some hubs to use Berd's spokes, if you don't mind voiding your hub's warranty.

Spokes come in round and bladed, or flat, shapes, and the latter is more aerodynamic. They're threaded on the end that inserts into the rim so that a wheelbuilder can thread a *nipple* — basically, a nut for the spoke bolt — and secure the spokes in place.

A spoke's thickness is called its *gauge*, and it can be straight gauge or butted:

» **Straight gauge** spokes have a uniform thickness from end to end. These are usually on basic bikes and heavy-duty touring or aggressive mountain bike wheels because they can be stronger or stiffer — but also heavier.

» **Butted spokes** change thickness from end to end. A double-butted spoke has thicker sections at the hub and rim, but the middle is thinner. For example, the diameter might taper from 2.0mm to 1.7mm to 2.0mm. A triple-butted spoke has different thicknesses at either end, say 2.0mm to 1.7mm to 1.8mm. Reducing the spokes' gauge saves weight, and butting allows them to keep more material at the ends and remove it where it's under less stress.

Most wheels use either j-bend or straight pull spokes (for a comparison, see Figure 5-12), and the difference is the shape of the spoke where it attaches to the hub. Both versions slide through a spoke hole on the hub's flange and have a flattened head to prevent it from pulling all the way through. The key difference is that J-bend spokes are bent at the ends (sort of in a 'J' shape), and straight pull spokes are straight with an end that looks like the head of a nail.

FIGURE 5-12:
Straight pull
(left) versus
j-bend spokes.

The act of wheel building is as much art as science, getting the right spoke tension, bracing angles, and choosing the correct spoke thickness. You could have identical rims and hubs, but a good wheelbuilder can make them perform quite differently using careful spoke selection and building.

A wheelbuilder also considers spoke count. Fewer spokes are lighter, but produce less laterally stiff wheels. Higher spoke counts are heavier, but make stronger wheels. Most wheels are laced with 24 to 32 spokes, but some heavy-duty wheels have 36 or even 48 spokes.

Most wheels are laced with the spokes reaching the rim in an alternating left-right sequence. But some brands, like Rolf Prima, uses a paired spoke pattern where spokes from the left and right sides of the hubs meet at almost the same point on the rim. This allows them to build lightweight wheels that are surprisingly stiff and strong, too, but they look different, and some cyclists prefer to let their bright neon team clothing (not their wheels) do the talking.

Bracing angle

In the earlier section, Hub widths, I mention that a wider hub often allows for a stiffer, stronger wheel, and here's why: It allows for a better bracing angle (see Figure 5-13).

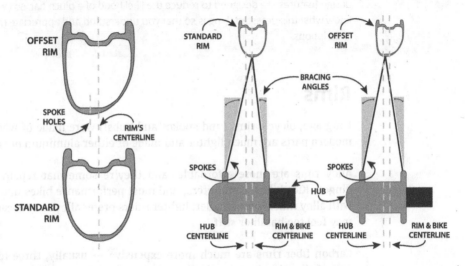

FIGURE 5-13: Bracing angle and rim offset.

The *bracing angle* is the angle of the spokes as they stretch from the hub to the rim. If the hub is wider, it has wider spoke flanges, and so the angle gets bigger. (Imagine a vertical line being 0 degrees, and the more the spokes lean toward the rim, the larger the angle becomes.)

Imagine standing up perfectly straight and someone trying to push you over. Now step one foot forward and brace yourself against your back leg — it would be much harder to push you over, right? It's the same with spokes — the more they're leaning in, the better they can resist lateral forces, so the stiffer the wheel will be. See notes at the end of this chapter for more fun facts and ways to improve bracing angles.

YIKES — A SNAKE BITE!

Before we dive into rims and tires, you need to know about snake bites, or pinch flats, which occur when you run into an object hard enough to compress the tire all the way to the rim.

When this happens, the tire's sidewall (and tube, if you have one) are pinched between the rim and the ground, often cutting two holes in the tube and/or sidewall and immediately letting all the air out of your tire. That's why it's called a pinch flat, and the two holes look like a snake bite.

The best way to prevent this problem is to keep your tires properly inflated — and not run into square-edged obstacles like curbs and rocks. As you'll see, some rim and tire design features are designed to reduce the likelihood of a pinch flat, so I want you to know what this detested thing is so that you understand and appreciate my descriptions.

Rims

Long ago, bicycle rims (and spokes and hubs!) were made of wood. Fortunately, modern parts are much lighter and made of either aluminum or carbon fiber.

Alloy rims are more affordable, and they're somewhat repairable if they get dinged. Kids bikes, commuters, and most performance bikes under $3,000 come with alloy rims. Some smaller, lighter riders prefer alloy rims because carbon rims may feel too harsh or stiff.

Carbon fiber rims are much more expensive — usually, three to five times the cost of alloy, but have much greater stiffness and strength-to-weight ratio. They also allow for a greater variety in rim shape profiles, or cross sections (see Figure 5-14), which has given us stiffer, tougher, more compliant, and more aerodynamic wheels.

Rim depths and widths

Rims typically provide two width measurements: internal and external (shown in Figure 5-15). For bikes with rim brakes, the external width is measured at the brake track to ensure it fits between the brake pads. That number doesn't matter for disc brake bikes, but the internal width as measured inside, between the bead walls, does matter, because it's the measurement that helps dictate proper tire fit. (You'll see how this all comes together in Figure 5-19, a chart with recommended rim-to-tire width combos.)

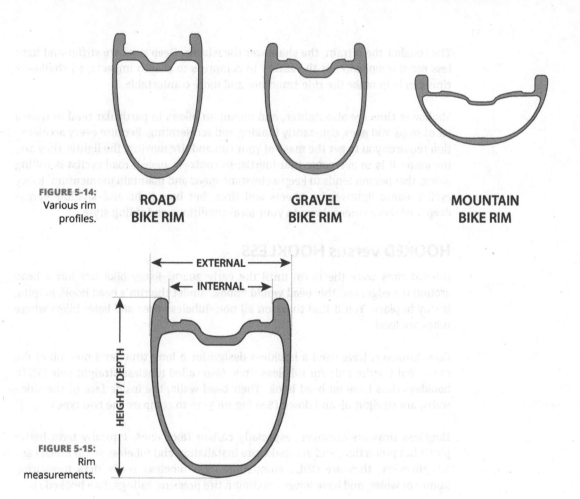

FIGURE 5-14: Various rim profiles.

ROAD BIKE RIM

GRAVEL BIKE RIM

MOUNTAIN BIKE RIM

EXTERNAL

INTERNAL

HEIGHT / DEPTH

FIGURE 5-15: Rim measurements.

The other measurement is *depth*. Before full carbon rims entered the picture, you rarely saw aerodynamic rims deeper than 55mm, because they required a lot of aluminum, which was heavy. Then some brands added carbon fiber fairings to shallow alloy rims to make aero wheels, but now they're pretty much all full carbon fiber.

Deeper rims are typically more aerodynamic, and most use an elliptical shape that makes the leading edge and trail edge similar when a tire is mounted on them, so that they're equally aerodynamic at the front and rear of the wheel.

Here are the common rim widths and depths for modern performance bikes:

>> **Road bikes:** 21mm to 24mm wide (internal), and 30mm to 80mm deep

>> **Gravel bikes:** 22mm to 26mm (internal), and 30mm to 50mm deep

>> **Mountain bikes:** 25mm to 32mm (internal), and 22mm to 30mm deep

The rougher the terrain, the shallower the wheels. Deep rims are stiffer and have less *radial compliance*, or the ability to compress to absorb impacts, so shallower rims can help make the ride smoother and more comfortable.

Shallower rims are also lighter, and mountain bikers in particular tend to have a lot of stops and goes, constantly braking and accelerating. Because every acceleration requires you to get the mass of your rim and tire moving, the lighter they are, the easier it is to overcome that inertia. In contrast, once a road cyclist is rolling along, that person tends to keep a constant speed and maintain momentum. Every cyclist wants lightweight wheels and tires, but how light-and-shallow versus deep-and-aero comes down to your local conditions and riding style.

HOOKED versus HOOKLESS

Hooked rims were the norm until the early 2020s. Every bike tire has a bead around the edge, and this bead would "hook" under the rim's bead hook, helping it stay in place. You'll find these on all non-tubeless tires and basic bikes where tubes are used.

Cars, however, have used a hookless design for a long time, and now bikes do, too — but they're only for tubeless tires. Also called tubeless straight side (TSS), hookless rims have no bead hook. Their bead walls, the inside face of the sidewalls, are straight up and down (See Figure 5-16 to compare the two types).

Hookless rims are stronger, especially carbon fiber ones, typically have better pinch flat protection, and are make tire installation and tubeless setup much easier. However, they are ONLY compatible with tubeless-ready tires measuring 26mm or wider, and have lower maximum tire pressure ratings than hooked rims!

FIGURE 5-16: ETRTO rim width to tire width recommendations.

HOOKED (CROTCHET) RIM

HOOKLESS (STRAIGHT SIDE) RIM

Wheel sizes

Wheel sizes employ a weird naming scheme: They are named for the approximate outside diameter of the tires installed on them, not the actual rim diameter. This strategy is helpful for determining the expected height of the wheel with the tire on it (because you won't ride it without a tire on it, right?) even if it does little to tell you the rim size.

Wheel sizes use a mix of imperial (inches) and metric (millimeters), and the metric ones have a letter after them (700c or 650b, for example). Let's start with the common options, and then I'll explain the numbers.

Here are the most common wheel sizes, by bike type:

>> **Kids:** 12, 14, 16, 18, 20, 24, and 26 inches

>> **BMX:** 18, 20, 24, 26, 27.5, and 29 inches

>> **Adult mountain:** 27.5 and 29 inches

>> **Adult road:** 650b, 700c

>> **Cruiser and commuter:** 26 inches, 650b / 27.5 inches, 700c / 29 inches

Road and gravel bikes are the only categories where metric sizes are the norm, and they're almost all 700c or 650b. The number 700 refers to a 700mm outside *tire* diameter (the rim's actual diameter is 622mm), and the c was part of an old, now obsolete a/b/c/d naming scheme that referred to width and slight variations in diameter based on the tires you wanted to use. This originated back when you had few options and you chose one of four widths. Nowadays, we specify rim and tire width in millimeters and have tons of options, but the 700c and 650b names have stuck.

So, if you say "road bike wheels," everyone assumes you mean 700c. The 650b size is for shorter riders on smaller bikes where 700c wheels/tires wouldn't fit or would create dangerous *wheel/toe overlap issues*, where your toe would be past the trailing edge of the front tire at the front of your pedal stroke.

The rest of the bikes, and the rest of the world (yep — a 20-inch bike is still a 20-inch bike in Europe, the UK, and elsewhere) use inches.

Tires (and Tubes)

Bicycle tires mostly come in three varieties — tube-type, tubeless-ready, and tubular — with lots of options and sizes for each. Let me run through these along with their construction terms and materials and some common terminology first, and then we'll get into sizes. Here's the scoop on tires:

>> **Tube-type:** Tube-type tires require an inner tube inside them to hold the air. You'll find these on most commonly available bikes. Typically, if you have a flat with one of these, you simply replace the tube and reinflate and then you're back in business. Just make sure to (carefully) feel around the inside of the tire to confirm that nothing sharp is left poking through to puncture your new tube, too.

>> **Tubeless-ready:** Tubeless-ready tires don't need inner tubes, but they do use a tire sealant to aid in air retention (see the nearby sidebar, "Tubeless tire sealant"). These tires typically use a little more rubber so that they're more airtight, which adds a bit of weight, but considering that you're not adding a 100g to 150g tube, they're lighter overall. Removing that extra friction between tire and inner tube also makes them more compliant and reduces rolling resistance, so they perform better, too.

>> **Tubular:** Tubular tires have the ends sewn together (which is why they're also sometimes called *sew-ups*) with the inner tube inside, forming a tube (or *tubular*), and are then glued onto a tubular road bike rim. These are typically used only by pros because they require more work, and if you have a flat, you're basically out of luck. Though they offer arguably superior performance, they're becoming more rare as modern tubeless-ready tires have matched or even exceeded tubular's performance while being much more user-friendly. As such, I'll leave it at that and recommend that you go with tubeless tires if you want the best performance.

Valve types

You put your pump on two common types of valves: Schrader and Presta (see Figure 5-17). Schrader is bigger and usually found on kids', commuter, and cruiser bikes. These valves are coated in rubber, and that keeps them snug inside the hole on the rim.

Performance bicycles have the thinner Presta valve stems, and almost every tubeless valve stem is Presta. Presta valves are metal (usually, steel or aluminum) and use a nut that threads onto them from the outside of the rim to keep it securely positioned on the rim (and not rattling around in their hole!). Most tubeless valve stems have a removeable core, the little part that depresses to let air in or out, to create an unrestricted airflow path, which makes setting up tubeless tires easier. (I tell you more about setup later in this chapter.)

 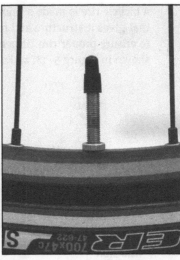

FIGURE 5-17:
Schrader (left) and Presta (right) valves.

TUBELESS TIRE SEALANT

Tubeless tire sealant is a liquid that you pour into your tubeless tires and serves two purposes:

- First, it coats the inside and creates an extra barrier layer to prevent air from leaking out through the tire's carcass.

- Second, it squirts out through any punctures and coagulates to seal the hole before the tire loses all its air.

Sometimes it works so well that you don't even notice and don't have to stop riding. At other times, it slows things down enough that you can stop and manually plug the hole before too much air escapes.

Most sealants are latex based, and some use added filler materials to help it clog a hole and seal it faster. A few tires are just tubeless rather than tubeless-ready. Though these do not require sealant to hold air, I still recommend adding sealant to plug any punctures.

The type of valve stem is dictated by the rims; less-expensive or basic rims typically have the larger Schrader-sized holes, and high-performance rims have smaller, Presta-sized holes.

Materials and terminology

A bicycle tire is made of more than just rubber with some tread. Inside is a casing that gives it structure and may add some flat protection, and all tires have a bead to ensure proper rim fitment. The common materials are assembled in layers, as shown in Figure 5-18, so let me show you what they do.

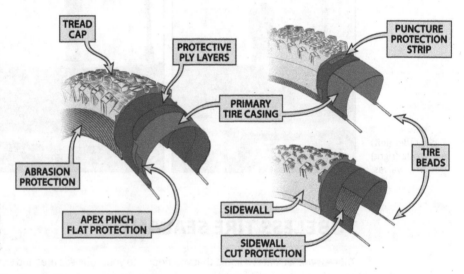

FIGURE 5-18: A typical performance tire casing construction.

Rubber

A bicycle tire's main material is rubber, and (for now) most brands are using natural rubber. The tires get their color from black carbon, which helps them last longer, too. Other ingredients are added to improve longevity and UV stability, and each brand has its secret formula to produce the desired *durometer*, or the hardness of the rubber.

A tire's durometer is largely responsible for how grippy it is, and also how long it lasts. A higher durometer rubber is stiffer, and a lower durometer means that it's softer. Typically, a softer rubber is more grippy because it can deform more easily to mold to the ground, but it wears out faster. Harder rubbers last longer, but don't grip as well.

TECHNICAL STUFF

Most bike tires range from 62a (soft) to 70a (firm) durometers. Some high-quality bike tires add silica, graphene, or other performance enhancers to enhance grip and durability, and some even make them slower to rebound, which further enhances traction and control.

Tread cap

The *tread cap* is the thicker section of rubber in the middle of the tire that has any tread on it. Even road bike tires with no apparent tread pattern have a tread cap, and even if it's perfectly smooth, it's likely 2mm to 5mm thicker there to help increase the tire's life span and reduce punctures.

Casing

Most bicycle tires use a nylon casing under the rubber to help keep it all together and prevent it from stretching out of shape. It's usually a woven material — commonly, with 30, 60, or 120 threads per inch (TPI). Lower TPI casings are a little heavier and stiffer, but they're tougher, so you'll find these on basic bike tires and some aggressive MTB tires.

Higher TPI casings are lighter and more supple, but can tear and puncture more easily. Road, gravel, fat bike, and XC mountain bike riders like a more supple tire because those bikes have less suspension to soak up the small bumps, and that softer casing molds to the shape of the ground more easily. Some top models and pro-only tires can be 170–200 TPI, and they're amazing, but also quite expensive and not as durable.

Some very-high-end road bike tires also use cotton casings, which are softer and more supple than nylon for a supremely smooth-riding tire. They're less durable, though, because cotton isn't as tough as nylon. If you want the best ride quality, a 320 TPI cotton casing tire is simply amazing.

Breaker

Some tires add a Kevlar, aramid, and/or extra nylon breaker layer on top of the casing. Sometimes the extra layers are on the sidewalls for better cut protection from sharp rocks. Others are under the tread cap to protect against punctures from thorns, rocks, nails, screws, glass, and other culprits. And, some tires combine those qualities to create tough mountain bike tires or highly puncture-resistant commuter bike tires.

Bead

The *bead* is a wire or thin Kevlar rope that runs around both ends of the tire. Cheap tires have a heavy metal wire bead, and performance tires have a lightweight, folding Kevlar bead. Both are there to do the same thing — prevent the tire's circumference from changing where it meets the rim. This is critical to having a safe, standardized interface between tire and rim, and it's what keeps the tire securely on the rim.

Apex

Wrapped around the bead might be a bit of extra rubber or dense foam called the *apex*. If you hit something hard enough to flatten the tire's sidewall against the rim, the apex acts like a cushion against pinch flats and snake bites — hopefully, preventing the sidewall (and tube) from being cut by the rim's edge.

Treads and siping

Tires range from smooth-as-a-baby's-behind to extremely knobby. Tread *blocks* are the bumps of tread sticking up from the tire, and each block is a knob. So a *knobby* tire is one with lots of tread, but it's also a colloquialism for any mountain bike tire.

Treads have various shapes and names (shown in Figure 5-19). The following list should help you discern which is best for your terrain and type of riding:

FIGURE 5-19: of treads, from left to right: sipes, file tread, semi-knob, and knobby.

>> **Sipes:** On road bike tires, sipes are small grooves in the rubber that help evacuate water so that you don't lose grip when riding in the rain or through a puddle. On knobbier tires, sipes are tiny slits in the knobs that allow each individual knob to squirm in a particular direction. This gives tire

manufacturers the ability to fine-tune performance beyond just tread block shape, size, and height.

» **File tread:** A file tread looks like an exaggerated woodshop file, with small, raised diamond- or pyramid-shaped nubs. Most brands using this tread place it in the center, with slightly smaller knobs on the edges for better cornering grip.

» **Semi-knob:** A step up from file tread, semi-knob tires have small, low-profile (short) knobs on them. They provide more grip but still roll quickly. For dry, hardpack terrain, this is a useful option. These, too, often put slightly bigger, taller knobs on the edges to improve cornering grip.

» **Knobby:** Most mountain bike tires are full knobbies, with bigger, taller knobs all over. Knob height, size, and shape vary by intended use. Generally, the center knobs are a bit smaller to squirm and deform around the terrain for maximum grip. Side knobs, also called shoulder knobs, are usually bigger and may run deeper onto the sidewall for better structural support to hold your line when leaning the bike way over in a corner.

Some tires use medium-size transition knobs between the center and shoulder sections to progressively increase grip as you lean the tire into a corner. Other tires leave a clear gap between center and shoulder knobs, which (theoretically) gives you a tangible indication of when you're reaching the limits of traction. Personally, I don't like the micro slip that comes during the transition from straight to cornering, but some riders do.

» **Mud spikes:** At the extreme end of knobby tires are mud tires, which use tall spikes of rubber to poke through the mud to grab firmer ground underneath. These spikes are widely spaced so that mud and crud can quickly fly off the tire and so that the tread doesn't get caked up with mud and lose its ability to grip.

You'll find a similar strategy of wider knob spacing on some all-conditions trail tires, which is a great choice if you ride in areas prone to mud and slop.

Sizes and widths

Another thing you need to know is tire size, and, as with rims, you have a mix of inches and millimeters. When listed in metric dimensions, their naming scheme is based on rim diameters, too, which can add a bit of confusion because wheel sizes are named for tire sizes. Honestly, it's kinda weird, but that's the way it is.

HOW TO SET UP A TUBELESS TIRE

Tubeless tires create a seal on the rim by securely locking the tire's bead into a shelf on the rim. Whether your rim is hooked or hookless, it usually has a small, flat shelf leading up to the bead wall.

As you inflate your tire for the first time, you'll hear it pop (and I do mean pop!) into place. That sometimes-quite-loud sound is the bead snapping onto the shelf. Even if you get a flat and lose all of your tire's air, the tire's bead tends to stay locked onto that shelf. If you can plug the hole, reinflating the tire is quick and easy.

Sometimes, though, it takes a bit of work to get those tires to seat and seal. Some people use air compressors to blast a lot of air in at once. Others use Booster floor pumps, which let you inflate a secondary chamber to about 160psi and then release it all at once into the tire to pop it into place.

If neither of those options works after several tries, you may just need to put a tube in there and inflate it to pop the tire onto the rim. Leave it inflated like that overnight to help mold the tire to that shape, and then deflate and remove *only one* side of the tire from the rim so that you can pull the tube out and then add sealant and reinflate.

Road and gravel tire sizing

For road and gravel bikes, tires are usually measured in millimeters, and you'll often find the size listed after the wheel size. For example, a "700c x 28mm" would be a tire that's 28mm wide designed for a 700c wheel.

However, on the tire's sidewall, you may also see the numbers 28–622, which is technically accurate because it's a tire that's 28mm wide designed to fit a 622mm diameter rim.

Mountain bike tire sizing

Mountain bike tires are often listed in both inches and millimeters. In the United States, people often refer to them in inches, but where the metric system is more prevalent, some riders are more familiar with millimeters. So most mountain bike tires will have both measurements specified on the sidewall. For example, a 29 x 2.4" tire will likely also have 61–622 stamped on it.

MY TIRES DON'T MEASURE THE SAME AS THEIR SPEC!

Though tire and rim manufacturers follow certain standards for bead seat diameter and rim wall height to make products easily work together, there is no standard rim width. The International Standards Organization (ISO) has ranges of recommended rim widths for ranges of tire widths, but they are just that — ranges and recommendations, not standards.

So, if you mount a tire that's 28mm wide on a rim with a 21mm internal width, it will measure narrower than if you mount it on a rim with a 24mm internal width.

And, every tire manufacturer makes tires differently, so one brand's 28mm may measure 27mm while another brand's is 29mm after you mount and inflate them. When choosing a tire, keep in mind that its actual width will vary, so it's a good idea to check some reviews on the brand's website or online retailers to see what others have experienced. Then pay it forward with a review of your own to help others in the future!

Other bikes' tire sizing

Other types of bikes, from kids' bikes to commuters to cruisers, use one or both of the naming schemes I mention here.

Typical tire widths by bike type

Tire widths cover a huge range. I mention some specific recommendations and common sizes for each type in Chapter 7, and Figure 5-20 shows the ETRTO's official recommendations, but here's a basic range for each main bike category:

>> **Road:** 23mm to 35mm

>> **Gravel:** 38mm to 50mm

>> **Mountain:** 2.0 inches to 3.0 inches

>> **eMTB:** 2.4 inches to 2.8 inches

>> **Fat:** 4.0 inches to 5.0 inches

>> **Commuter:** 35mm to 50mm, or 1.5 inches to 2.4 inches

RECOMMENDED TIRE SIZES BY RIM WIDTH

INTERNAL RIM WIDTH (mm)

TIRE WIDTH (mm)	15	16	17	18	19	20	21	22	23	24	25	26	27	28	29	30-31	32-33	34-37	38-40	41-45	46-50	51-64	65-71	72-78	79-83	84-89	90-96	97-100
20-21	✓	✓	✓	✗	✗	✗	✗	✗	✗	✗	✗	✗	✗	✗	✗	✗	✗	✗	✗	✗	✗	✗	✗	✗	✗	✗	✗	✗
22-24	✓	✓	✓	✓	✓	✗	✗	✗	✗	✗	✗	✗	✗	✗	✗	✗	✗	✗	✗	✗	✗	✗	✗	✗	✗	✗	✗	✗
25-27	✓	✓	✓	✓	✓	✓	✓	✓	✓	✓	✗	✗	✗	✗	✗	✗	✗	✗	✗	✗	✗	✗	✗	✗	✗	✗	✗	✗
28-34	✓	✓	✓	✓	✓	✓	✓	✓	✗	✗	✗	✗	✗	✗	✗	✗	✗	✗	✗	✗	✗	✗	✗	✗	✗	✗	✗	✗
35-39	✓	✓	✓	✓	✓	✓	✓	✓	✓	✓	✓	✓	✓	✗	✗	✗	✗	✗	✗	✗	✗	✗	✗	✗	✗	✗	✗	✗
40-46	✗	✗	✓	✓	✓	✓	✓	✓	✓	✓	✓	✓	✓	✓	✗	✗	✗	✗	✗	✗	✗	✗	✗	✗	✗	✗	✗	✗
47-54	✗	✗	✗	✗	✓	✓	✓	✓	✓	✓	✓	✓	✓	✓	✓	✓	✓	✗	✗	✗	✗	✗	✗	✗	✗	✗	✗	✗
55-57	✗	✗	✗	✗	✗	✓	✓	✓	✓	✓	✓	✓	✓	✓	✓	✓	✓	✗	✗	✗	✗	✗	✗	✗	✗	✗	✗	✗
58-63	✗	✗	✗	✗	✗	✓	✓	✓	✓	✓	✓	✓	✓	✓	✓	✓	✓	✓	✗	✗	✗	✗	✗	✗	✗	✗	✗	✗
64-65	✗	✗	✗	✗	✗	✗	✗	✓	✓	✓	✓	✓	✓	✓	✓	✓	✓	✓	✓	✗	✗	✗	✗	✗	✗	✗	✗	✗
66-71	✗	✗	✗	✗	✗	✗	✗	✗	✓	✓	✓	✓	✓	✓	✓	✓	✓	✓	✓	✓	✗	✗	✗	✗	✗	✗	✗	✗
72-83	✗	✗	✗	✗	✗	✗	✗	✗	✗	✓	✓	✓	✓	✓	✓	✓	✓	✓	✓	✓	✓	✗	✗	✗	✗	✗	✗	✗
84-99	✗	✗	✗	✗	✗	✗	✗	✗	✗	✗	✗	✗	✓	✓	✓	✓	✓	✓	✓	✓	✓	✓	✗	✗	✗	✗	✗	✗
100-113	✗	✗	✗	✗	✗	✗	✗	✗	✗	✗	✗	✗	✗	✗	✗	✗	✗	✗	✓	✓	✓	✓	✓	✓	✓	✗	✗	✗
114-132	✗	✗	✗	✗	✗	✗	✗	✗	✗	✗	✗	✗	✗	✗	✗	✗	✗	✗	✗	✓	✓	✓	✓	✓	✓	✓	✓	✓

FIGURE 5-20: ETRTO rim width to tire width recommendations.

Wider tires: The better choice

Around 2019, as road-tubeless gained mainstream acceptance and brands embraced it by launching more and better products, wider rims and tires also showed up. For decades, roadies swore by 19–23mm tires pumped up to 100–110psi, but road-tubeless ushered in the wider-tire, lower-pressure era of improved comfort, better traction, and reduced rolling resistance. Now, most riders are running 25mm tires as the narrowest, and many are on 28–32mm tires — some even at 35mm wide!

Mountain bikers, meanwhile, have always liked wide tires, and in the mid-2010s, the bike world got a little carried away with 2.8 to 3.0-inch-wide Plus-sized tires, even putting 2.6-inch tires on some kids' bikes. What everyone quickly realized was that the extra weight of all that rubber sucked out some of the enjoyment, though it did shift most riders from 2.0- to 2.2-inch tires up to 2.25- to 2.4-inch tires, with more aggressive riders and eMTBs using 2.5- to 2.6-inch tires.

Gravel bikes run a wide gamut, depending on the scenario. Racers want lighter weight and may experiment with a size as narrow as 38mm, but mostly running 40–42mm tires for normal courses. When the route gets rough, most riders find that a 45mm tire is the perfect balance between weight, comfort, grip, and performance. For gnarly courses, desert sand riding, or bikepacking trips, you may want 50–55mm tires (if they'll fit in your bike) to smooth out the ride.

TIP

For more information about brake pads, rims, and tires, visit Dummies.com/go/bikingfd.

» **Shifting through drivetrain options and how they work together**

» **Cranking away at the various standards**

» **Spinning the bearings**

Chapter **6**

Drivetrains

This chapter covers the parts of the bike that you pedal and shift. They're the parts that turn your leg motion into forward motion, from the pedals and crankset, through the chain and derailleurs, to the gears on the cassette.

I dive deep into drivetrains because, well, they have (literally) a lot of moving parts. They're complex, and knowing how all the parts work together (or don't) is helpful when deciding what type you want on your next bike. It also helps you troubleshoot when something goes wrong. And, when it's time to upgrade, it's helpful to know what makes some parts better (or, at least, more expensive) than others and where it makes the most sense to spend a little more.

With all of that said, most of this discussion enters the realm of advanced nuance. If you just want to hop on and pedal, that's fine. Think of this chapter as a reference for when you want to learn how drivetrains work and which details matter for advanced bike fit, performance, and upgrades. If you just want to see the bikes, skip ahead to Chapter 7, and then come back to this one when you fall in love with biking completely and want to geek out on the details.

A bicycle *drivetrain* consists of the parts that turn your pedal strokes into forward motion and the shifters that control gear selection.

Here's a list of the common parts of the drivetrain (displayed in Figure 6-1):

>> Crankset and crank arms

>> Bottom bracket (sometimes abbreviated as BB)

>> Chainrings

>> Chain

>> Cassette (possibly freewheel, or single cog)

>> Derailleurs

>> Shifters

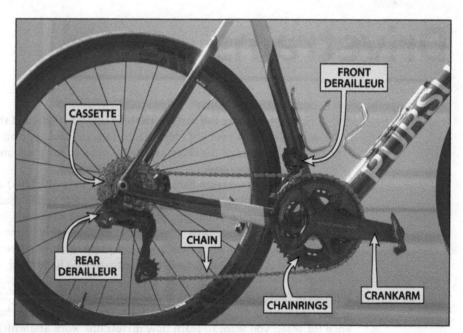

FIGURE 6-1:
The main
components of a
bicycle drivetrain.

First Things First: Systems versus Components

Ready to learn about the parts of a drivetrain? Sorry — I need to compare systems with components first because that's the world we live in now. Don't worry if these next couple of paragraphs use words you're not familiar with — the point here is to give you a top-level understanding of how modern drivetrains do and don't work together. Trust me: This knowledge will come in handy throughout the rest of this chapter.

Most modern drivetrains from the big three manufacturers (Shimano, SRAM, and Campagnolo) and the smaller players (MicroSHIFT, SunTour, TRP) are now designed and sold as complete *systems* that are optimized to work best together.

From the middle tier and up, all three major brands are focusing on wireless or semi-wireless electronically shifting groups, where the shifter levers are completely untethered and the derailleurs either have their own individual batteries (SRAM, Campagnolo) or are connected to a main battery (Shimano).

Each brand uses its own wireless communication protocol, so there's no mixing of brands, but you can mostly mix parts from the *same* brand to build a system to your liking.

Most bikes in the middle tier and higher now use hydraulic disc brakes. On road and gravel bikes (any model with a curved drop-bar-style handlebar), this means the brake's lever, master cylinder, and hose are combined with a shifter lever into a single part. Sometimes called a brifter (because it's a *brake-lever-and-shifter* combination — get it?), it basically means you're stuck using whatever brakes come supplied with that lever.

Crankset

The crank*set* (see Figure 6-2) is a unit that combines the crank arms and the chainring (or chainrings). Some units are sold together or, more often at the high end, separately, allowing you to choose arm length and chainring sizes independently. The three main terms you need to know in order to talk about crank arms are material, spindle diameter, and arm length, all described next.

Crank arm material

Crank arms typically come in aluminum (or *alloy*) or carbon fiber, with some cheap bikes and BMX bikes sporting steel ones. Some boutique manufacturers make titanium cranksets, too.

Carbon fiber crank arms are typically lighter and stiffer but also more expensive. Alloy crank arms are tougher and run the gamut from entry-level to high-end, with the best ones nearly rivaling carbon's weight and stiffness.

FIGURE 6-2:
A typical road
bike crankset.

The spindle

The *spindle* is the tube connecting the left- and right-side crank arms to each other. Most brands permanently fix the spindle to one arm or the other, but a few (like some from Race Face, Rotor, and BMX "three piece" cranks) are completely modular systems that let you attach each arm separately. Spindle diameters are now mostly 24mm, 30mm, and something called DUB. These are explained along with bottom brackets later in this chapter.

Spindles come in different widths and diameters, with the width dictated mostly by the frame's bottom bracket width. Road bikes have the narrowest bottom bracket shells, and thus the narrowest spindles and cranksets. Mountain bikes get a little wider, mainly to make room for bigger tires, and fat bikes have the widest. Gravel bikes vary from brand to brand, using either road or MTB widths.

Crank arm length

The *crank arm length* is usually determined by rider height or, more specifically, femur length. Common sizes range from 165mm to 177.5mm for adults, and from 140mm to 155mm for kids' and youth bikes. Most adult bikes come with 170mm–175mm arms, depending on frame size, but most e-bikes come with shorter 165mm crank arms. Why? Because, with a motor assisting you, you don't need as much leverage and crank-to-ground clearance becomes more important. But when it's all you, longer crank arms give you more leverage to help you drive the pedals downward more easily, which can be helpful on climbs and sprints.

However, many riders are switching to shorter crank arms because they reduce the total circumference of your pedal stroke, and thus also decrease the total vertical distance your foot travels up and down on each rotation. The effect is that it feels like you're spinning more easily, but it can also (perhaps counterintuitively) help you stay in a more powerful sweet spot of leg extension.

TECHNICAL STUFF

Stand up and squat halfway down, stopping when your knees have a 90-degree bend, and then jump up quickly. Now squat half as far and jump back up. The second one felt easier, right? That's because most of us are stronger near that end range (top half) of a squat, so if you don't have to bend your legs as much with each pedal stroke (which is what happens with shorter crank arms), you'll stay in a more powerful zone of leg extension. True, you'll have less leverage, but unless you're trying to maximize every possible watt for racing, shorter cranks will likely feel better and easier in most situations.

Despite all that, it's nuance. If you're just getting started, whatever crank arm length comes supplied on your bike will work just fine.

Bottom Bracket

The *bottom bracket*, or just *BB*, is the part that holds the bearings that your crankset's spindle spins on. It mounts into the frame's aptly named bottom bracket shell, and there are several BB standards and measurements worth knowing about.

Older bikes, low-end bikes, and kids' bikes often have a bottom bracket that has the spindle built into it, and the cranks simply bolt onto it. The original design was called a *square taper* BB (see Figure 6-3) because it had square-shaped prongs that would taper slightly so that the cranks would fit more tightly on them as you tightened their mounting bolts.

You'll still find these items on inexpensive bikes and kids' bikes, and they work perfectly fine for those applications. In 2000, bottom brackets switched to a larger axle design with the unfortunate name of ISIS, and Shimano introduced a similar standard called Octalink. Both improved the crank arm-to-bottom bracket interface, but their larger spindles meant smaller bearings, and both designs suffered from extremely poor reliability.

FIGURE 6-3:
You can see – from left to right – square, taper, Octalink, and ISIS bottom brackets.

That poor reliability led to a new, spindle-less design and the four primary standards used today on every performance bicycle:

>> Threaded bottom brackets

>> Outboard bearings

>> PressFit bottom brackets

>> 30mm spindles

Figure 6-4 shows a threaded outboard and PressFit bottom brackets.

FIGURE 6-4:
Threaded Outboard (left) and PressFit (right) bottom brackets.

Outboard bearing BBs use an oversized housing on either side of the frame's BB shell to fit much larger bearings, with this added benefit: Their wider stance offers better support to the crankset and created a stiffer system.

Because outboard BBs don't contain the axle that the cranks spin on, the spindle was added to the crankset and made those stiffer. Overall, this combo was a dramatic improvement in performance and durability, all built around 24mm spindles.

Then came 30mm spindles. Figure 6-5 shows the difference between 24mm and 30mm spindles. These required new BB standards to fit the larger bearings necessary to fit around these larger spindles. Some of the early designs weren't great. Others were good but never really went mainstream (I'm looking at you, BB386EVO). DUB is a newer standard that's 28.99mm in diameter. If that seems really close to 30mm, it is, but as you'll soon learn, every millimeter counts with bearing size.

FIGURE 6-5:
The 24mm versus 30mm spindles, both shown on modern cranksets with integrated spindles.

The two that stuck and work across a wide variety of frames are PressFit (refer to Figure 6-4) — which is a *design* standard rather than a *size* standard — and threaded bottom brackets — which now have a larger standard called T47 that fits modern 30mm spindles. These are the two main BB standards now found on performance bicycles. So, what's the difference between them?

PressFit bottom brackets (PFBBs) are bearings captured inside a nylon cup that's pressed into the frame. Some designs use sleeves that thread together to create a single unit to improve bearing alignment. Threaded bottom brackets screw into threaded metal inserts in the frame. These typically last longer and are easier to install and replace, but are a little heavier overall.

Two last tidbits about bottom brackets you should know: bearing material and bottom bracket width.

I touch on bearing material later in this chapter because bearings affect every part of your bike that spins, from cranks to pedals to wheels to derailleur pulleys — even the headset that connects the fork to the frame.

The width of your bike's bottom bracket is about the width of your frame's BB shell, which varies based on the type of bike you have and how wide the tires are that will typically fit into it. Honestly, this is a confusing rabbit hole, and it's a lot easier just to ask your shop's personnel for the right standard when it comes time to replace or upgrade. Basically, BB shells get wider along this spectrum:

Road/Gravel (68-86mm) < MTB (73-92mm) < Fat Bike (100-121mm)

However, there are exceptions for these width ranges, too. Even seasoned industry veterans still have to look at charts and graphs to order the right part, so there's no shame in just asking someone at the shop.

For non-performance categories like cruisers, commuters, and kids' bikes, most of them use a standard 68mm BB shell, but it's still worth asking.

Chainring

The chainring drives the chain forward, and it comes in a wide variety of sizes, shapes, and quantities. As simple as the chainring may look, it has a lot going on.

Modern chainrings come in two varieties: direct mount and spider mount, shown in Figure 6-6.

FIGURE 6-6:
Spider chainring (left) versus direct mount chainring (right).

CHAINRING QUANTITIES AND SPEEDS

Modern bikes have mostly done away with *triples*, which are cranksets with three chainrings, because they're heavy and they rarely shift well.

Nowadays, most road bikes have *doubles*, with two chainrings, also referred to as 2x (pronounced "two by"), and sometimes combined with the number of gears in the rear. So, a 2x11 ("two by eleven") would have two chainrings and an 11-speed cassette, for a total of 22 gears.

You may remember when a 21-speed bicycle was a big deal. In the 1980s and '90s, bikes were combining a triple chainring with a 7-speed cassette (3x7), yielding 21 distinct gear combinations, or "21 speeds."

Though road bikes switched from triples to doubles long ago, mountain bikes held on to them until the late-2000s, when 2x drivetrains became popular. Then, in 2016, the first official 1x ("one by") MTB drivetrain launched and quickly became the default standard. Now it's almost impossible to find a mountain bike over $500 with anything but a 1x.

Many mountain bikes now have 1x12 drivetrains, making them "12-speeds," with low and mid-tier models getting 1x9, 1x10, and 1x11 options. This may sound like a down-grade from 21 speeds, but as you'll see when we get to cassettes later in this chapter, modern wide-range cassettes offer a better total gear range in a lighter, simpler, better performing design.

The spider is a set of smaller "arms" that mount behind or are attached to the drive side crank arm (it's arms on arms — confusing, I know), and the chainring(s) bolt to spider. Various bolt patterns exist, referred to as the bolt circle diameter (BCD), or the diameter of a circle passing through the center of the bolt mounting holes. The most common standards are 110BCD and 104BCD.

Many modern cranksets now use direct mount (DM) chainrings, meaning the chainring(s) and spider are a single piece that mounts directly to the crank arm. This simplifies installation, is less likely to have bolts work loose, and can create an overall lighter, stiffer system. But there are a lot of different interface standards, as you can see in Figure 6-7.

The chainrings' shift quality is largely determined by the amount of tooth shaping, ramping, and pinning they have — basically, the attention to detail. Cheap bikes come with cheap stamped-steel chainrings with basic tooth shaping. Higher-end ones are forged and CNC-machined out of lightweight aluminum to achieve precise tooth profiles, with ramps and pins on the back to guide and carry the chain upward for smooth, effortless upshifts and well-timed downshifts. Premium chainrings are also stiffer and have special surface treatments to improve durability.

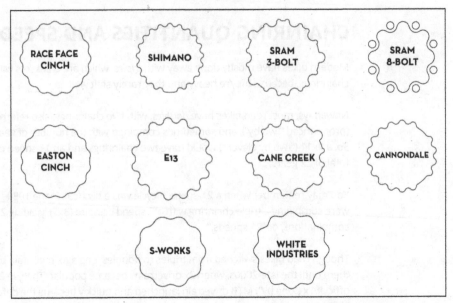

FIGURE 6-7:
Most of the
different
direct-mount
standards for
chainrings.

RACE FACE CINCH

SHIMANO

SRAM 3-BOLT

SRAM 8-BOLT

EASTON CINCH

E13

CANE CREEK

CANNONDALE

S-WORKS

WHITE INDUSTRIES

Courtesy of Wolf Tooth Components.

Narrow-wide chainrings

The advent of 1x drivetrains, which don't need a front derailleur, created a new issue with chain retention. As clunky as front derailleurs were on mountain bikes, they did help keep the chain from bouncing off the chainring, which always happened at the worst possible time.

So brands created *narrow-wide chainrings*, which have chainring teeth with alternating narrow and wide profiles that precisely slot into the alternating narrower or wider gaps between chain links. By filling that space more completely, the chain has a harder time bouncing off. Combined with a clutch on most rear derailleurs (explained a little later in this chapter), it's an effective chain management method for most riding short of extremely aggressive mountain biking, where riders will often add a chain guide over the top of the chainring.

All chainrings have a certain offset to achieve an ideal chainline, which is illustrated in Figure 6-8. This keeps the chain as straight as possible as it moves through the gears, minimizing noise, friction, and wear. This is achieved by matching the correct chain offset with your bottom bracket width, hub width, and drivetrain type. Honestly, it would take pages to explain all the options, so it's best to just check with your local bike shop to ensure you're getting the right part.

Chainrings are usually round, but there are also ovalized designs that can improve pedaling efficiency by maximizing your leverage where you're strongest.

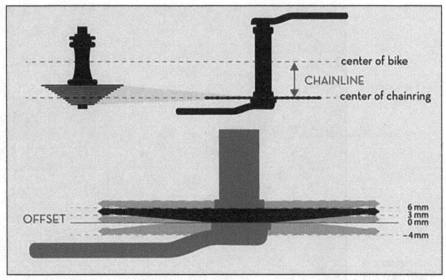

center of bike

CHAINLINE

center of chainring

OFFSET

6 mm
3 mm
0 mm
–4 mm

FIGURE 6-8:
An example of
chain line and
chainring offsets.

When it comes to gearing, the larger the chainrings, the faster you can go, but the harder they are to pedal, so riders typically pair chainring size(s) with a cassette size (explained in the section Cassette (or freewheel) below) that lets them stay in the bottom two-thirds of the cassette for most riding, saving the bigger, easier gears for the climbs!

Chain

The chain (refer to Figure 6-9) connects the chainrings to the cassette, looping through the derailleur(s). Though it looks simple, the inside and outside of the links are all shaped to help it glide up and down a cassette and to shift gears smoothly and reliably. To a point, the more expensive the chain, the smoother and quieter it is. After that, you're paying for a lighter-weight chain with better surface treatment.

The visible links are the inner and outer plates, which are connected by pins, which are surrounded by rollers. The rollers are the round gizmos you see between the links, and they're what nestle into the dips between the teeth on the chainrings and cassettes.

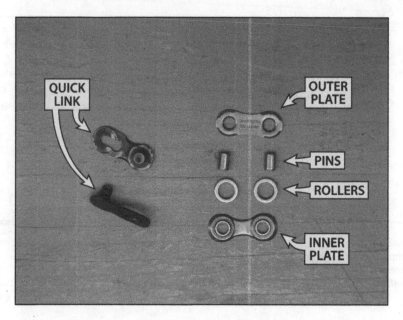

FIGURE 6-9:
Chain parts and
a quick link.

Chains are made of steel, and, depending on the quality of the chain, may have different surface treatments to make them smoother or more rust-resistant. Higher-end chains may have hollow pins and/or holes stamped out of the outer links to save weight.

Most mid- to high-end chains now use quick links to connect them, which allow you to break the chain apart and reconnect it without tools (though quick link pliers make it much easier). This makes it easier to degrease the chain off the bike for proper cleanings, but you should know that all chain brands consider these quick links to be single-use items. Personally, I reuse them multiple times (as does everyone I know). You do you. Either way, it's a great idea to keep a spare in your toolkit in case you break a chain while you're out on a ride.

WARNING

Chains are designed specifically for the number of "speeds" of your drivetrain, so only put a 12-speed chain on a 12-speed group, for example. And make sure your spare quick link is the same brand and speed as your chain, too!

Cassette (or freewheel)

The *cassette* is the cluster of cogs, or gears, sitting on the rear wheel's hub. Some teeth are shaped to help move the chain onto or off of a cog whenever you shift, so you'll notice that some teeth look different from others on the same cog.

Freewheels and cassettes can range from 6 to 13 speeds, with kids' bikes and entry level adult bikes usually having 6, 7 or 8 speed freewheels and modern road, gravel, and mountain bikes having up to 12 speed cassettes. The move from 11 to 12 speeds on these three categories started around 2016 and finished in late 2023, so if you're shopping used, you will still see nice bikes with 11-speed groups.

The last main thing you should know about the cassette is its *range*, or the spread from the smallest cog to the largest.

Most road bikes have a narrow range cassette, often ranging from a 10- or 11-tooth small cog up to a 23- to 32-tooth large cog. The narrower the spread, the closer the *gear steps*, or tooth count differences from cog to cog. For example, on a narrow range 12-speed cassette, the tooth counts might look like this:

11-12-13-14-15-16-17-19-21-23-25-27

The example above would be called an 11–27 cassette, because we use the smallest and largest cogs to name them. Figure 6-10 shows narrow- versus wide-range cassettes. Notice how the first seven cogs have one-tooth jumps. This means there's minimal difference between them, which helps riders keep their cadence similar from one gear to the next, which is more important on the smaller half of the cassette.

FIGURE 6-10: Narrow- versus wide-range cassettes.

Why? Because you're usually shifting into the bigger (easier) cogs when you're climbing, so getting to an easier gear is more important than maintaining the ideal cadence. But most riders have a specific cadence at which they're most efficient, so the better they can maintain it, the better they can ride. Despite that, you usually choose the cassette based on the lowest (easiest) gear you need for whatever climbing you're doing, because no one wants to painfully grind uphill in a too-hard gear.

Mountain bike cassettes have a much wider range. Most modern MTB cassettes have 10-50, 10-51, and 10-52 spreads. Gravel bike cassettes often range from 10-36 up to 10-45, depending on whether they have 1x or 2x cranksets.

Gravel bikes sit somewhere in the middle — bikes with a 2x crankset have a narrower range (like a 10-36) cassette, and 1x bikes have a 10-42 to 10-45 — unless they have a *mullet* build, which pairs a gravel-size chainring with a mountain-bike-size cassette. This is a popular setup for riders tackling big mountain roads with steep, chunky climbs and singletrack adventures.

Derailleur

The *derailleur* is the gizmo attached to the frame that the chain rolls through. As you click the shifter, the derailleur moves to guide the chain from one cog or chainring to the next.

Front derailleurs are simple because they're only shifting between two, maybe three, chainrings by moving a cage to guide the chain from one chainring to the next. Regardless of chainring size, their designs are quite similar across all brands.

Rear derailleurs (see Figure 6-11) have more varied designs to accommodate the wider range of cassette sizes. The bigger the cassette, the more chain you need. So, especially on mountain bike derailleurs, you'll find longer pulley cages with offset upper pulleys to give it the room it needs to articulate across a wider arc. A clutch-type mechanism prevents that long pulley cage from bouncing forward when you hit a big bump, which could cause your chain to come loose.

Some modern mountain bike derailleurs now use a direct-mount design that attaches directly to the rear axle and frame, offering improved alignment with the cassette and a much stronger part.

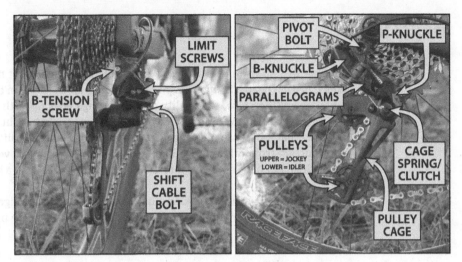

FIGURE 6-11:
The rear
derailleur's parts.

Shifter

The last pieces of the drivetrain puzzle are *shifters,* which are used to change gears. These come in two main variations — levers and triggers — but with the growth of electronic shifting, you can add paddles and buttons to that list.

Originally, bikes shifted with mechanical levers physically attached to the chain. Modern shifters came about with small levers on the downtube. These friction shifters, so called because there was enough friction in their pivot to hold them in place after you moved them, pulled or released a cable attached to the derailleur. Eventually, these switched to indexed shifters, which had individual clicks to indicate each gear, making shifting much easier and more precise.

Nowadays, almost every flat bar bike (one with flat handlebars) with a mechanical drivetrain uses a *trigger shifter.* It's usually a combination of a paddle and a small trigger mounted under the bar — the paddle pulls the cable to shift to a larger gear and the trigger releases the cable, letting the derailleur shift to a smaller gear.

Drop bar shifters (like those on road and gravel bikes) work in a similar fashion, relying on ratchets, levers, and paddles built into the brake levers to pull and release the cable.

Bearings

Anything that spins on the bike is spinning on bearings — that means the hubs, cranks, pedals, headset, and little pulleys hanging off the bottom of the derailleur. As with everything else, the quality of the bearings goes up with the price of the bike, but most bikes (even *very* expensive ones) stop somewhere in the midrange of bearings. That's because midrange bearings are *good,* and the differences in friction reduction from midrange to high-end to ultra-premium is very low in terms of total drag. But before we dive into that topic, let's look at what a bearing really is.

The term *bearing* usually refers to a unit called a sealed cartridge bearing (SCB), but can also refer to an angular contact bearing (ACB). Both are made up of these five parts:

- » **Bearings:** The little round balls
- » **Races:** The inner and outer surfaces that the balls roll on
- » **Seals:** The things you see on the side that keep crud out and grease in
- » **Grease:** A type that varies by use case and quality of bearing
- » **Retainer:** A plastic retainer that keeps the balls spaced apart evenly

The balls and races are usually made of steel, with higher-end models using harder and/or higher-quality steel used for both. The harder the steel is, the less likely they are to pit or deform or wear out, and better-quality metals won't corrode or rust — or at least not as easily. Some, like Enduro's XD15 nitrogen-infused stainless steel, are virtually impervious to everything.

Ceramic bearings also have grades. However, when it comes to bicycle parts, they're all extremely hard and smooth, so they roll well with virtually no drag — *when they're new.* How long they maintain that feeling and their durability are determined more by the race's material and how well they're protected from outside elements. If a little dust or dirt gets in there or the race's metal is dramatically softer than the ceramic material, they can wear down the race and things will start to feel sloppy even if the ceramic balls are still perfect.

It turns out that size does matter

The reason that so many ISIS BB's failed was because when the spindle diameter grew from 17mm on Square Taper BBs to 22mm on ISIS BBs, the ball diameter got *much* smaller. See Figure 6-12 for a visual comparison.

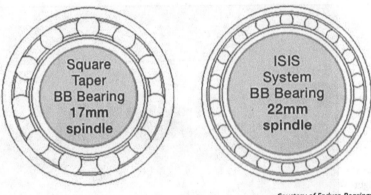

FIGURE 6-12:
Ball bearing
size versus
spindle size.

Courtesy of Enduro Bearings.

Bigger balls have two key advantages: They roll more slowly at a given speed, and they have a larger contact patch to better support the load placed on them. The thickness of the race matters, too, because more material makes them stronger. So, when ISIS tried to cram a bigger spindle into the fixed amount of space inside bottom bracket shells, the races got thinner and the balls got smaller, and they wore out quickly.

Pedals

Like everything else that spins on your bike, pedals spin on bearings — very small bearings, which is why better ones also add needle bearings or bushing bearings to improve durability. And like everything else, you get what you pay for. Cheap bikes come with cheap pedals that often fail or break quickly. If you're going to be putting in the miles, or riding hard, jumping, or doing tricks, invest in a good set of pedals!

Installing pedals

This statement is important: Each pedal threads onto the crank arm in a different direction (see Figure 6-13), and if you do it wrong, you can strip the threads in your crankset and ruin it.

Here's an easy way to remember how to thread pedals correctly: The top of the pedal's axle (or *spindle*) should roll forward to install (toward the front wheel), and then roll backward to remove it.

FIGURE 6-13:
Left and right
pedal threads
move in opposite
directions.

So the right side (or *drive* side) pedal, as viewed from the drive side of the bike, installs with the normal righty-tighty-lefty-loosey pattern like every other bolt you've ever used. The left side (or the *non-drive* side) is the opposite.

Put them on the correct side

Make sure that you're putting the correct pedal on the correct side. Look at the threads and it should be obvious (many pedals have L & R identifiers), but if it's not threading in easily, don't force it. *Cross threading*, or forcibly threading a pedal into the wrong side, will strip the threads on your crankset, effectively ruining the entire crankset.

Avoid overtightening them

You do *not* need to overtighten the pedals. I usually thread them on until they're *finger tight*, or as tight as I can get them using only my fingers, and then use a wrench to snug them a little. Some people may disagree, and I've seen some folks make them very tight, but those people also end up struggling to get them off. I've used my method for more than 20 years and ridden thousands of miles and never once had a pedal come loose.

Use the proper tools

Many pedals have flat sections near the threads that fit a 15mm wrench, so you'll need that (or an adjustable wrench) to snug or remove them. Higher-end pedals may also (or only) have a 6mm or 8mm hex wrench socket on the back of the spindle, which you access by sliding the tool into the backside of the hole on the crankset that the pedal threads into.

Differentiating types of pedals

A bicycle can have one of two types of pedals: flat or clipless. For info about each type, read on.

Flat pedals

Flat pedals (see Figure 6-14) come supplied on most bikes, so named because they're flat. You might hear them called *platform* pedals, too. Most have little nubs or pins on them to add traction so that your feet don't slide off. If they start feeling crunchy or don't spin freely, or if your kids have bent them from jumping off homemade ramps, spend a little extra here to make your bike safer and more enjoyable!

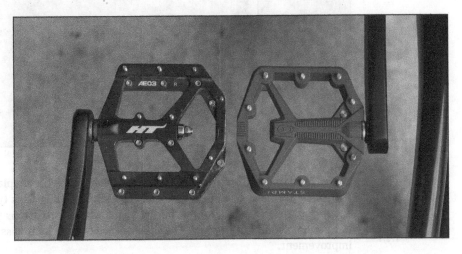

FIGURE 6-14:
Flat pedals.

Flat pedals are perfect for kids, commuters, cargo bikes, fitness bikes, and general riding on any type of bike. I put them on one of my gravel bikes that I use for ripping around town, because they work with any type of shoe.

Some mountain bikers prefer flat pedals because they can move their feet off quickly to catch themselves before a wreck, or just to put a foot down in a corner so that they can whip through it faster.

Clipless pedals

Clipless pedals are the ones you see serious cyclists using, with special cleats on the bottom of special cycling shoes that attach to the pedals.

Oddly enough, you clip into clipless pedals (see Figure 6-15). Those cleats on the bottom of cycling shoes click into place and lock the shoe onto the pedal. This not only aids efficiency (see the nearby sidebar, "Pedaling perfect circles") but also helps keep you attached to the bike over rough terrain, which sounds scarier than it is. In fact, I'm more timid riding a mountain bike with flat pedals than I am with clipless pedals because I feel like my feet will fly off over every jump, drop, and bump unless my shoes are securely attached to my pedals!

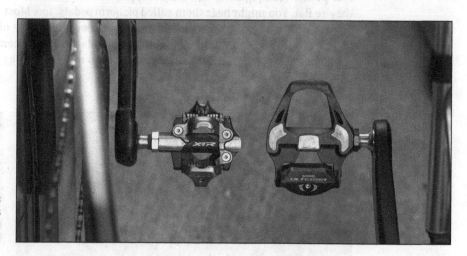

FIGURE 6-15:
Clipless pedals for MTB (left) and road (right).

TECHNICAL STUFF

Clipless pedals get their counterintuitive name because they replaced the toe clip that riders formerly used to secure their feet to the pedals. This type of clip had a small cage that formed around the toe of the shoe, with straps you could cinch tight to hold your foot in place. Toe clips worked okay, but clipless pedals are a big improvement.

Clipping in, for most pedals, involves a motion similar to dipping your toes into a pool: Simply step your foot onto the pedal with your toes pointing downward so that the front of the cleat slots into the front of the pedal, and then press your heel downward to "click" into the pedal. It sounds weird, but it's easy to master.

TIP

For more information about spindles, bottom brackets, gear range, and more, visit Dummies.com/go/bikingfd.

2

Buying a New Bike and Other Gear You Need

IN THIS PART . . .

Purchasing your bike.

Getting the necessary gear and equipment.

Chapter 7

Finding the Perfect Bike

I n the purest sense, the perfect bike is the one you have. Though this concept is in line with Zen philosophy, the reality is that there is no one perfect bike that excels at everything. There are, however, some bikes that do lots of things pretty well, and others that do one thing exceptionally well.

Whether it's commuting to school or work, running errands or grocery shopping, hitting the bike path with friends, getting in shape, joining the group road rides, or exploring local mountain bike trails, you can find a bike for every situation.

In this chapter, I walk you through the types of bikes available, which may help you figure out which one you need. At the end, I describe the four frame materials — steel, aluminum, titanium, and carbon fiber — and the pros and cons of each type.

We'll start with an overview of the different categories of bicycles. You may be surprised by how many categories there are. But you can keep yourself from feeling overwhelmed by maintaining your focus: First, think of where you're most likely to ride your bike, and then focus on those categories to see what best fits your plans. (And, of course, breathe in, breathe out).

Don't worry if all of these choices seem like too much right now. As an enthusiast, I like having "horses for courses," because it means I can find a bike that excels at a particular type of riding. But within each broad category — such as road bike or mountain bike or commuter bike — some bikes are terrific all-around performers, no matter how you want to use them, and I point out how to find them.

Think of it this way: A compact SUV serves most drivers really well by offering a good mix of performance, safety, fuel economy, and interior space. You can certainly buy a model that's bigger or sportier or more efficient, but each of those specializations comes with more trade-offs. As you'll begin to see while reading this chapter, it's the same with bikes!

The focus here is on the bikes themselves. I cover the components and related technologies in chapters 3 through 6. So if you run across a few words or topics you don't understand yet, don't worry — I'll get you there.

Road Bikes

A *road bike* is designed to quickly and efficiently cover long distances on paved surfaces. It has skinny tires and rounded *drop* handlebars (see Chapter 3), offering a variety of hand positions.

Modern road bikes come with 20 to 22 speeds with shifters integrated into the brake levers, and newer models are going wireless or semi-wireless with shifting.

Though racers as recently as the 2010s were still riding on skinny 23 millimeters (mm) wide tires at high pressures, most bikes now are designed to fit tires that are 28–35 millimeters wide. And most roads bikes have disc brakes now. (I don't recommend buying any new bike with rim brakes — they're basically obsolete; I discuss brakes in Chapter 5.)

Integrated or semi-integrated cockpits are becoming the standard, and higher-end bikes often come with more aerodynamic and/or ergonomic handlebar shapes.

WHAT'S AN INTEGRATED COCKPIT?

Internal routing is basically standard on road and gravel bikes, as well as some mountain bikes — it simply means that any brake hoses, shifting cables, wires, or other control lines (for dropper seatposts and suspension lockouts, for example) that you typically see on the outside of the frame are hidden inside the frame.

Semi-integrated routing means that these control lines are visible at the handlebar and then feed into a sleeve under the stem and through a headset port rather than loop down into a hole on the bicycle's frame.

Fully integrated (or *stealth*) routing means that those lines run inside the handlebar and stem, through the headset, and directly into the frame and fork. You basically don't see any cables or wires anywhere on the bike, which looks amazing but makes it harder to service.

Unless you're frequently packing your bike in a box for travel or constantly swapping handlebars, drivetrains, or brakes, there's no need to fear integrated cockpits. They look great, and they're more aerodynamic than other types.

Racing

When most people think of a road bike, they're imagining what the Tour de France racers are riding — in other words, a race bike that's designed with an emphasis on efficiency and speed.

Modern race bikes have blended aerodynamics with lighter materials, helping them do well on long, flat stages and higher-elevation climbing stages. They're stiffer than other types of road bikes to maximize efficiency, but not so stiff that they beat up riders after hours in the saddle day after day.

They typically have sharp handling and put the rider in a somewhat aggressive position, with geometry designed to favor power output and a low, aerodynamic position that works well for professional racers. However, these features work less well for weekend warriors who aren't racers.

I WANT WHAT THE PROS RIDE, RIGHT?

The old NASCAR maxim was "Win on Sunday, sell it on Monday" — and it seems to apply to cycling, too. A lot of casual riders will ask their bike-shop employees for the same bike their favorite pro is racing in "Le Tour."

That's generally a mistake, and here's why: Most riders are not racing their bikes for a living. Most of us have desk jobs that have diminished our flexibility. Most of us don't need to sacrifice comfort and stability for the marginal gains of an extra 3% efficiency.

(continued)

(continued)

The UCI (cycling's global racing governing body) mandates that any bike raced in World Tour races — such as the Tour de France, Giro d'Italia, or Vuelta a España — must also be for sale commercially to consumers. Thus, brands make race bikes work for the pros and then also for regular riders, in that order.

The takeaway is this: Race bikes are for racers, and just because your favorite pro rides a certain model or uses a certain setup doesn't mean you should, too.

Fortunately, many brands have figured out how to make an excellent race bike that's also fun to ride. If you have good flexibility, if most of your rides will be in a fast group, and if you might enter a race a few times per year, a modern road race bike is probably the right one for you.

All-Road / endurance

The *all-road* bike is the true all-around performer and generally the best option for most people wanting a road bike.

Most models have some aerodynamic shaping and good performance, but the winning attribute here is prioritizing comfort over long distances and predictable handling on varied road surfaces.

Don't confuse comfort with sluggish, Lazy Boy-like relaxation. These are still performance bikes, but with geometry that puts you in a slightly more upright riding position that's more comfortable during hours in the saddle. The rear of the bike usually has more vertical compliance built into it to reduce vibrations and mitigate small bumps.

Steering is relaxed and the wheelbase is a bit longer, which improves stability and makes it easier to cruise along in a straight line without feeling like you have to be constantly attentive to where you're heading.

Where race bikes typically max out at with tires that are 28mm wide, all-road bikes fit tires up to 35mm wide, which helps tame rough tarmac. Some come with fender mounts or even a rear rack mount and extra water bottle cage mounts, making them useful for all-day rides or quick commuter trips during the week.

Also known as *endurance* or *gran fondo* (Italian for "big ride") bikes, the all-road bike is a great choice for anyone just looking to hit the open road, ride with friends, join some group rides, or complete a *gran fondo* or charity ride now and then.

Aero

Here's where we start to get into more specialization. Though most race and all-road bikes have become more aerodynamic, some pure *aero* road bikes are still optimized for aerodynamics over comfort and weight.

These typically have wing-like tube shapes with deeper cross sections, teardrop-shaped seatposts, and they sometimes tuck the stem deeper into the top tube and head tube of the bike, all in an effort to reduce drag so they slice through the air more easily.

Aero bikes look cool, but their unique shapes often make them very stiff, with a less lively ride quality and a harsher feel over bumps.

If you're constantly battling headwinds or riding solo without friends to draft behind, and if you preferably have smoother roads, an aero bike can be a lot of fun and make you feel like you're coasting really, really fast!

Climbing

Even more of a specialty these days is a pure climbing bike. This type prioritizes a low-weight frame and a stiff lower section around the drivetrain.

The lightest frames can drop below 700 grams, which is about 200–300 grams lighter than most standard road bike frames. That's anywhere from half a pound to almost a full pound lighter, just from the frame, which is a lot, but it comes with trade-offs.

Many of the lightest climbing bikes have rider weight limits, and they don't feel as stiff or precise as other types of bikes. But if your goal is to build the lightest possible bike and own the *KOM/QOM* (King or Queen of the Mountain) leaderboard, a climbing bike is a logical place to start.

Crit

The *crit* bike is a purpose-built, short-track race bike. *Crit* is short for *criterium*, which is a closed-circuit race usually held in a downtown area, with riders racing at more than 30 miles per hour (mph) around a city block, with tight corners and constant attacks and accelerations.

Crit bike handling is precise, with quick steering that requires constant attention but allows a rider to whip around competitors and sprint for the finish.

The crit bike is often made of aluminum because a lot of people crash in crit races, so you want a bike that is inexpensive and can take a beating and still make the lineup the next week for another round.

This bike is helpful for its intended use, but that's about it. It isn't what you'd want for standard road riding, because it tends to be stiffer and can feel a bit twitchy when riding in a *paceline*, or tightly packed group of riders.

But if you're going to race crits, a crit bike is an excellent second bike to have around so that you're not risking your road bike.

Track

Like a crit bike, a *track* bike is purpose-built for racing, but on the track. This fixed-gear bike has no freewheel (see Chapter 5), so if its rear wheel is turning, so are the cranks. Basically, either you're pedaling it or it's pedaling you.

The track bike also lacks brakes because, when you're done racing on the track, you just pedal more slowly until you can safely pull off the track and dismount.

Some riders have co-opted track bikes as fixed-gear (or "fixie") city bikes and learned to skid to a stop, but these aren't bikes you'd want to use for a proper road ride, because that would be dangerous and, honestly, not fun at all. But if you want to race on the track, you need a track bike.

Triathlon

A pure *triathlon* bike is purpose-built for putting the rider into an aerodynamic tuck that minimizes overall system drag on the rider-bike combo.

I'm grouping the triathlon with the road bike because you can really only ride a triathlon bike on the road, and because it's also a niche bike that few people need — most amateur triathletes or the tri-curious, who may participate in one or two races per year, can get by just fine with a regular road bike by attaching aero bars (see Chapter 3) to them.

The "tri bike" comes with bullhorn-shaped handlebars that stack aero extensions on top, letting you rest your elbows on pads to give you the slimmest profile possible.

The triathlon bike is made for going as fast as possible in a straight line, so its slow speed handling can be a little wonky. Fortunately, most triathlon courses have few turns, which is good because the brake levers are on the bullhorns. But you're mostly resting on the aero bars, so in order to slow down, you have to sit up (not aerodynamic at all!), move your hands (not aero!), and brake (not fast) so that you can turn (not aero or fast).

If you've completed a few triathlons and you love them enough to <gasp!> consider doing more, a triathlon bike is a great additional bike for racing.

TIP

You may find yourself training alone with your tri bike. Most road cyclists do *not* want you riding it in their group ride precisely because of the triathlon bike's diminished handling and braking characteristics, which makes them less agile and thus less safe in a tightly packed peloton.

Gravel Bikes

The *gravel* bike is similar to a road bike, but more capable. It's designed to cruise along unpaved surfaces like gravel forest-service roads, dirt access roads, unmaintained country roads, and even smooth dirt trails.

This category of bikes has reinvigorated road cycling because it gives you most of the speed and handling of a road bike, but lets you get farther away from traffic. Their off-road ability also gives you the confidence to explore those "I'm not sure where this goes, but it looks like a shortcut" backroads, which is always fun (and sometimes a real adventure!).

The category arguably started with the launch of the Salsa Warbird in 2012, which was the first mainstream drop bar bike that had bigger tires and revised geometry to help it handle rough dirt roads. Fast-forward a decade and almost every brand now has a gravel bike (or five), and this includes a lot of options for everything from racing to adventure.

Gravel bikes look like road bikes but have a slacker head angle and longer chainstays for better stability. Gravel bikes can also fit tires up to 55mm wide, and they usually come with wider, flared handlebars and wide-range gearing. (See Chapter 2 for an explanation of head angles and bicycle geometry.)

The racier versions are taking on the same internal routing and integrated cockpits as road bikes, but the more adventurous bikes are sticking with non-integrated or even full external routing to make repairs and field service easier.

And now I'm even bundling *touring* and *bikepacking* bikes in this category. Whereas both types used to be considered road bikes, modern touring and bikepacking bikes more closely resemble gravel bikes, and more people are using them to explore unpaved backroads, so they fit better here.

Basic gravel

The *basic gravel* bike is equivalent to the all-road endurance road bike in that it can do fairly well most of the things you want a gravel bike to do. If you're on a budget, it also makes a perfectly good road bike simply by swapping wheels and tires.

This type may lack some of the extra mounts of an adventure bike, but it generally clears a 48mm tire, and that's enough for most activities.

Popular (and recommended) features are top-tube bag mounts, which let you add a bit more storage for snacks, and a third or fourth water bottle cage mount, because hydration is extremely important when you're heading out for a long journey.

If you just want to get off the roads or you have the option to take random turns and explore new roads of any type, a basic gravel bike is a fantastic option.

Racing gravel

Serious racers prioritize speed over options, so a *gravel race* bike will usually forego extra mounts for fenders and racks and have internal or fully integrated routing to make it more aerodynamic.

Some even skip the top-tube bag mounts, though most models have them and they make a helpful place to stash fuel — especially important because most gravel races are 80 miles or more (and some are 350 miles!).

Tire clearance is usually smaller, with many maxing out at 42-45mm wide tires, and that's because wider rubber adds weight and racers like to have the lightest possible bikes (and lowest rotational mass). For racing, most riders can get by with 38-42mm tires, so it's not that big of a deal. It just means that your bike will be less capable on rougher terrain.

If you're focused on racing over exploring and you don't mind a pared-down, slightly rougher ride, a gravel race bike is the one for you. And, if you do split your time between road and gravel but if your toy allowance only has enough for one bike, this gravel race bike might be the right way to go.

Adventure gravel

An *adventure gravel* bike typically has the most tire clearance, the most mounts, and a bit longer wheelbase to add stability when loaded down with bags and gear. These features add a bit of weight, and the bike won't be the quickest, snappiest bike around, but it makes up for it by being more fun!

Many of these bikes will fit 29-inch mountain bike tires up to 2.25 inches wide (57mm), which helps them roll over almost anything. That extra tire volume also makes them more comfortable over rough terrain, making these bikes an excellent choice for multiday trail riding on, say, the Great Divide Mountain Bike Trail, a 2,700-mile route that crisscrosses the Continental Divide from Banff, Canada, all the way to the Mexican border.

These bikes are also often suspension-corrected (or at least have fairly tall forks), making it easy to add a suspension fork to the front of the bike without messing up the geometry or handling.

If you're looking for a drop bar bike that can do anything, carry anything, and make every ride a blast, an adventure bike is for you.

Bikepacking / touring

The category of *bikepacking* (think biking plus backpacking) and *touring* bikes will typically have all the mounting points for racks, bags, cages, and fenders, but with smaller tire clearance than an adventure bike. That's because if you're not going on an off-road adventure, a touring/bikepacking bike will be more efficient and narrower tires will be a lot lighter and faster rolling.

The geometry will be a little more upright, keeping your torso, neck, and head from having to lean over so far, like on a racier bike. This keeps you more comfortable over long miles and lets you enjoy the scenery, too!

Look for a bike with mounts for a rear rack and three mounting points on each fork leg (often referred to as "anything cage mounts"), as well as fender mounts. You may also want wiring ports for a front hub dynamo, allowing you to power your headlights and taillights simply by riding. (See Chapter 9 for more about bike accessories.)

Most of these bikes will clear a 42mm tire, and maybe more, but the important number to look for is tire clearance *with fenders installed*. If you're heading out for a multiday tour (or weeks or months), you'll want fenders unless you like getting your gear (and your pants) wet every time you hit a puddle. All bikes have a maximum tire size they fit, and fenders typically reduce tire clearance by 4–6mm. So a bike that fits 700x42 might only fit 700x36 with fenders. For the best experience, be honest about where you're riding and outfit your bike accordingly.

If the bike has external cable routing, make sure it won't interfere with the Velcro straps and other attachment points for any frame bags you plan to use. Many tourers carry spare cables and small parts, so make sure the cable/hose/wire routing on your bike isn't so complicated that you can't fix it by the side of the road or require proprietary tools.

If you're looking to hit the open road — paved or not — for some self-supported bicycle touring, a touring/bikepacking bike is for you.

Cyclocross Bikes

There's not really a recreational form of *cyclocross* (also known as *CX* or *'cross*); it's just racing. Think of it as obstacle course biking, like a cycling *steeplechase*. Cyclocross bikes look like road bikes, but with slightly bigger tires (up to 33-35mm wide), that are designed to race on grass, dirt, mud, and sand.

Races are short but extremely intense — imagine a 30- to 60-minute full-gas interval. There's varied terrain, off-camber turns, and even barriers and stairs to jump over and run up.

For this reason, a 'cross bike's geometry is designed for quick handling and maximum power transfer. Comfort is *far* down the feature list because, honestly, there's nothing comfortable about racing 'cross. They're like off-road crit bikes, but with higher bottom brackets so that you don't clip your pedals on roots or rocks.

They also lack mounts for anything except a bottle cage (maybe two, if you're lucky), but you really don't need much to drink in such a short race. (Good luck finding a chance to drink anyway!)

Before gravel bikes came along, most people used CX bikes for riding dirt roads. They still work for that purpose, and CX bikes make fast urban commuter bikes, too, as long as you don't need to carry gear on them.

For casual 'cross racers who can't justify buying another bike, a basic or racing gravel bike works just fine — just mind the pedal clearance. Gravel bikes have lower bottom brackets to keep you "in" the bike, whereas cyclocross bikes' higher bottom brackets keep you riding "on" the bike. The difference may only be a centimeter, but it has a huge effect on handling.

The only reason to buy a cyclocross bike is that you're going to race cyclocross frequently enough to justify a purpose-built bike. If the idea of buying a very specific bike for a sport where spectators line the course blowing air horns, yelling, jeering, cheering, and likely drinking beer while you bury yourself in pain seems ridiculous, it is. It's also extremely fun and addictive!

Mountain Bikes

A *mountain bike* (MTB) is designed to ride on trails, usually *singletrack*, or trails built just for riding and just wide enough for a single mountain bike.

Mountain bikes got their start when a few rowdy folks in California put balloon tires on their cruiser bikes and started racing downhill. The bikes came to be known as *clunkers* because they were cobbled together with whatever parts could handle the abuse. People would ride them down a dirt road that came to be known as Repack Road because, after a couple of runs, the coaster brake rear hub had to be repacked with fresh grease!

These riders included Joe Breeze, Gary Fisher, Tom Ritchey, and others who were the first to make bicycles specifically for riding off-road. Originally called *all-terrain* bikes, or ATBs, mountain bikes started out with 26-inch wheels before jumping to 29 inches and some experimentation with 27.5 inches (also called *650B*).

MTB wheels, suspension and geometry

Before we get to the different types of mountain bikes, it's helpful to know a little about the commonly used wheel sizes, suspension, and geometry so that you can better understand the category as a whole.

Wheel sizes

I discuss wheels and tires in depth in Chapter 5, but here are the basic stats for mountain bikes: They now mostly use 29-inch wheels (called *29ers*) for adult bikes, with some smaller-size frames for shorter people using 27.5-inch wheels. Kids' and youth bikes range from 20 inches to 24 inches to 26 inches to 27.5 inches.

Some bikes, particularly e-mountain bikes and some enduro, freeride, and downhill bikes use mixed wheel sizes, putting a 29er up front and a 27.5-incher in the rear. Sometimes called *MX* or *mullet* builds, the idea is to help the bikes roll over rough terrain more easily in the front but provide a lighter, nimbler rear end for whipping the bike through challenging terrain.

Suspension

Modern mountain bikes come in categories based on the amount of *suspension* travel they have. A bike without rear suspension is called a *hardtail* (because the "tail" of the bike is rigid and hard), and those with rear suspension are called *full suspension* because they're fully suspended, front and rear. The primary goal of suspension is to keep the tires in contact with the terrain (as opposed to bouncing off the rocks and roots) so that the tires maintain traction, and to absorb the impact when landing a jump or dropping off a ledge.

The more aggressive a bike's intent, the more travel its suspension will have. You'll hear them called *short travel* or *long travel* accordingly, and I explain next the typical range with each category of mountain bike. See Chapter 10 for a deep dive on how bicycle suspension works and how to set it up.

Geometry

A mountain bike's geometry is optimized for the type of riding its suspension travel allows for. Typically, the biggest change from short to long travel is the head angle. (See Chapter 2 for more about a bike's geometry.) For example, short-travel cross-country (XC) race bikes have shorter suspension travel and a steeper head angle, giving them sharper handling and snappier acceleration. But long-travel downhill (DH) bikes have a longer wheelbase and slacker angles that help it remain stable on steep, high-speed descents.

Below, I break down the mountain bike category by suspension travel, moving from shortest to longest, and explain what types of terrain or riding style each is best suited for. Then I close out the chapter with a few specialty types of mountain bikes that are less common.

It's worth noting that all good mountain bikes these days come with 1x drive-trains, and most come with dropper seatposts. If they don't, it's usually a good sign that they're a lower quality or very-low-budget bikes.

WHAT'S A 1X DRIVETRAIN?

If you remember back when mountain bikes came with a triple chainring (head to Chapter 6 for a refresher on drivetrains), with three speeds up front, then you've been doing this for a while. Those mountain bike *groups* — the combination of crankset, chain, chainring, cassette, front and rear derailleurs, and shifter — were the norm for decades.

In 2009, SRAM introduced its XX group as the first 2x10 drivetrain, reducing the front chainrings to two and expanding the *cassette*, or rear cluster of gears (called *cogs*) to ten speeds. These were called *2x10* (or two-by-ten) groups, with the numbers simply referring to the number of gears on either end of the bike.

A few years later, these were replaced by 1x11 groups with larger cassettes and just a single chainring. These new groups were lighter and simpler and still offered about the same total gear range as the earlier 2x10 groups.

These 1x ("one-by") groups also eliminated the front derailleur, which was always a clunky, misbehaving part on mountain bikes, and that freed designers to make more radical frames with better suspension kinematics and fit wider tires, all of which led to higher-quality mountain bikes for everyone!

Nowadays, MTB cassettes have 12 speeds with massive, 50- to 52-tooth large cogs, and 1x12 groups have become the default on most bikes costing more than $2,000. Below that, you may still find 1x10 and 1x11 groups, but for all but the cheapest bikes, a one-by drivetrain is the standard.

Cross country (XC)

Cross-country (or XC) mountain bikes typically have between 0mm and 120mm of rear-wheel travel. Almost every mountain bike now comes with a suspension fork unless you specifically seek out a rigid fork, and for XC, these usually have 100–120mm travel.

Rear suspension is usually 100mm for this category, though some bikes have as little as 30mm, by using flexible frame members rather than shocks, or they may combine those to achieve 60–100mm of travel.

Typically, the shorter the travel, the more efficient the suspension. More efficiency means more of your pedaling effort goes into forward propulsion, as opposed to compressing or extending the suspension, which is an unfortunate side effect of having rear suspension. Most modern bikes from quality brands have sophisticated designs, though, that minimize this pedaling-induced "suspension bob."

Yes, you can still find hardtail XC bikes (they have no rear suspension), and these are often more affordable or good for racing in flatter states like Florida or Texas. But most pros now race on full-suspension bikes for most courses, and having some suspension makes your bike more capable, should you venture onto bigger trails now and then. Plus, as you age, suspension is definitely (definitely!) your friend.

XC geometry puts the rider in a powerful pedaling position and provides quick, nimble handling, but modern designs are surprisingly capable on the descents, too.

Most XC bikes come with flat handlebars and stems between 60mm and 90mm long. Dropper seatposts come supplied on some, but not all, XC bikes, though the frame should at least offer cable routing that allows you to add one later.

These bikes are optimized for pro athletes racing XC Olympic (XCO) courses at the World Cup level and, yep, at the Olympics. So, these high-performance XC designs work well for those who race frequently or for riders who live in flatter areas and don't need a lot of suspension.

Downcountry / light trail

If you like the speed of an XC bike but want something a little more capable on rougher terrain, this in-between category is a nearly perfect bike for most riders.

Light trail bikes, more recently dubbed *downcountry* (a term that people either love or hate, but we're stuck with it now), usually have 120–140mm of rear travel with matching forks.

This amount of travel lets you bash through root and rock gardens and take little jumps and drops while still pedaling well and remaining fairly lightweight. You typically see riser bars make their appearance here (almost all XC bikes come with flat bars), and stems get a bit shorter. From here on up to AM/FR bikes (described in the later section "All mountain / freeride (AM/FR)," this one should definitely come with a dropper seatpost installed.

Unless you're routinely hitting big drops or going after steeper, gnarlier terrain, a light trail bike is a great choice and what most people think of when they think of a mountain bike.

Trail

The *trail* bike bumps up rear travel to between 130mm and 150mm, with forks that match or may have 10mm more travel than the rear. Yes, there's some overlap with downcountry bikes here, with the key difference that a trail bike generally has tougher components, a longer travel fork, and bigger, knobbier tires.

A trail bike is a suitable option for many riders, especially ones who live in mountainous terrain where you spend equal time climbing and descending.

In this travel range, the bike still pedals well but is incredibly capable on the descents and technical terrain. The geometry is balanced between climbing and descending, with a slight bias toward going downhill but still able to pick its way through tight sections at lower speeds.

If your local trails have bigger obstacles or rougher terrain, a trail bike is an excellent all-rounder that's fun to ride almost anywhere.

Enduro (EN)

An *enduro* event is like turning mountain biking with friends into a race: The event has multiple timed downhill segments that you race down, but then pedal up to the start of the next segment at your leisure. It's like riding up the hill with your buddies at a conversational pace and, then racing each other to the bottom and doing it all over again.

As such, the *enduro* bike is optimized for downhill speed and capability, though you still need to pedal back up the mountain without being completely gutted.

An enduro bike can have anywhere from 150–170mm of rear travel, with 150–180mm forks. It's a little burlier than a trail bike, and a little slacker up front for more stability on high-speed descents, but it often has a steeper seat angle so that you can get over the pedals when you're climbing.

Many enduro frames have lower standover heights and longer-travel dropper posts, so you can get low behind the bike on steep sections.

Chances are good that a proper enduro bike won't be your first mountain bike, but if you plan on jumping straight into the races, it's purpose-built for that.

All mountain / freeride (AM/FR)

Freeriding became a thing in the 1990s and 2000s, characterized by riders shredding through the woods, down mountainsides, and over wooden ramps and other manmade technical trail features built (often illegally) deep in the woods, often forging new "trails" by skidding their way down.

If you've heard of North Shore riding, that's freeriding in a nutshell, and fortunately it has gone legit, with thousands of legal trails and increasingly difficult obstacles, both natural and manufactured. Just search online for the term *north shore freeriding* for an endless supply of entertainment.

Also called all-mountain bikes because they're capable enough to ride "all of the mountain," these bikes typically have 170–190mm of travel with 170–200mm forks, sometimes even getting a burlier dual-crown fork.

This type of bike is made to handle huge jumps, hucks, and drops, both in the woods and at bike parks. It's designed primarily for going downhill, and it isn't much fun to pedal uphill. As such, this bike is the kind you buy when you and your friends shuttle each other to the top of the mountain in a vehicle, or ride lift-served bike parks.

If you ride parks, hit massive jumps, or huck 20-foot drops and don't mind sliding down nearly vertical rock faces, an all-mountain/freeride bike is the one for you. (But, you know, maybe you should work your way up to this one?)

Downhill (DH)

The downhill (DH) bike is designed for one thing and one thing only: to get you down the mountain as quickly as possible, no matter what the terrain.

These bikes usually have 190–210mm travel with dual-crown forks (where the fork legs extend to the top of the head tube and are captured by an upper and lower crown to increase stiffness), very slack head angles, and no mounts for any accessories — not even a bottle cage. If you want water while you're shuttling back to the top, wear a hydration backpack.

The downhill bike also sports extremely short rigid seatposts — no droppers here. That's because you're standing on the pedals the entire ride down and there's no sitting and pedaling on a downhill bike. If you're pedaling at all, it's a sprint out of the gate and through any flatter sections so that you can maintain maximum speed.

You'll find DH downhill bikes being ridden at bike parks, which often host downhill races because they have the steep terrain and chairlifts and gondolas to transport you back up to the top for another lap.

If you're going to race downhill, get a downhill bike. Otherwise, one of the other options will be more versatile (and fun) for regular trails.

Fat bikes

Fat bikes were originally created for riding in the snow, with huge, 4-inch-wide tires that could float over packed powder. Now the fat bike has evolved, with tires up to 5 inches wide and wheel sizes up to 27.5 inches, and people ride them on sand, snow, and regular trails.

Many fat bikes have rigid forks because those massive tires offer plenty of cushion (and gobs of traction — good luck ever sliding out unless you're on ice!). But some have suspension forks, and there are a handful of full-suspension models, too.

Fat bikes have extra-wide axle spacing, and the cranks (and therefore pedals) sit wider than on normal bikes, which is necessary to create room for those monster-truck tires.

Because of all that traction and cushioning, some riders love this style for extended bikepacking, particularly in winter or deserts. The bigger tires add a lot of rotational weight, however, so you face the usual trade-offs.

If you find yourself often riding on soft sand or snow, a fat bike is a fun way to extend your riding season or float across otherwise challenging surfaces.

Dirt jump / slopestyle

Dirt jump bikes are like oversized BMX bikes, except that they're designed for *jump lines* (downhill trails with lots of jumps) and *pump tracks* (short loops with whoops and jumps that you "pump" the bike through using more momentum than pedaling) rather than street tricks and race tracks.

Most are hardtails (described in the earlier "Suspension" section) that come with 80–100mm travel suspension forks, riser bars, and short, rigid seatposts. As with downhill bikes, you're never sitting and pedaling, only standing and pedaling and pumping the bike through the berms and ramps.

Slopestyle is an event where you're racing three or four other riders down a smooth, groomed trail with huge bermed turns, jumps, and bumps. *Dual slalom* (DS) is similar, but you're racing only one other person on a separate-but-parallel track. Both slopestyle and DJ bikes are very similar, and very purpose-built for the inended use – they don't make great mountain bikes for riding on regular trails.

If you have a pump track or jump line nearby, or if you want to race DS or slopestyle frequently, grab a dirt jump bike. It gets bonus points in that it's usually a one-size-fits-most, so you really need only one for the entire family, and then everyone just takes turns.

Trials

Perhaps the most specialized bike style of them all is the *trials* bike. Bicycle trials are best searched for online to truly understand the sport, but imagine a course where you have to jump up, onto, over, and off of 4- to 5-foot obstacles, hop from log to log, balance across long, narrow planks that abruptly change direction at sharp angles, and hop up steep, root-filled, completely unrideable hillsides, all without ever taking your feet off the pedals. That describes trials, and the bikes for it are extremely specialized (and weird-looking).

Commuter Bikes

Any bike can be used to commute around town, but purpose-built commuter bikes typically have features that make it easier to bring your possessions with you (like books, laptops, or clothing), or to pick up groceries or other products and bring them home. Look for mounts for a rear rack, which will let you add *trunk bag* or *pannier bags* (purpose-built bags that clip onto a front or rear rack).

Bonus features include extra mounting points on the front of the bike or fork legs, full-coverage fenders, a chainguard to cover the chain so that you don't spatter grease on your pant legs, and dedicated light mounts. Some include a bell, which comes in handy in congested areas, and some even have integrated security locks for the rear wheel (or mounts so that you can add one later).

Most have a more upright riding position, which helps you stay alert when riding in city traffic — and stay comfortable. The saddles have more padding and are a little wider than performance bikes. Tires are a little fatter — usually, 35mm to 45mm wide — and ideally with puncture/cut protection features and reflective sidewalls.

Fitness/Hybrid Bikes

A *fitness* bike looks like a cross between a commuter bike and a road bike. It combines the benefits of both models — hence the term *hybrid*. It has flat handlebars like a commuter, but skinnier tires and slightly *taller* (or harder) gearing so that you can go faster, like on a road bike. Most of these come with alloy frames, but you'll find a few boutique carbon fiber ones, too.

The hybrid is designed for riding quickly, but with a more upright position that's safer on bike paths and city streets. It should have two or more bottle cage mounts, but rarely has extra mounts for carrying cargo. If you're looking for a bike that lets you get a good workout but you don't plan to join group rides — or if you simply prefer the flat handlebars and more comfortable seating position — then a fitness bike is the right choice. These make for speedy commuter bikes, too, if you don't need the rack and accessory mounts.

Cruiser Bikes

The most popular bike in the cruiser category is the beach cruiser, with its curvy tubes, oversized handlebar, and cushy seat. But cruisers can also have frames with straight tubes, and some have funky designs that look more like choppers than bikes.

Regardless of the frame's design, they're all designed for cruising along at a casual pace. Most are single-speed, and most use coaster brakes. You'll find some with internally geared hubs and rim or disc brakes, but rarely with a derailleur and cassette. Their big, balloon-like tires work well on packed sand for riding on the beach and — combined with wide, thick seats — offer a comfortable ride.

Cargo Bikes

The cargo bike is purpose-built for hauling gear and people, and you can find it in two basic types: standard and bakfiets.

Standard cargo

Standard versions (see Figure 7-1) have cargo platforms in the back and range from short-tail to long-tail, depending on how far back they stretch from the saddle. Some use the same wheel size, front and rear, and others have a smaller rear wheel that brings down the platform for a lower center of gravity, which is helpful when you place a heavy load on it.

Most models come with a bare platform and let you add the accessories you want, from bags to boxes and from seats to footrests. If you're trying to carry people, a padded seat for bigger kids and adults or a complete child carrier for toddlers are useful additions.

A few brands also make *utility bikes*, which are like compact cargo bikes that have shorter wheelbases and less cargo capacity. Some of these put the main cargo basket in the front with a smaller front wheel to keep the weight low. Utility bikes are good if you don't have room for a larger cargo bike, or just don't need as much capacity or room for passengers.

FIGURE 7-1:
A standard
cargo bike.

Bakfiets cargo

The Dutch term *bakfiets*, which comes from "baks" (container, like a box) and "fiets" (bicycle), refers to cargo bikes that have a large container or platform between the rider and the front wheel (see Figure 7-2). These are useful for bigger cargo loads because the platform can be flat like a trailer, and it keeps the weight low. But handling is vastly different from a typical bike because the front wheel is so far in front of the rider and there's a learning curve to riding them.

The bakfiets cargo bike is also useful for kids because you can add a container (usually made of wood or high-density EPS foam) with one or two seats and seat-belts. This gives your passengers a better view and lets them relax (or nap), because they don't have to hold on to handlebars like they do when riding on the back of a standard cargo bike (or should do, anyway — my kids liked to stand and "surf" the bike while I gave them rides to school).

Most cargo bikes of every type nowadays are e-bikes, which I highly recommend. Because they have payload capacities topping 400 lbs., you'll appreciate the electric assistance a motor provides. The e-bikes cost more, with good mid-drive motor versions starting around $3,500 to $5,000 — but if you're looking to replace your car, the price is well worth it, in my opinion. Some hub-motor models start at less than $2,000.

WorkCycles

Because of the added weight (the bikes themselves typically weigh 60 to 80 lbs.), disc brakes are the way to go. Most come with durable, puncture-resistant tires, and I recommend inflating them with about 10 to 15 pounds per square inch (psi) more air pressure than you would for a tire of the same size on a normal bike. Trust me: Changing a flat tire on a cargo bike is no fun whatsoever, and my kids have popped plenty of them by riding around town with their friends on the back and not enough air in the tires to support their shenanigans!

e-Bikes

With few exceptions, every type of bike listed in this chapter is also available as an e-bike. In this section, I spell out a few key points, but for a deep dive on e-bike technology, types, and the facts you need to know before buying one, visit Dummies.com/go/bikingfd.

In the United States, e-bikes come in Class 1 (up to 20 mph assist) and Class 3 (up to 28 mph assist), and both are *pedal assist,* which means you must pedal in order to make the motor kick in. In Europe and most of the rest of the world, e-bikes are limited to 25 kilometers (km) per hour (or 15.5 mph) in most situations.

There's also a Class 2 in the middle spot that adds a throttle, letting it propel you without having to pedal. Sometimes, the throttle assistance is limited to 20 mph (or 25 km/h), and at other times it pushes you all the way to 28 mph. Because a throttle basically makes it a moped, this model isn't legal everywhere, so ask your local bike shop or research local laws before using it this way.

An e-bike has either a hub motor or a mid-drive motor. A hub motor puts the motor in the rear hub (or, rarely, the front hub) and is typically much less sophisticated. The mid-drive motor is in the middle of the frame, and the crankset attaches directly to it. This type typically has better electronics and smoother power delivery, but it costs more.

Most e-bikes have a remote control on the left side of the handlebar, so you can cycle through modes to change the level of assist, but sometimes the controls are on the top tube, and sometimes they're in both spots.

Recumbent Bikes

A *recumbent* bicycle is one where you sit back in what looks like a lounge chair and the pedals are located out in front of you. Some are two-wheeled, which require some quick leg work to start and stop, and some are tricycles, where the front or rear can have two wheels and the opposite end has only one. Basically, you just sit back and pedal while holding a handlebar to steer.

A recumbent bike can go very fast because you're lower to the ground with a smaller total frontal profile, so they're far more aerodynamic. Some models add *aero fairings*, or panels to smooth airflow, or complete enclosures to make them extremely aerodynamic. The downside is that they create a smaller visual presence and are often shorter than the hood of most cars, so they're harder for drivers to see. That's why many riders install a tall pole with a bright orange flag on it.

If you're looking for something different, or faster, or if you are physically limited or unable to support your upper body weight on traditional bicycle handlebars, recumbent cycles are worth a look.

Adaptive Bikes

Adaptive bikes are specialty bikes, often custom made, for people with limited physical capabilities. The most common are handcycles, for people who've lost the use of their legs — or who have no legs. These bikes usually look similar to recumbent bikes, sometimes with more upright seating (particularly if it's made for mountain biking, because you need to be able to see the terrain better).

Adaptive bikes have normal cranksets, chains, and other drivetrain parts, but they have handles instead of pedals, and riders "pedal" with their arms rather than their legs.

Adaptive road bikes are mostly normal, analog (lacking e-bike motors) models, but most adaptive mountain bikes are e-bikes, providing an electric assist so that they can ride *up* the trails, too. Fortunately, more and more mountain bike parks and even some regular trails are starting to add adaptive trails that are wide enough for these bikes to ride!

Kids' Bikes or Balance Bikes

Most types of bikes are also available in kid-size versions, with wheel sizes ranging from 12 inches up to 27.5 inches to fit all ages. Most also come in only one frame size per wheel size, but those frames are sized according to the anticipated rider's height.

Unlike adult bikes that come in small, medium, and large sizes, for example, or by frame size, like 56 centimeters or 59 centimeters, kids' bikes are referred to by wheel size, in inches: 12, 14, 16, 20, 24, 26, or 27.5. Given how quickly kids grow, and how varied their heights are from kid to kid, there's no real guide to say, "At this age, they need a 16-inch bike." Instead, have your kid sit on the bike and make sure they can easily reach the handlebars and put one or both feet flat on the ground while seated on the saddle. When it looks right and they're comfortable, that's probably the right bike size.

If you're buying a kid's bike from a good bike shop, you probably won't find training wheels on them, and that's a good thing! Why? Check the end of Chapter 11 for tips on how to teach a kid to ride a bike and you'll see.

Balance bikes are the best model for young riders who are just learning. These bikes, also called *scoot* bikes because kids sit on them and kick their feet to scoot along, have no pedals or cranks on them — and *definitely* no training wheels.

Once the kid has mastered balancing and handling, which happens surprisingly fast, it's time to get them on a bike with pedals, and you have lots of options.

The main thing to think about is keeping it simple, especially for the youngest riders. Coaster brakes are OK, but a single rear brake teaches them better technique (and they work better). And stick to one speed so there are no gears to shift. Let the kid focus on pedaling and combining that propulsion with the handling and balance they just learned. As they progress, the bike they ride can become more sophisticated.

Many small kids' bikes add suspension and other accessories because it looks cool, but until they're shredding mountain bike trails with you, you can skip these extras (even if your kids are begging you for them). Those items add a lot of weight, and on cheap kids' bikes, they rarely work well, if at all. They're only making the bike heavier and harder to pedal, and adding more things to go wrong.

Think about it this way: If your kid weighs 50 pounds and their bike weighs 20 pounds, that's already 40% of their weight. Add 5 pounds of low-quality suspension, and now it's 50% of their weight. Adding 5 pounds to an adult's bike makes it feel heavy. Adding it to a kid's bike makes it feel like a tank.

Bikes by Frame Material

After you have an idea of how many types of bikes are out there, you're probably starting to think about which one makes the most sense for you. In Chapter 8, I help you narrow down your choice to get the best one for you. But first, you should also think about what you want the frame to be made of. Though bicycles can be made from a variety of materials, these are the primary options:

>> Steel

>> Aluminum

>> Titanium

>> Carbon fiber

You can also find exotic materials like scandium, magnesium, and even wood. They're rare, though, so I focus on the four that you're most likely to find at your local shop, because they cover 99.9% of all bicycles on the market.

Steel

Steel is the original bicycle frame material, and you'll often hear fans say, "Steel is real!" Though most performance bikes have switched to carbon and aluminum, steel remains popular among bikepackers, touring riders, and gravel riders.

Typically, steel bikes are more affordable than the other options, but also a bit heavier. People love steel for the ride quality because it's good at damping vibrations, it has just a bit of "give" to smooth harsh terrain, and it has a lively feel that gives a bike some character.

Steel is also easy to repair, which is why touring riders love it for heading out into the unknown for days, weeks, or months at a time. Chances are good that you can find someone who can weld just about anywhere in the world, and they can repair your bike if it breaks.

Steel is also popular for inexpensive bikes and kids' bikes, but there's a massive difference between these and the quality steel bikes coming from premium brands.

The cheapest bikes use *high-tensile* (also known as "hi-ten") steel, which is heavy but strong. For basic kids' bikes or something you're only going to ride around the neighborhood, it's fine.

Chromoly is a more premium-level steel, and certain varieties of it range from good to ridiculously good. When you see two steel frames that cost $800 and $1500, the difference lies largely in the quality of material and how much shaping, butting, and working the tubes have received.

At the top of the rung are stainless steel frames. Some say these have a crisper ride quality, but beyond being more resistant to corrosion, they have little extra benefit over a high-quality chromoly steel frame other than aesthetics and bragging rights. Some brands, particularly custom builders, use stainless steel for high-wear/high-stress areas like dropouts and head tubes.

A good-quality steel road bike frame weighs between 1,600 grams and 2,400 grams.

SHAPING? BUTTING? WORKING?

Metal bicycle tubes are no longer just round. Advanced processes allow manufacturers to make shapely tubes that, at a glance, can be indistinguishable from carbon fiber's fluid shapes.

This is sometimes done with *hydroforming*, or using high-pressure water to press a tube against a mold to stretch it into various shapes. This can be done to make a box section (imagine a cross section of the tube being square-ish) for more torsional stiffness, or to flatten a section to create a bit of flex.

Butting is the process of creating thinner sections in the middle of a tube where less material is needed. The ends of a tube need a certain *wall thickness*, or thickness of the material, in order to be welded to another tube, but the middle section can be thinner to save weight.

(continued)

(continued)

> *Working* a tube generally means rolling, bending and shaping it in *mandrels*, special tools for curving and reshaping metal tubes. Sometimes this is done purely for aesthetics, but usually it's to shape a tube around the tires for more clearance or to create a bit of vertical compliance to take the edge off bumps — or all of the above.
>
> All these processes add time and expense, so frames with this extra work cost more, but they also usually have a better ride quality.

Aluminum

Aluminum bikes, colloquially called *alloy,* are lighter than steel bikes, but typically stiffer. Technically, almost every metal is an alloy, or a blend of metals, but I (and virtually every cyclist everywhere) use the term here to refer to aluminum frames. Like steel, there are different grades of aluminum.

Aluminum bikes grew in popularity starting in the early 1980s, when bike manufacturer Cannondale introduced bikes that were much lighter than the steel bikes offered at the time. This innovation set off a space race among brands to introduce their own alloy bikes, which quickly replaced steel at the premium level.

Alloy bikes typically have larger tube diameters, which is necessary to achieve the desired strength-to-weight ratio, and can also have advanced shaping and butting on higher-end models. Most modern alloy bikes have at least one or two main tubes with hydroformed shapes.

Compared to steel, an alloy bike's ride quality is usually a little harsher, though the best frames overcome aluminum's inherent stiffness with good design features.

Though most steel bikes have antirust coatings applied inside and out, aluminum is virtually rustproof, making it a helpful option for beach cruisers and for anyone who lives near the coast or rides on salted roads in the winter. (You should still rinse off sweat and saltwater after your ride, though, because it can eventually corrode the metal.)

A good-quality aluminum road bike frame weighs between 1,260 grams and 1,500 grams.

Titanium

Titanium is the Goldilocks metal for bikes. It has the ride quality of steel and is also:

>> Almost as light as aluminum

>> Mostly easy to repair

>> Nearly impervious to rust or corrosion

If you want a bike for a lifetime, get one made from titanium (and then pray the standards don't change. . .again!).

The only downside to titanium is its price — expect to pay a pretty penny. It's far more expensive than steel or aluminum, often starting at $3,500 for a frame, but usually closer to $5,000 or more. (*Note:* There's always an "or more" option if you really love spending money.)

Because of titanium's price, few major brands still offer a stock titanium bike; they're mostly offered by smaller, boutique brands and custom frame builders — which only adds to their allure.

Though steel bikes can be fixed anywhere you can find a welder, titanium requires special equipment to weld because it has to be done in an oxygen-free environment. Builders do this by spraying argon gas inside the tubes and around the area being welded. This means your average auto shop mechanic can't make an emergency repair for you. But you can still find quite a few custom bike builders who can — you just have to ship your frame to them.

That shouldn't be a deterrent, because titanium frames are tough — and because they're a specialty item these days, it's rare to find one that's made poorly.

Titanium comes in two varieties: the more common 3/2.5 and the higher-end 6/4, with the numbers referring to the percentages of added aluminum and vanadium. (Yep, titanium is an alloy, too!) The key difference is that 6/4 is lighter, stronger, and more expensive, but both yield a similar ride quality. Most frames are made with 3/2.5, some use 6/4 for certain tubes or sections, and almost none is completely made of 6/4.

A good-quality titanium road bike frame weighs between 1,200 grams and 1,600 grams.

Carbon fiber

Carbon fiber bikes started showing up in the 1990s and quickly replaced aluminum on the top rung (which pushed it down to the low- and mid-tier, which mostly pushed steel out of the big-brand catalogs by the 2010s).

Though carbon fiber as a frame (and component) material had some growing pains early on, modern carbon fiber bikes are fantastic. The top models from major brands are incredibly light (some dipping under 700 grams!), yet strong and stiff enough to handle the power output of top professional cyclists.

Carbon fiber allows nearly infinite shaping possibilities, which has allowed bikes to become more aerodynamic and integrated.

Because it's laid up in pieces, and those pieces can be cut into any shape and individually layered in various orientations and quantities, designers can fine-tune the stiffness in any plane — lateral, vertical, or torsional, for example — to give a bike the exact performance and ride-quality characteristics they want.

This means bikes can be stiff at the head tube and crankset to handle the forces you're putting into it, but compliant and forgiving elsewhere to make it comfortable to ride. And carbon does an excellent job of damping vibration, too, so you'll feel fresher after a few hours on a carbon bike than on a comparable metal one.

Various grades of carbon fiber exist, too, with higher-quality materials having better stiffness-to-weight ratios. Naturally, the better materials can produce a lighter bike, but they cost more, and not just because of the materials. It's also because it takes more engineering and expertise to make an ultralight bike just as strong and stiff as a less expensive one.

Naysayers joke that these are plastic bikes, with the typical complaint that if a carbon frame breaks, it often fails catastrophically (versus a metal bike, where a crack might take quite some time to cause the frame to completely break). Though that point is occasionally true, a catastrophic failure is also exceedingly rare and usually (okay, almost always) due in some large part to a bike being ridden in extreme circumstances outside of its intended use or because of a freak accident. Good frames don't just fail randomly, but the key words are *good frames*. (In Chapter 8, I explain how to avoid buying a poor-quality bike.)

Most of my personal bikes are composed of carbon fiber, and I love them. It's my preference because of its weight, ride quality, and looks. And now that carbon bikes have been out for a while, the technology has trickled down to reasonable price points, too!

A good-quality carbon fiber road bike frame weighs between 860 grams and 1,200 grams. Higher-end bikes are almost always under 1,000 grams, and some premium models venture into the range of the low 700s; however, these often come with rider weight limits and caveats like "Don't sit on the top tube."

TECHNICAL STUFF

All the typical weights listed here are for road bikes. Gravel bikes are similar — usually, 100 to 150 grams heavier because they're a little beefier, and mountain bikes can range from around 900 grams for a lightweight race hardtail up to 3,000 grams for a long-travel alloy full-suspension bike. If you're comparing weights, pay attention to the details of how they're listed so that you're truly comparing apples to apples. Some list their weights with or without frame hardware (like derailleur hangers, bottle cage bolts, and thru axles), with a rear shock or not, and the frame size. Some brands even list the raw frame weight *before paint*, so always look for those asterisks!

Now that you're likely leaning toward one or two types of bikes and maybe have an idea of which material you'd prefer, it's time to drill down and pick the one that will work best for *you*.

Chapter **8**

Purchasing Your New Set of (Two) Wheels

irst things first: There are no bad bikes. There are bikes, and then there are much, *much* better bikes. But any bike you ride is a good bike if it gives you joy, provides transportation, or simply expands your freedom.

The point of this chapter is to illustrate that where you buy your bike matters, and that some options will deliver a bike that gives you more joy, makes transportation easier, and allows for more freedom.

Considering Your Favorite Type of Riding

Will you ride mostly on a bike path? Run errands or commute around town? Ride country roads on the weekends? Or hit the trails in the mountains?

You probably have a pretty solid idea of which type of riding you'll do 90% of the time. Cross-reference that idea with the types of bikes described in Chapter 7 and find the category (or categories) that overlap the most, and then start there.

"But I want to ride lots of different ways and places," you say. That's great! But in that case, you need to either buy multiple bikes (always my preference!) or go with the model that's most capable.

What do I mean by *most capable*, you ask? I mean that you should look at which type of riding you'll be doing that will demand the most from your bike and then buy the one that'll handle the job. Table 8-1 lists a few scenarios.

TABLE 8-1   **Bike-Buying Scenarios**

If You Want to Ride On	Buy This Bike
Road and gravel	Gravel bike
Gravel and XC	XC mountain bike
Trail and enduro MTB	Light enduro mountain bike
Trips for commuting and errands	E-cargo bike

Finding Where to Buy a Bicycle

If you have already read Chapter 7 or browsed for bicycles, you know that you have a lot of choices when it comes to buying a bike. Any combination of factors can make a bike the perfect one for you. Maybe it's lighter, works better, needs less maintenance, has someone to service it, or just fits you and your needs better because someone cared to help you get the right bike *for you*.

REMEMBER

With that info in mind, the best place to buy a bike is, hands down, your local bike shop.

You have other options, too, from big-box department stores (Walmart, Target, sporting goods specialists) to online retailers to direct-to-consumer brands. Each has its pros and cons, and each meets the need of a certain type of customer.

In the following sections, I describe the differences between them so that you can pick the best place to purchase your next bicycle.

From your local bike shop to online shopping, *where* you buy your bike is just as important as *what* you buy. The following sections present an overview of the options and what you're likely to find from each.

REI: A LOCAL BIKE SHOP ON A NATIONAL SCALE

REI is the exception to the rule in that it's built like a department store or sporting goods store, but it's also much like a local bike shop.

Not only does the store carry high-quality bikes from major brands, but its Co-op house brand is excellent, too, and offers a great value. Plus, most if not all locations have a full-service bike shop inside, so the bikes are properly assembled and tuned up before purchase, and you can take one for a test ride to help get your bike fit dialed in.

Plus, REI can provide repairs and tune-ups after the sale, and it sells all the gear and accessories you need in order to outfit yourself and upgrade your bike, too — just like your local bike shop does.

The Local Bike Shop

If you're looking for the highest-quality bikes and a knowledgeable staff to help you choose the best bike for you, head to your local bike shop, (which includes REI, see the nearby sidebar, "REI: A local bike shop on a national scale").

The local bike shop typically has the widest selection of bikes for all types of riding, from gravel to road to mountain to commuter. Some specialize in a certain type of bike, but most carry a little (or a lot) of everything and have it in a wide range of sizes at a wide range of price points.

That said, excluding kids' bikes, most of what you'll find at your local shop starts around $500 or $600 and can go up to $10,000 or more. Some shops also have a good selection of used bikes they've taken on trade-in, so it's worth checking before seeking deals elsewhere.

The big-box store

If you're looking for the cheapest possible bike, department stores like Walmart, Target, and Dick's Sporting Goods are the place to go.

The word *cheapest* usually means *affordable*, but sometimes it does mean cheap. (See the later section "An online store" for more on this topic.)

REMEMBER

As with most things in life, you get what you pay for.

Quality varies a lot by store and by the brands that are carried, so it's helpful to know what to look for — and what to avoid.

Plenty of bikes have some sort of brand name imprinted on them, like Magma or Next, but these are typically the least expensive and of the lowest quality. They're also the heaviest and the quickest to wear out and need repairs. While these bikes often come fully assembled from the store, it's still recommended to take them to your local bike shop for a safety check.

But you can certainly find some gems.

Walmart's Ozark Trail house-brand is a step up from other bikes typically found there. The frames and components are of higher quality, with thoughtful specifications (often referred to as *specs*) that make the bikes more user-friendly.

And once-venerable brands like Schwinn, Mongoose, Nishiki, and others now mostly make affordable bikes sold at sporting goods stores. This situation is helpful for consumers in that the designs are coming from manufacturers who know their bikes, but their specs save consumers money wherever possible. The bikes are still very much low-end budget bikes, but they're better than the even cheaper models.

Decathlon, a French retail chain with locations in Europe and Canada (and sold online elsewhere), stands out for offering a huge variety of good-quality bikes, all designed in-house and made specifically for the chain.

Decathlon's better brands include Rockrider and Van Rysel, with others coming in at lower price points but still having better overall specifications and designs than typical big-box store bikes. These range from a few hundred up to thousands of dollars, but typically represent a great value even for more advanced riders. In fact, they're fielding a UCI World Cup MTB race team with Olympic ambitions, and those athletes are racing on the same frames they're selling in store!

The Downsides of Really Cheap Bikes

When shopping on price, it's worth thinking about what goes into a $150 bike. Considering the store probably paid $90 for it at wholesale, if you keep working backwards to the distributor, then the assembler, then the manufacturer, you quickly get to a point where every part on that bike cost anywhere from a few cents to a few dollars. And the whole thing was made for about $35 or less.

So, when you're putting your kids (or yourself) on that bike, realize that the materials are the heaviest and lowest-quality options, the designs and technology are decades old, and tolerances and tuning are an afterthought at best. And then it's all assembled by an untrained minimum wage employee.

I don't say this to scare you. Plenty of folks ride these very affordable bikes without issue. But they won't last long, and the repairs and replacement parts often cost more than the bike is worth. Many of them quickly end up in landfills, which is a shame. Expanding your bike budget by even a few hundred dollars will get you a much, much better bike!

An Online Store

Online bike stores are sport-specific online stores (check the list of sites later in this chapter). I am not talking about Amazon or department store websites, although some major bike brands (like Raleigh) do sell via Amazon.

Online stores are useful if you already have a good idea of the size and type of bike you want and are familiar with the specifications and components. The selection is virtually limitless, and there are deals to be found. But customer service ranges from nothing to chat support to FAQ sections, and there's no way to touch and feel the bike in person until it's shipped to your door — which means if it's not right, you also have to repack it and ship it back. And if it is right, you have to assemble it yourself — or pay your local bike shop to do that for you.

Direct-to-consumer brands

Direct-to-consumer brands typically offer a comparably equipped bike at much lower prices because they eliminate distributor and retailer markup and pass that savings along to consumers.

European brands Canyon and YT Industries built their entire business model around shipping directly to consumers with no retail presence. Ari (formerly Fezzari) is one of the leading US-based direct-to-consumer brands, the Icelandic brand Lauf switched to this model in 2022. Many boutique and custom brands and builders, such as Alchemy Bicycles, also only sell direct.

Even Specialized and Trek, two of the world's largest and most popular bike brands, started selling direct to consumers with a mixed model of also selling through local bike shops (albeit at normal retail prices, but with wider availability to consumers living in remote areas).

"MADE IN ASIA" IS A GOOD THING

Most bicycles in the world are made in Asia — specifically, China and Taiwan — partly because labor is less expensive, but also because they're just *really* good at it.

Taiwan produces some of the best bicycles in the world, with cutting-edge alloy and carbon fiber manufacturing plants and technology. Many of the best factories located in mainland China are owned by Taiwanese companies, too, so a label saying "Made in China" doesn't tell the whole story.

More broadly, other factories have been growing in capability and expertise in the Phillipines, Vietnam, Myanmar, and Indonesia, among others, and these factories are used by some of the biggest and best brands in the world.

So, if you're looking at a high-end bike and it's "made in Asia," chances are good that it's a really good thing.

Knowing What You Can Expect to Spend

It's always good to know what you're getting into before you start dreaming of a custom titanium gravel bike with the best parts. Sticker shock is real when you're looking at the top models, but, fortunately, trickle-down tech is also very real, and beginner bikes are so good these days that you might wonder why anyone needs to spend more.

Breaking down cost

What does a bike cost these days? The short answer? They range from $80 to $25,000. The better answer is to break that down into price ranges:

Price ranges will vary based on where you're shopping. You can pick up a bike at Walmart, Target, Dick's, and similar stores for about $80 to $300 for basic no-name-brand models. Well-known bike brands that might sell in these stores range from $300 to $600, with a few reaching $1,200.

Bike shops and good brands that sell direct or via online retailers (look for examples throughout this chapter) also sell beginner and kids' bikes starting from $250 up to $900. Mid-level bikes, which have better components and frames but are still targeted at newer riders and those who aren't looking to ride too fast or hard but still want something nice for bike paths, commuting, or general fitness usually range from $900 up to $2,000.

You might be thinking, "Whoa — $2,000 for a bike?" Yes, but today's $2,000 bike is basically a $4,000 bike from a few years ago. New bikes are so good these days, rest assured that you're getting a truly decent bike at $2,000 that will work well for many years to come. Go higher than $2,000 and you get into bikes designed to be ridden harder and more often. Here's how these upper-level bikes break down:

$2,000 to $3,500: These have good general performance and quality parts but are heavier with basic features and fewer adjustments. Frames will range from aluminum at the low end to basic carbon at the high end.

$3,500 to $5,000: The frames are slightly better, with mid-tier carbon layups and lighter alloy tubes. Wheels get progressively better with mostly tubeless-ready designs. Drivetrains are mid-tier, which work nearly as well as top-tier groups with only minor weight penalties. Some even have wireless or electronic shifting.

$5,000 to $8,000: This is the sweet spot for high-performance riders. Wheels and tires are lighter and better, drivetrains are near the top tier, and all (or almost all) cockpit parts are carbon fiber. Suspension will have all the adjustment options.

$8,000 to $13,000: These top-level production bikes are usually spec'd out with team replica components and livery. They get the best drivetrains, wheels, tires, and cockpit parts, with all the standard bells and whistles. Some even have electronic suspension controls!

$13,000 to $22,000 and higher: These are the bleeding-edge bikes — the super-cars and trophy trucks of the cycling world, where top brands and custom builders push the boundaries of what's possible and then deck them out with the most premium parts.

The benefits of bike shops

Supporting your local bike shop is kind of like supporting yourself. Your bike will perform better and last longer than a department store bike, which means you'll enjoy riding it more and spend less money and energy to do it.

Here are a few good reasons to buy a bike from your local bike shop:

Service after the sale

If something goes wrong with your bike, whether it's new or a decade old, your local bike shop probably has the knowledge and parts to fix it.

Many shops offer a service period where they'll perform free tune-ups and fits on new bikes, and they're equipped to perform almost any repair. From tune-ups to upgrades, they can also help with any warranty issues or recalls, often swapping parts or even calling in a replacement bike for you. Bike shops can even help pack and ship your bike if you're taking it on vacation or traveling to a race.

Experience matters

The folks who work at bike shops are almost always avid riders themselves, and most of them geek out on the latest bikes and components and trends, too.

This makes them helpful resources for asking questions about brands, components, and which upgrades make the most sense for you. They'll even be able to suggest the right accessories, like helmets, lights, locks, or bike rack for your car.

Local knowledge

Want to find a group ride? Safe, low-traffic routes or bike paths? Local singletrack? Your local bike shop will know where to go and how to find them, and can point you in the right direction.

They can also help you choose the right bike for local conditions, from tires and wheel size to suspension and handlebar shape. Getting a bike that will handle local roads and trails well could be the difference between your riding once a month and your loving it so much that you're pedaling every day!

YOUR NEW FAVORITE BIKE SHOP

Choosing a bike shop is like choosing a hair stylist or masseuse: You need to feel comfortable with them and trust them to do right by you.

Most of us have a built-in radar, or gut feeling on this, and it's usually clear within a few minutes of being in a bike shop whether it's a good fit for you. The shop's vibe should mesh with your personality.

The employees should be helpful and attentive without being pushy. Don't be afraid to say you're "just looking," but also don't be afraid to ask questions — lots of questions, if you have them.

And don't feel pressured to buy something you don't want or that doesn't fit you. It's okay to say "No, thanks" or "Let me think about it" and walk away.

You may end up buying another brand of bike from a different bike shop (and you should definitely shop around to find the bike that works best for you), but when the time comes to address parts and service, the shop you like best is the best shop to use.

Taking a chance by buying online

Sticking to reputable cycling-focused online retailers (check our list of good ones later in this section) often delivers a great experience and gets you a quality bike and parts.

But, as you're poking around the Internet, you'll probably find tons of options that might look good. Since we can't possibly list every retailer, the best thing you can do is to make sure the brand of bike you're looking at is a good, high-quality brand.

So, how do you know whether a brand is any good?

Locating high-quality brands

One way is to search the bike brand's name (and a bike model name if you're looking at something specific) and see what comes up. The best thing to look for are reviews of something from that brand by the top cycling media.

These sites' editors provide experienced third-party coverage and reviews of good brands. Though they may not all cover every model, chances are good that you'll at least find a few things from the same brand you're considering.

Here are some reputable sites to look for in the search results:

- Bicycling
- Bikepacking
- Bike Radar
- Bikerumor
- Cyclingtips
- Gearjunkie
- Gravel Cyclist
- The Loam Wolf

- The Lunch Ride
- MTB-News.de
- MTBR
- Outside
- Pez Cycling News
- Pinkbike
- Road.cc
- Velo

This is only a partial list. Other helpful cycling media are out there, too, so what you're scanning for is consistency. If you see legit-looking cycling websites, YouTubers, bloggers, and social media influencers consistently talking positively about a brand, that's a great sign that it's a brand worth considering for your next bike.

Locating high-quality online retailers

Once you've found a few brands you like, you'll want to find a good retailer.

This task is a bit easier, especially if you start by searching for the brand and model you want. Most of the best online bicycle retailers advertise using brand names as their keywords, so you'll usually find them at the top of any search results page in the Shopping recommendations.

Alternatively, if you're not sure which brand or model you want and you just want to shop around, here are some of the top online retailers for bikes and cycling components and gear:

- » Backcountry
- » BikesOnline
- » BikeTiresDirect
- » Competitive Cyclist
- » EvansCycles
- » Evo

- » PerformanceBike
- » JensonUSA
- » RAcycles
- » REI
- » TheProsCloset
- » WorldWideCyclery

This list provides just a small sample of sites, but it's a good place to start.

WARNING

If you find a site with pricing that seems too good to be true, or with bad grammar or obviously poorly translated content, then there's a decent chance that those sites are either non-authorized resellers who probably won't offer any after-sale service or returns or, worse, they're selling counterfeit products.

BEWARE OF COUNTERFEIT BICYCLES!

Counterfeit bicycle frames are a serious issue because those frames, forks, and parts are often made using the same molds as the real thing (even coming out of the same Asian factories, in some cases), but their design, quality control, and materials can be vastly different.

No brand is safe from this threat, but the bigger, more popular brands tend to have more knockoffs. Specialized, Shimano, and Pinarello, in particular, have seen thousands of knockoff products being sold through trading sites like Alibaba and eBay.

The most obvious warning sign is the price. If it's too good to be true, it probably is. And riding a counterfeit bike (especially one made of carbon fiber) can pose a serious safety risk to you and those riding with you.

Buying a Used Bike

Riding a bike is a *green* (environmentally friendly) way of commuting, so why not take that concept a step further and buy a bike that someone has already loved?

You are not only saving money but also probably helping someone else make a little money off a bike they're no longer using.

The following sections spell out what you need to know as you start shopping around for a used bike.

Determining whether a used bike is right for you

If you're looking for something specific, or you want the latest and greatest, then a used bike is probably not your best option.

But if you're just looking for something to ride occasionally, hit the greenway, or test the waters before investing in something more expensive, then a used bike is a great choice.

Your choices will vary quite a bit, and the previously mentioned tips apply here for finding the right type of bike from a quality brand. As you scour the classifieds and shops and online marketplaces, search online for the model and brand of anything you find, to see whether it's a good bike. If you can add the model year to your search, you'll likely find media reviews that can clue you in to whether it was a popular bike in its day. At the very least, if you see a lot of results for the brand/model showing up in cycling media outlets' coverage, it's likely a high-quality brand and model.

Knowing where to find a good used bike

As with new bikes, you can find plenty of different places to buy a used bike, each with their own pros and cons. This section lists where to look and how to shop them.

Your local bike shop

A good start is to call your local bike shops and ask if they have used bikes for sale. Explain what type of bike you're looking for, the type of riding you plan to do, and tell them how tall you are, and they'll let you know if they have anything that's a good fit. (They may also ask what your budget is because they may have a new bike that fits your needs and your budget, too.)

Local online marketplaces

Craigslist, OfferUp, and Facebook Marketplace are obvious places to look because they've basically replaced the classified section of our local newspapers and are a great place to check for an affordable used bike. Because it's free to list a bike, people will list, quality and variety here will be all over the spectrum, from junk to decent and some may need some major repairs — so use caution when considering a used bike.

The Pro's Closet

Now referred to simply as TPC, The Pro's Closet started out as a place for professional cyclists to sell their bikes, gear, and kits from the previous race season, letting you score a deal on a high-end bike with a bit of pedigree. Now they've expanded to allow anyone to ship them their used bikes and equipment, even clothing, and TPC will clean them, tune them up, and list them for sale. This means it's a great place to hunt for higher-quality bikes and components that have been checked over by an expert. Then, if you buy it, it's professionally packed and shipped to you. This means the bikes here may cost a bit more, but (say it with me) you get what you pay for.

Bike Exchange

Users pay a fee to list their bikes at Bike Exchange, which basically means you'll see only higher-quality bikes because no one's going to pay $20 to $40 to list a $50 to $100 bike. The bikes are photographed, sold, and shipped by their owners, so an element of trust is required that what they list is what you get, and that they can properly pack and ship it.

Bicycle Blue Book

Bicycle Blue Book is a combination marketplace and buyer that will estimate the current market value of your bike, let you list it for sale, or let you trade it in for credit toward something newer or better. Or, they'll offer you a price at which they'll buy it from you. This makes it an easy place to sell bikes, which means it's also a good place to buy bikes, with a typically higher-end inventory of road, mountain, and gravel bikes to choose from.

TIP

For more information about bike shop etiquette and buying a used bike, visit Dummies.com/go/bikingfd.

» **Taking care of your vision**

» **Lighting your way**

» **Locking it down**

» **Making noise to stay safe**

» **Keeping your balance**

Chapter **9**

Getting the Necessary Gear and Equipment

H elmet, sunglasses, and lights — check! I take these three safety items with me on every ride. I consider them to be essentials because they protect two of my most important organs (brain and eyes) and help others see me so that they don't run me over. Depending on where I'm going, I also bring a lock, and sometimes I have a bell on my handlebar.

This chapter covers the basic safety gear you'll want to buy to protect you and others while you ride. I also discuss the basic items that can make each ride a little more comfortable, with tips based on different scenarios, such as road riding, mountain biking, and commuting.

In this chapter, I cover these main areas of concern for acquiring gear for your bike:

» Safety — helmets, eyewear, and lights

» Locks

» Noise

» Comfort and hydration

>> Tools

>> Items that are nice to have

>> Common accessories for different types of riding

If you read this entire chapter, you'll be well equipped for whatever the road or trail may bring. (Also check out Chapter 13 for basic maintenance tips and repairs so that you know how to use all this stuff!)

Safety for Your Head: Helmets

Helmets come in several varieties and can range from $20 to $400+. Different styles work better for different types of riding, but the goal is the same: Protect your head, and thus your brain, from injury.

Proper helmet fit is critical to the helmet's ability to protect you, so review the tips in Chapter 12 to make sure your helmet fits your head and is adjusted properly. In this section, I focus on the designs and features and tell you what to look for.

Bicycle helmets range from simple and inexpensive to complex and *expensive*.

The basic helmets at big-box stores are fine if you just want something simple and affordable. Every helmet sold has to pass Consumer Product Safety Commission (CPSC) safety tests in the United States and/or European Committee for Standardization (EN) safety tests for countries in the European Union. Other safety tests are out there, but most of the world uses one of these two, so all helmets with either rating on them will meet those minimum safety standards.

TIP

You'll also see helmets with a European "CE" rating, which means that the helmet has not only passed the required EN-1078 test, but also met any higher standards that the manufacturer set for that helmet.

More expensive helmets usually have more vents, less weight, advanced fit and retention features, and additional safety equipment — and, honestly, they look cooler. Some are more aerodynamic, and some have deeper, fuller coverage for more aggressive riding (like mountain biking).

Helmet types

Let me talk the basic categories first, and then I'll talk features. Helmets fall into one of the five basic groups described in the next few sections.

Kids' helmets

The term "made for kids" means that you'll find sizes for toddlers up to youth. Some of the better ones have extremely good-yet-simple retention systems that make it nearly foolproof to get a good fit. Two of my favorite brands for kids' helmets are Kali and Lazer, but Bell, Giro, and others are great, too. If your kid is riding in a bike trailer, make sure to buy a helmet with a slim, flat/round rear so that it's not pushing the kid's head forward and down if they sit in a trailer.

Commuter / basic helmets

If you're riding for transportation, you should know that commuter helmets typically have a simpler design that looks more "normal" than sporty, so they fit with an urban environment. Having fewer vents helps keep your hair from getting messed up or frizzy, but that also means less airflow, so this type can be a bit warmer. Good ones have vents that can open or close depending on the weather, and some have integrated rear flashing lights.

Road bike helmets

Road bike helmets tend to have more vents and be lighter and more streamlined for aerodynamics. More vents means more airflow for cooling, which is important, and a lighter weight matters — you'd be surprised at how much more strain a couple of extra ounces can put on your neck when you're riding for more than a couple of hours! Gravel and XC riders often use road helmets, too. Some aerodynamic helmets reduce the number or size of the vents to reduce drag, so they're often a bit warmer, which makes them useful for winter riding (although some still have a surprising amount of airflow inside).

Mountain bike helmets

MTB helmets range from barely-bigger-than-road helmets to full-face moto-style helmets. XC helmets are sometimes nothing more than a road model with an added visor. Pretty much every MTB helmet has a visor, which can help deflect tree branches and glare. Riders hitting bigger obstacles prefer helmets with a deeper rear section that extends lower to cover more of the back of their head and temples, and those racing Enduro or Downhill, or riding the bike parks, usually wear full-face helmets.

Many full-face helmets have fewer vents because they have to meet Downhill Mountain Biking safety standards, which has rules about objects not being able to penetrate those holes. But you can find more ventilated full-face helmets that meet regular MTB standards, too. Some have removable *chin bars*, the piece that comes down around your mouth and chin, letting you disconnect it for regular riding and better breathability and then lock it into place for the descents.

TT/triathlon helmets

These specialty helmets are usually teardrop-shaped and have only a few vents. They're typically used only during races because they're aerodynamic but not practical when you're just out riding normally. Some have integrated visors, and most of them look pretty goofy.

Helmet features

Modern helmets have a lot of fancy features, and most brands have their own trademarked names for certain designs, but the basics are the same for most. As with most products you buy, more and fancier features typically means more expensive, so choose only what you need (versus want) if budget is a concern. This section describes some of the key helmet features and their options:

>> **Buckle:** Most helmets use a simple plastic clip to connect the straps under your chin, and these work well.

>> **Straps:** Straps are made mostly from a nonabsorbent material (like nylon). The main difference from model to model is how they connect under the ears.

>> **Padding:** Inside the helmet you'll find padding. Often the padding is removable so that you can wash it (because it absorbs sweat, which eventually stinks) or replace it.

>> **Foam:** Most helmets — like, 99.9% — use expanded *polystyrene* (EPS) foam (like those disposable coolers, only firmer) as their base. This foam crushes under impact to absorb the forces before they reach your brain.

TECHNICAL STUFF

Some helmets use multiple-density foams, adding a softer layer to help absorb more force. Others use multilayer foam with cone-like shapes between them to dissipate the force across a larger area. Internal structures made of plastic or carbon fiber can also spread forces around, which means less of a blunt point of trauma, and these skeleton-like structures inside the foam also help keep the helmet from breaking apart during impact.

>> **Shell:** The term *shell* usually refers to the outer hard layer plus the EPS foam as a unit, but specifically it's the plasticky layer that covers the foam and protects it from nicks and dents.

>> **Rotational impact layer:** If you wreck and hit your head, the standard tests only require that a helmet manages direct, linear impact forces. Multi-directional Impact Protection System (MIPS) was developed to address that problem by adding a slip plane, or sliding layer, inside the helmet. This layer allows the shell of the helmet to rotate a few degrees

independently of your head to reduce the total amount of rotation that reaches your brain.

>> **Retention mechanism:** At the back of the helmet is a cradle that works with the straps to keep the helmet on your head. Many of these retention mechanisms have an adjustment dial to close it in around the back of your skull.

Helmet care

Your helmet is an investment. Here are six tips to get the most out of your helmet:

>> **Don't leave it in the sun:** Heat and UV can degrade the EPS foam, so don't leave it lying around your yard or in your car.

>> **Don't drop it:** I know, your helmet is supposed to handle impacts, but you don't want that impact to come from your dropping it on the ground and ruining a perfectly good helmet.

>> **Check for cracks and dents:** If you do drop it, check the foam for cracks. If you see any, its integrity is compromised and it may not protect you in a wreck. Throw it away.

>> **If you wreck, throw it away:** Even if you can't see any damage, if you wreck and hit the helmet in any way, it's toast — even if you can't see any damage. Cracks can be under the shell or invisibly small, so better safe than sorry.

>> **Rinse it off:** If you're a heavy sweater, or one of those folks with extra salty sweat, rinse your helmet after each ride and let those pads dry completely (*not* by putting it in the sun!!).

>> **Replace it:** Every helmet has a shelf life, and most rands recommend replacing it every three to five years. EPS foam degrades over time, and even though it may look fine, it may not have the same impact resistance it did when new.

Brain safety: A game of millimeters

WARNING

Though a few degrees of rotation, or a few milliseconds' more time before impact forces reach your brain, may not seem like much, they can literally be the difference between a concussion and no concussion. The G-forces from an impact drop off rapidly with even a few extra millimeters of foam in the helmet, and a well-designed helmet can spread those forces laterally while also reducing them dramatically.

The vital five-star rating

All helmets have to pass government tests to be allowed for sale, but Virginia Tech takes it a step further and adds more impact angles and considers rotational impact. The group tests hundreds of new helmets every year, with the best receiving a five-star rating. If you want the safest helmets around, check this list: https://www.helmet.beam.vt.edu/bicycle-helmet-ratings.html

Safety for Your Eyeballs: Sunglasses and Eye Protection

No matter where you're riding, eye protection is important. Even if you're slowly rolling along a bike path, a bug can fly in your eye. If you're riding behind someone, dirt or water can fling up from their tires, and if you're mountain biking, branches, bugs, dirt, mud, rocks, and other items can all end up in your peepers.

The style is up to you, but cycling-specific sunglasses perform better when you're riding faster. They're shaped to deflect the wind while also venting so that they don't fog up (as much) when you're huffing and puffing up a steep climb or stopped at a traffic light.

Some, like Oakley and Smith, offer specific lenses for road and mountain bikes, with tints that highlight certain parts of the spectrum to add contrast and detail, helping you see the road or trail more sharply. I like photochromic clear lenses that darken in sunlight — these work well when transitioning in and out of tree cover and tunnels, for example. They're clear when light is low, and darker when it's bright.

Polarized lenses can be good because they let you see through windshield glare. Commuters may find them helpful for predicting driver behavior, and they also give oil spots on the road a rainbow-like sheen, so they're easier to spot!

Personally, I've found that too-dark lenses are not ideal for performance cycling, but the tint, shade, and style are up to you. Try a few on, borrow some friends' shades, and see what works for your face shape.

TIP

Try on the glasses with your helmet on and make sure the top of the lens or frame has at least a 1-centimeter gap between it and the helmet's brow — you don't want those banging together while you're riding, because your helmet will continually push the glasses down your nose. It's *annoying*.

Also make sure that your sunglasses' arms fit around or under the helmet straps (I prefer *over* the straps so that they're not interfering with the helmet's function in an impact, but some designs work better under — try both) and under or below the helmet behind your ears. If you stick with paired brands, this is easier (for example, Smith helmet with Smith shades), but lots of brands mix and match perfectly well. Many glasses have adjustable temple tips so you can bend them to better fit your ears and helmet.

Safety Illumination: Lights and Reflectors

I talk about having reflectors and flashing lights in Chapter 12, and the gist of it is this: You should have front and rear flashing lights on your bike on every ride.

Flashing lights improve your visibility to others, which means you're more visible to other riders, drivers, and pedestrians, which means they're less likely to ride, roll, or walk in front of you — or hit you from behind.

The sad truth is that drivers quite literally get away with murder all the time. Few cases of a driver hitting a cyclist end up with the driver facing any punitive criminal action, even when they're clearly at fault. And sometimes the excuse is something as simple as "I didn't see them." So, having flashing lights front and rear not only makes that excuse far less plausible, it also means that the other person is less likely to hit you in the first place.

Check Chapter 12 for a bit more on the legalities and reasons for lights and reflectors. In this chapter, I focus on the features and tech products you should know about in order to choose the right lights for you.

Reflectors

Acquiring reflectors is easy — they usually come supplied on your bike, and are found on the pedals and wheels and somewhere on the front and rear of the bike (usually, the seatpost and handlebar).

Lights are usually added after the fact. Many commuter and city e-bikes have lights built in, powered by the bike's battery, but most other bikes, including road and mountain e-bikes, do not include them.

Lights fall into two categories: those that help you be seen and those that help you see. The former is not the latter, but the latter works for both, so if you plan to ride in the dark, get a headlight that is bright enough to let you see where you're going and works well for daytime use, too.

Headlights

Pretty much every light these days uses LEDs, not bulbs. Most list their brightness in lumens, and some, particularly in European markets, use lux. A *lumen* is a measure of output at the LED, and *lux* is a measure of brightness on the ground, which proponents say is a more useful measure, but it's also dependent on being measured at a specific distance from the light source.

Regardless of how you measure, my advice is get the brightest light you can afford. No one anywhere ever has said "I wish my bike light weren't so bright."

TIP

Most lights have multiple levels, letting you click through Low, Medium, and High modes, and most also have one or more flashing modes (wherever legal, which is pretty much everywhere except Germany). I recommend getting a headlight with a flashing mode because it draws more attention to you during daytime use.

If you're going to use the headlight for night riding and you need to see where you're going, pay attention to the beam pattern. Some have a simple round reflector that just throws the light forward; others use more sophisticated reflector shapes to cast a broader beam pattern with a flat cutoff so that it doesn't blind oncoming traffic.

Aiming the headlight

For daytime use, you can angle the headlight mostly level so that it's aiming directly at oncoming traffic. At night, angle it downward to illuminate the path in front of you. The faster you're riding, the farther out in front of you the light should hit the ground. Slower riders will want the light closer to them.

WARNING

Don't light up your front tire too much, especially with a very bright light, because it can become a visual distraction that makes it harder to see objects in front of it.

Mounting the headlight

For casual riding, mounting the light atop the handlebar is fine, and almost every light comes with a strap or clamp to do this. Niterider, Light & Motion, Trek/Bontrager and Knog are four of my favorites.

If you have a handlebar bag, cycling computer, or phone mount, just make sure the light is getting past those items and not lighting up the accessories on your bar, which can create a visual distraction. Similarly, if the light's LED or lens is visible, angle it downward so that it's not visible in your peripheral vision. You want to see what is being illuminated in front of you, not the light itself.

Performance riders should consider mounting their headlight under their cycling computer, which is likely on an out-front mount that's holding the computer out in front of the handlebar. Several brands (I'm partial to K-Edge, but you may like others) make adapters that bolt under your computer and use the GoPro-style two-prong mounting standard, and several light brands (Niterider, Light & Motion, Lightskin, and Knog, for example) make mounts or adapters to work with those. This arrangement keeps the light in front of anything that might block it, including your own drop bar handlebars, and makes you more visible from a wider angle. It's also more aerodynamic, but note that it may require mounting the light upside down, and some lights' reflectors have optimized their beam pattern based on being mounted right side up.

Taillights

A taillight usually straps around the seatpost, but a few of them have proprietary mounts for specific saddles and/or seat bags. Brighter is better here, too, because the main function is to draw attention to you so that cars don't hit you.

That said, if you're riding in a group, you don't want to blind your riding buddies, so look for a light that has a solid (nonblinking) mode or can be dimmed.

Some taillights cast light down and forward to illuminate your calves, which creates a lot of visual motion. When a driver can see your legs moving at night, it makes you seem more human (as opposed to an obstacle) and the driver is more likely to give you more space as they pass.

Some taillights have randomized flash patterns, too, and these tend to do a better job of attracting attention. A steady pulse pattern helps drivers better gauge their distance on wide open country roads, whereas an unpredictable flashing pattern works better in urban environments as it causes a driver to slow down a little to process it and thereby pay more attention to you.

Lock It Up

If you're riding your bike to a location where you need to leave it accessible but unattended, you need a bike lock. Locks come in four main styles, and a wide range of quality and theftproof-ness. Let's talk styles first.

U-locks

The U-lock probably isn't what you envision when you try to picture a bike lock. It's a U-shaped shackle that locks into a cylindrical crossbar. The good ones have a cover for the keyhole to protect it from water and dust.

This is usually the strongest type of lock, but it's relatively small, so many people combine it with a cable or chain that can run through both wheels while the U-lock is looped around the bike's frame and whatever object you're locking it to.

Chains

Chain locks are usually covered in plastic or fabric to prevent them from scratching the bike. They range from supercheap and completely ineffective to robust and nearly unbreakable. The best ones are also heavy — sometimes weighing 10 or 12 pounds! The Kryptonite brand's New York Fahgettaboudit model is a great example — it weighs almost 11 pounds and costs $160, but it's backed by a cash guarantee against theft.

Cables

Cables are convenient, but they almost always need to be paired with a U-lock, padlock, or something else. They range in length from just barely able to secure your other wheel to long enough to loop through front and rear wheels and frames on four bikes leaning against each other.

I use cable locks when leaving the bikes on my car's hitch rack, or when we ride as a family, so we only need one lock. Most cable locks offer only light-to-medium security, so if you live in a high-crime area, they should play a supporting role rather than serve as your main bike lock.

Folding locks

Folding locks use flat metal links that pivot on reinforced pins. They work similarly to a chain, but they fold down more compactly, making them easier to mount to your bike or carry in a bag, and they articulate better than a U-lock while also extending farther. This makes them a useful option, and the better ones are also quite strong. The pins that connect the links can be a weak point, so check the ratings and reviews before buying.

POSITION YOUR LOCK CORRECTLY

In high-theft areas, always position the lock so that the keyhole is facing downward, and, if possible, position it so that it can't be repositioned by thieves. That's because, if it's facing upward, crooks can easily squirt Superglue into the keyhole, which will quickly dry and prevent you from unlocking it. Then, when you're forced to leave your bike there, they'll come back in the middle of the night with an angle grinder, cut the lock, and steal your bike when no one's looking.

Some thieves don't even wait for the cover of darkness — they just cut the lock quickly and take your bike. Less-secure locks can be cut in minutes, and (sadly) most of us are so engrossed in our phone screens or afraid of conflict that we just look the other way as it happens. So, getting your lock positioned so that it's hard to cut or reach also helps prevent theft.

And, if you see someone cutting a bike lock, say something. Snap a photo or video with your phone and then call 911. Pay it forward and maybe someone will help save your bike one day, too!

Security ratings

Brands rate their locks differently, and better brands will recommend different ratings based on the intended use and environment. But you should look for a couple of standardized tests and ratings:

>> **Ice spray certified:** These locks can withstand being "frozen" by the output from compressed air cans, which emit a freezing-cold chemical spray of compressed chemical difluoroethane that can make some metal brittle enough to crack.

>> **Sold Secure:** This third-party certification ranks locks bronze, silver, gold, or diamond, working with police and insurance companies to stay abreast of the tools and tactics used by thieves so that they can rank locks based on their ability to resist them. A higher rating (diamond is the best) means the lock is harder to cut or break and will take more time to do so.

>> **ART label:** The ART label uses ratings from one to five stars and is exclusively used to rate locks for two-wheeled vehicles. A two-star rating means it's recommended for bicycles; higher ratings are for mopeds, scooters, and motorcycles. That said, with many performance bikes costing as much or more as a motorized alternative, a stronger lock might not be a bad idea.

Bike lock strength

Many crimes are crimes of convenience, so any lock that takes any effort to defeat is often all the deterrent that's needed. Areas that are known for crime often have sophisticated thieves with the tools to cut most locks in less than a minute, so if your lock is better than the one on the bike next to it, chances are it won't be your bike that's stolen.

Your best bet is to ask an employee at your local bike shop what's best for your area, consider the value of your bike, and then find a product that fits your needs and budget.

How to lock up your bike

How securely you lock up your bike depends on your area, how long you'll be leaving it unattended. For quick trips into a store, locking the frame to a bike rack is plenty.

For longer absences, the most secure way to lock up your bike is to slide a U-Lock through the frame, rear wheel, and bike rack, with a cable running through the front wheel, too. Secure the loops on the cable to the U-Lock's shackle.

TIP

You can also find specialty bolts that use unique tools that make it difficult to remove seatposts, wheel axles, and other expensive components. Hexlox and Pinhead are two good brands.

Ah-Oogah! Horns and Bells

If you ride on shared paths, busy streets, or crowded trails, a bike bell or horn is a must-have item. It serves two purposes: It alerts others to your presence, and it tends to move them to move out of your way.

For kids' bikes, a horn can be fun, but for adult bikes, you probably want to stick to a bell. They're sleeker and less obnoxious.

WARNING

When riding, ring the bell well before you ride up on pedestrians or other riders. If you're approaching from behind, ring the bell when you're 30 to 50 feet away so that they have time to react safely. At that distance, the sound is softer but still audible, so you won't startle them, like you would if you ring it immediately behind them. Do that to someone and they might jump right in front of you! It also helps to give a verbal indication of your passing before doing so — most bike trails in the U.S. instruct you to say "on your left," so the person being passed knows you're coming around their left side.

Mount the bell near the grips so that you can reach it with your thumb without having to take your hand off the grip. Especially in crowded areas, you want to have full control of your bike and be able to brake.

You can find inexpensive bells at big-box stores and bike shops alike. If you want to get fancy, Spur Cycle makes some nice all-metal bells that look gorgeous and sound wonderful!

Items Made for Comfort

After you have the safety and security items ready to go, consider a few items that can make you more comfortable on the bike.

Water bottles

If you're riding for more than 20 or 30 minutes, bring something to drink. Some mountain bikers and gravel riders wear a hydration pack, but for most rides and riders, a simple bottle on the bike works best.

You can find a basic water bottle at any bike shop, but some of the more popular ones come from Specialized, Polar, and Camelbak.

Any water bottle intended for biking is sized to fit into a standard bicycle bottle cage, so pick one up as opposed to trying to stuff a single-use plastic water bottle in there, which will just rattle around and fall out (though there are bottle cages that are size-adjustable to fit multiple bottle sizes).

When you're done drinking the water, empty the bottle and dry it out between uses. If you're putting a sports drink or anything other than water in them, rinse them well, including squirting clean water through the spout. Give them a scrub once in a while or shake a (diluted!) bleach solution through them. They can get gross and moldy if you don't keep them clean!

Bottle cages

Most bikes have one or more mounting points for bottle cages, but few bikes come with the cages installed. Ask your shop or find them in the bicycle section of big-box and sporting goods stores. The cages range from $4 to $20 in most places, but some ultralight carbon fiber or titanium ones can easily top $80 or more!

For cruising around town, any basic bottle cage will do. The main difference between basic and fancy bottle cages, other than weight, is how tightly they hold the bottle, what angle you can remove the bottle, and how adjustable they are. When choosing a cage, consider where it will be positioned inside the frame and how large of bottles you plan to use — some cages offer vertical adjustment so you can reposition them to make room for larger bottles.

For road cycling, most cages are fine, too, but if you live in area with lots of pot-holes or rough roads, a product that holds a bit tighter is good — but not so tight that you're wrestling with your bottle to remove it.

For gravel cycling and mountain biking, you want a cage with a good, strong grip on your bottle. It might be slightly harder to pull it out, but you won't lose the bottle over rough terrain. My favorite cages are from Blackburn, and you can find options for every budget. I also like those from Silca, Wolf Tooth Components, and PRO Bike Gear.

Bike shorts

Of all the items in a cycling-specific *kit* — which is what we cyclists call our collection of cycling apparel, such as gloves, socks, and related items — padded bike shorts are the most important.

The nice thing about padded bike shorts is that they add a little cushion between you and the saddle, and you can simply wear regular shorts or pants over them if you're not quite ready to roll out in full Spandex.

Bike shorts offer other benefits, too. The compressive material helps reduce muscle fatigue, and it's more aerodynamic. Loose, baggy clothing creates a lot of aerodynamic drag, but tighter clothing lets you slip through the air and reduces the amount of energy you have to expend to ride faster.

Some bike shorts have straps that fit over your shoulders, called *bibshorts*, or *bibs*. They offer more support and don't have restrictive waist bands, but some riders prefer just the shorts — particularly women because many bib designs make it harder to take potty breaks.

WHY IS IT CALLED A CHAMOIS?

Originally, bike shorts used a leather chamois (pronounced "SHAM-ee") in the crotch. It had to be conditioned with oils to remain soft, and its purpose was to reduce friction between the rider's skin and the saddle. If you've ever used a chamois to dry your car, you know how hard and scratchy the chamois is when it's dry, so you can imagine that these took some care to maintain.

Modern bike shorts use soft, slippery synthetic fabrics over various types and densities of foam, and sometimes gel padding, to provide cushioning and prevent friction. Many riders also use a chamois cream to further reduce friction, especially on rides lasting more than an hour. My favorite is Chamois Butt'r's Coconut formula, which uses coconut oil, but *lots* of other excellent options are available.

Some cool features to consider are *cargo* shorts or bibs, which add small pockets on the sides of your legs. I use these to carry my phone and small snacks, or to stuff wrappers in after fueling up with a gel or energy bar. Some bib styles also have small pockets on the lower back, too.

Yoga-style waistbands are wider and softer and not as tight around the waist, making them quite comfortable. Many shorts have a higher waist on the rear to cover your backside when leaning forward in the riding position. (Bibs are useful for this, too.) Others have silicone or compressive grippers on the inside of the leg openings to keep them from sliding up as you ride. Men's and women's shorts usually have different padding shapes and thicknesses, too.

Cycling gloves

Gloves are helpful for several reasons. First, they protect your hands if you wreck. Your natural human instinct is to throw your hands out in front of you when you wreck, and your palms can get scraped up if they hit, well, just about any surface you're riding on.

Gloves also provide better grip on your handlebars, especially if you're sweating a lot. Most gloves have a terry cloth panel on the thumbs, which works well for wiping away sweat in the summer (and snot in the winter).

Some gloves have padding in the palm, and others don't. Though you might think that thicker is better, gloves with too much padding make it harder to get a good grip on the bars. Some riders, particularly mountain bikers, prefer no padding because it gives them a better feel for the handlebars.

Maintenance Supplies

Even if you have no interest in becoming a home mechanic, there are a few essentials you need at home and on the bike to keep it in good working order and make basic repairs in a pinch. For the details, read on.

Floor pump

A bicycle floor pump is so named because it rests on the floor and you stand on its foot platform while you pump. This keeps it stable and lets you quickly inflate any tire.

Most good pumps have either a universal *pump head*, or *chuck*, which is the part you attach to the valve stem on your tire to inflate it, or a dual head. A universal chuck works on both Presta and Schrader valve stems, and a dual-head design has a separate hole for each one. However some pumps have reversible chucks that you have to manually switch depending on which type of valve stem your wheel has.

Most brands use a lever that you lift to secure the head to the valve. But, some thread onto the valve stem, which can be more secure, but you need to make sure your tubes or valve stems have threads on them. And make sure your valve cores are installed very tight so that you don't accidentally pull them out when removing the pump.

Pumps come in High Pressure (HP) for road bikes and High Volume (HV) versions for gravel and mountain bikes. HP will work for bigger tires, but HV pumps don't work well for thinner tires that need to go to higher pressures.

TIP

You can use many floor pumps to top off your car tires in a pinch! It may take a while, but it works – I've done it many times!

If you're setting up tubeless tires, an air compressor is best. If that's out of the question, look for a booster pump — it has an extra air chamber that you can inflate to 160psi and then release all of the air all at once to help seat your tubeless tires on the rim. These tend to work well and can save a lot of frustration.

Basic repair kit

In case you get a flat tire or need to make a quick adjustment or repair while you're out riding, this section presents some items you need to take with you. I keep mine in a saddlebag, but some folks have it all in a pouch or tool roll in their backpack, handlebar bag, or frame bag. The point is to have it easily accessible and stocked with the following items:

WHY DOES MY PUMP'S GAUGE GO TO 250PSI?

Modern performance bikes and riders are almost all using tubeless tires for road, gravel, and mountain bikes now. These allow for a lower tire pressure, which offers more grip, comfort, and efficiency (as explained in Chapter 5). Whereas many riders with tubes used to run 90psi to 120psi on their road bikes, most folks are now running 65psi to 80psi.

So, if we're all using a lower tire pressure, why do many bike pumps have gauges that show 250psi?

It's because, when you compress the pump to inflate your tire, you're creating a lot of pressure. Maybe your tire's only at 40psi, but when you press down, the needle spikes to 120psi or more. Inflate to 80psi and it might spike to 200psi or more. If the gauge couldn't allow the needle to move freely into these higher ranges, it could mess up its own calibration and reduce its accuracy. So, even though you're (hopefully) never inflating your tires to 200psi, your pump's gauge needs that wiggle room to operate correctly, which is why ASME recommends that gauge range should be twice the operating pressure.

Spare inner tube: Be sure to get the right size for your bike's wheels and tires. Even if you're running tubeless tires, you can always use a tube in a pinch.

Tire levers: Use these to remove the tire from the rim. I cover how to fix a flat in Chapter 13.

Mini tool: Make sure this tool has, at minimum, all the bits that fit all the bolts on your bike. Usually, this includes a T25 Torx plus 2.5/3/4/5/6mm hex wrenches. Some toolkits also include screwdriver bits, a chain breaker, CO_2 chuck, spoke wrenches, and more. It's really about weighing the what-ifs versus the size and weight of larger multitools.

Mini pump or frame pump: You need some way of inflating your tires, and a small portable pump is the best. A frame pump is usually longer and fits onto your frame, and it fills tires faster but is larger and heavier. A mini pump may also attach to the frame, but can also fit in a jersey pocket, hydration pack, frame bag, or (sometimes) saddlebag. The smaller it is, the more strokes you'll need to inflate a tire, and definitely get the right one for the job — high-volume for MTB and gravel and high-pressure for road.

CO_2: If you're racing, you will want one or two CO_2 cartridges and a CO_2 chuck to attach it to the valve stem. These items blow a concentrated blast of carbon dioxide into your tires and inflate them in seconds — perfect for getting back on course quickly (or reseating tubeless tires). But the cartridges aren't refillable, so they create waste, and they're expensive — so I use my pump whenever possible. Even if you have these on board, it's still a good idea to carry a pump, too.

Tire patch kit: A patch kit can be used on a tube (or a tire given the right kit), making them a useful addition to every kit, even if you're running tubeless.

Tire plugger: If you're running tubeless, a tire plug kit is the quickest way to get back up and running if you get a puncture that sealant alone won't seal. Similarly to a car tire repair kit, these use a metal prong to shove a tacky rubber stick into the hole in your tire, instantly plugging it. Some plug kits come with two plug sizes to fix different size punctures, plus the jabber prongs and a storage capsule. Some also include a small blade so that you can cut off the excess plug sticking out of your tire, which helps prevent it the plug from getting ripped out while riding. Some tire plug tools are designed to stick into the ends of the handlebars, making them quickly accessible — sometimes letting you repair the tire so fast that you don't even need to add much more air!

Chain lube

All new bicycle chains come with a tacky grease on them, which is mostly fine for casual riding. Eventually, though, the grease wears off and you need to lubricate the chain.

Before you buy whatever lube is available at the shop or spray WD-40 on there (don't do this — WD-40 is designed to loosen bolts, so it's a terrible chain lube), you should understand how chains work and why they need lube. If you haven't read Chapter 6, on drivetrains, I explain the parts of the chain in detail there. The point of chain lube is to create a lubricating barrier between not just the chain and the gears but also the plates, pins, and rollers of the chain itself. All that metal-on-metal action needs lubrication.

The lubrication has several jobs. First, it reduces friction. It also reduces wear and prevents rust. And the best lubes also resist contamination, actually helping to keep the drivetrain clean.

Let's look at the three main types of chain lube:

>> **Dry:** Intended for dry conditions

>> **Wet:** Intended for wet conditions, like rainy days

>> **Wax:** Works well in any condition

WARNING

The dirtier the chain becomes, the more it creates an abrasive slurry that wears away any protective coatings or slick finishes, and then eventually the metal itself. If you never clean your chain, you're basically creating a rough paste that's wearing down your entire drivetrain every time you turn the pedals.

What's the best way to lube my chain?

The bare-bones chain maintenance is just wiping down your chain with a clean rag now and then, especially after riding in wet conditions. Your front tire will spray your chain with all the dirt on the road or trail, so wiping it off after each ride is a good first move.

If you ride in clean, dry conditions, a standard dry lube will work fine. Just note that both wet and dry lubes are oil based, so any dirt, dust, or other stuff that flings up onto your chain will stick to it (see prior Warning for why that's bad). Wax lubes, however, coat your chain with a dry, waxy, flaky coating that sloughs off as you ride. That means any contaminants that stick to it are quickly eradicated, so they never have a chance to grind down your chain. Wax lubes take more work to apply, but they produce the fastest, cleanest, and quietest chains.

Regardless of what you choose, definitely use a bike specific chain lube. If you want to maximize chain life and performance, get a wax-based lube. Want to know why? Go down the rabbit hole of chain lube geekery at Zero Friction Cycling (www.ZeroFrictionCycling.com.au), it's fascinating!

Cleaning kit

A clean bike is a happy bike is a fast bike! As with any other mechanical product, if you take care of your bike, it'll last longer and work better. A quick wipe-down with a microfiber rag is often enough to keep the bike looking fresh, but when things start to get grimy, it's time to give it a proper cleaning. Isopropyl (rubbing) alcohol will take care of any little grease marks from around the chain area.

Dish soap and an old toothbrush work fine, but Park Tool, Muc-Off, and Mountainflow sell complete bike care kits with brushes that reach into all the nooks and crannies of a bike. These are the four key brushes you need:

>> **Cone brush:** Fits between the frame and the tires and the suspension linkages, for example

>> **Cassette brush:** Slim enough to fit between cassette cogs

- » **Big firm brush:** Helpful for frame, tires, and rims

- » **Chain cleaner:** Clips around the chain with brushes that spin as you rotate the cranks

These four brushes cover all the bases, especially when combined with an old toothbrush. Add an ecofriendly degreaser and bike wash and you're covered. Just note that the chain cleaner is best used after you've wiped off any surface grit and excess chain lube, and, ideally, thoroughly rinsed it with hot water to flush out any contaminants. Then follow the cleaning with more rinsing and let it dry completely before adding fresh lube. (I give you more cleaning and maintenance tips in Chapter 13.)

Common Accessories

A few other items that make rides better are specific to the type of riding you're doing. It goes without saying that a helmet should be on everyone's head, and flashing lights on any bike ridden on streets. And if you're a performance rider, you will want to switch to clipless pedals as soon as you're comfortable with them, especially for road and gravel. (Many MTB'ers still prefer flat pedals.)

Here are my suggestions for accessories and gear for commuters, roadies, gravel grinders, mountain bikers, and cargo bikes.

Commuter gear

Adding a rear rack and pannier bags to your bike makes it easier to carry a lock, books, your laptop, a change of clothes, and other items you may need at work or school. Most standard bikes can accept universal-mount racks, which clamp onto the seatstays and seat tube, and many city, commuter, gravel, and other bikes have attachment points for bolt-on racks.

Most of these racks use a standard design that pannier bags attach to, making it easy to choose from a wide variety of shapes and sizes. Ortlieb is known for high-quality waterproof bags, in case you need something for rainy days.

Check the load rating for the rack and bag, and for your bike's frame, and make sure you don't exceed it. Some pannier bags have hideaway clips and extra shoulder straps that let you wear them like a messenger bag or backpack, and some are oversized for hauling groceries. Check all the options, because there's something for almost anything you'd need to do. Many also have reflective panels and clips for lights to add more visibility.

Rack bags attach to the top of the rear rack and can be used alone or in conjunction with panniers to add more storage. Some bikes can mount front racks to their frame or fork, too, letting you put the bags up front instead, or add those along with the ones in the back. A simple crate lashed to the top of a rack is also an incredibly effective carrying device.

If you do ride in the rain, invest in a good pair of waterproof pants, jacket, and overshoes (or rain boots). Showers Pass and Endura are two good brands, and many of their pieces will fit over standard clothes and have side zips on the legs so that you can pull them on and off without removing your shoes.

Road cyclist gear

Invest in a couple of good cycling kits and you'll not only feel faster — you'll *be* faster. You don't need to spend much. Brands like Pactimo offer killer products at reasonable prices. As you start riding more, adding a few pieces like a windbreaker and arm/knee warmers will come in handy.

I like the compact wind jackets that roll up small enough to fit in a jersey pocket, which is useful for taking along if the sky looks suspect, or pulling off if things heat up.

A thin beanie or cycling cap will help keep your head warm under your helmet, or just provide a visor for helping keep the sun out of your eyes.

Most road bikes are sold with tubes in them, even if the tires and wheels are tube-less ready. Switching to tubeless will let you run lower pressures for more comfort and traction, and it can reduce the likelihood of flatting from a puncture (because you add sealant to the tires, and that plugs the hole before much air can escape). Going tubeless also saves about 100 grams of rotational weight, which makes you feel even faster when sprinting or climbing!

Most bikes also come with basic handlebar tape, so upgrading to a product with more cushion or grip (or both) will make it feel like a new bike. Supacaz bar tape is universally loved (it's my favorite) and comes in a wide variety of awesome colors.

Gravel cyclist gear

All the recommendations for road cyclists apply here, with the reminder of how great a top tube or handlebar bag is. The spirit of gravel riding is about getting off the main roads and venturing out farther from civilization, which means you'll want to have some extra snacks and maybe even a small first aid kit. Definitely bring a wind or rain jacket.

For all my performance bikes, I like to carry lightweight TPU tubes. (Ask your local shop or search online — Pirelli, Tubolito, and others make them.) They fold up in half the space of standard butyl tubes, weigh half as much, and are tougher. These are comforting backups in case of a flat, especially on rougher surfaces like gravel and mountain bike trails.

Most gravel races are 50 to 100 miles long (some are as long as 350 miles!), so the top racers wear slim race vests that have a few pockets on the front shoulder straps for snacks and a small reservoir on the back for water. This lets them skip most of the feed stations, which saves time, but that means they sometimes miss out on bacon and candy bars – which begs the question, are they really getting their money's worth?!?

Mountain bike gear

Where roadies and gravel grinders can get away with form-fitting clothing, most mountain bikers want clothing that's a little baggier because they're moving around more. A good rain shell with oversized hood that fits over your helmet is useful, and the lighter-weight ones work fine even if you're just trying to block the wind. Look for those with PFAS-free DWR treatments or proper waterproof membranes like those from GoreTex or Polartec.

A hydration pack or hip pack is a good way to carry more water and a jacket, especially helpful if your full-suspension design limits you to one (sometimes small) water bottle.

Many riders use hidden tools on their bikes to stash accessories inside the handlebar or stem cap or adjacent to the water bottle cage. Others strap a spare tube to the top tube or under the saddle.

WARNING

If you're storing anything under your saddle and you have a dropper seatpost, make sure the rear tire won't hit it if your seat is dropped all the way down and your suspension is fully compressed!

A good pair of mountain bike shoes will help keep you feeling fresher, too. Compared to sneakers, MTB shoes have stiffer soles that support your feet better on the pedals, whether you're riding clipless or flat pedals (see Chapter 6 for more about pedal types). They range from very walkable to completely rigid, with XC and fast trail riders and racers preferring the latter for maximum efficiency.

Cargo bike gear

Most cargo bike brands offer a wide array of accessories, which is good because most are sold without much of anything attached to them. The good news is that you can then customize them to suit your needs. The bad news is that the accessories often add $200 to $1,000 or more to the cost of the bike, and most are proprietary to that brand of bike, so you're kinda stuck.

I've had three cargo bikes, and the two most useful things I added was a front basket and rear seating, which included pads, an extra handlebar, and footrests. These bikes have let me make grocery runs and take my kids to school. I've also added rear pannier bags, which are huge, which has let me use it for full, family-size Costco runs!

I've also found that many cargo bikes use lower-tier drivetrain components. That, plus the fact that you're moving a heavier bike loaded with cargo and you're likely going to wear out the chain, cassette, and chainring faster than on a normal bike. Some E-cargo bikes will wear it out even faster because of the extra torque from the mid-mount motor. So be prepared to replace the cassette and chainring if you can (and possibly upgrade to higher quality parts).

Now you're all set for any type of ride. With these basics, you can ride through all the seasons and make basic repairs.

TIP

For more information about bike locks, chain lube, and other accessories to have on hand, visit Dummies.com/go/bikingfd.

3

Using and Maintaining a Bicycle

IN THIS PART . . .

Preparing for your first ride.

Understanding the basics of riding a bike.

Exercising sound bike safety.

Repairing and maintaining a bike.

Finding great places to ride.

Chapter 10

Preparing for Your First Ride

T his chapter will help you get the bike ready for your first ride, and the tips here provide a useful mental checklist to run through before every ride, just to make sure everything's in good working order — and that *you* are ready, too!

Before Your First Ride

Before you take off on your bike for the first ride, you need to make sure that the bike fits you properly, the controls are set up correctly, and the tires are properly inflated.

The sizing guide in Chapter 2 can help you choose the right bike size, and now it's time to get your fit dialed in so that you're as comfortable as possible. The proper size isn't just about comfort, though — being able to easily reach the brake levers and drop a foot to the ground when you stop will make you a *safer* rider, too.

Here's a quick checklist to complete before your first ride:

>> Check and adjust the saddle height.

>> Make sure the brake levers are angled so that you can reach them easily.

>> Make sure the brakes are working properly.

>> Press down on the handlebars to make sure they're tight.

>> Spin the grips a little to make sure they're tight.

>> Stand over the front wheel and trap it between your legs, and then try to turn the handlebars to make sure the stem is tight.

>> Check the tires for proper inflation.

>> Put on your helmet.

>> Pedal up and down the street to make sure the chain and cranks turn smoothly.

>> If they do, keep pedaling and shift the gears to make sure they shift correctly.

>> Turn on your bike lights.

After you complete all these tasks, roll on out and start having fun!

Knowing what to do if something isn't right

If any part of your bike fails these tests, check this book's table of contents for that part of the bike or fit procedure to get it (and you) ready to ride. You'll find maintenance and repair tips in Chapter 13.

Not quite sure how to properly fit and adjust your helmet? Check Chapter 12 for tips.

Adjusting the saddle height

The first thing to adjust is the saddle (the bike seat) height, but first you should know how to measure the saddle height (see G in Figure 10-1) on the bike. Take a tape measure and place one end at the center of the bottom bracket (the gizmo that your cranks spin on) and extend it upward along the seat tube to measure the distance to the top of the saddle.

If your bike has a weirdly angled seat tube, measure from the center of the bottom bracket through the center of the clamp that's holding the saddle on the seatpost, but be sure to measure all the way to the top of the saddle, not the clamp.

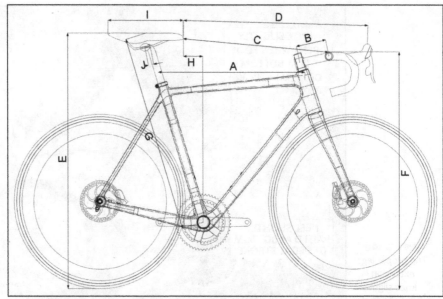

FIGURE 10-1:
Bike
measurements
(the seat
height is G).

Credit: Pursuit Cycles

Now make sure the top of the saddle is level with the ground (flat), and then determine your ideal seat height.

TIP

A good starting position is to stand next to the bike and adjust the top of the saddle even with your hips.

You can also set the seat height two or three inches shorter than your inseam (not the inseam measurement on your pants, but your *actual* inseam, measured from crotch to floor when standing barefoot).

This strategy will get you pretty close, and then it's time to hop on the bike. If you can't do this in front of a mirror, have a friend watch you slowly pedal past them and ask them to note the angle of your knee when the crankarm is pointing straight down.

Your knee should have a slight bend (as shown in Figure 10-2), somewhere around 35 degrees when that leg's pedal is at the bottom of the stroke. That sounds like a lot, but it *looks* like it's barely bent, especially when you're looking down at it while seated on the bike.

And, you should achieve that angle while your ankle is slightly flexed — your foot shouldn't be flat or the heel dropping lower than the ball of your foot.

This process will give you a clean and efficient pedal stroke.

KNEE SLIGHTLY BENT WHEN FOOT IS AT BOTTOM OF PEDAL STROKE*

140° to 150°

HEEL SLIGHTLY RAISED AT BOTTOM OF PEDAL STROKE

*measure angle from ankle bone to center of knee to hip bone

FIGURE 10-2: The proper leg extension is knee slightly bent and foot slightly flexed.

If your legs are too straight, lower the saddle a bit. If they're too bent, raise it a bit. Make small adjustments; you'd be surprised by how much of an impact even 1 centimeter of extra seat height can make — or by how much of an improvement even 2 millimeters can make!

WHERE SHOULD I PLACE MY FEET ON THE PEDALS?

Whether you're using a clipless pedal (the type where your shoe clicks into the pedal and is mechanically connected), or flat pedals, (like the ones that come on most bikes), the ball of your foot should be centered over (or a few millimeters in front of) the pedal's *spindle*, or axle.

What you *don't* want to do is use your instep or heel to pedal the bike. I see a lot of kids and newbies make this mistake, and it leads to poor form and bad fit. It also takes your calf muscles out of the equation, so you're not getting all available power (or working those calves for some great-looking legs!).

If things *look* good but still don't *feel* quite right, here are four signs you need to make a few more adjustments to the saddle height:

>> **Your knees rise up too high.** If you're an adult and hop on a kid's bike, notice how your knees stick up high? Though your position might not be quite that exaggerated, if your seat's too low, it overworks your quadriceps and you don't get good power to the pedals.

>> **You can put your feet flat on the ground while seated.** Unless it's a BMX bike or a beach-cruiser-style bike that's designed to keep you low, you probably want to raise the saddle if you can put both feet flat on the ground while seated. However, you should be able to reach the ground with your toes and safely lean to one side and support yourself with one foot.

>> **Your legs have to straighten out to complete the pedal stroke.** If the seat is too high, your legs will be too straight at the bottom of the pedal stroke. This decreases power output, but more importantly, the saddle is likely putting too much pressure on your perineal area (some of the sensitive bits between your legs), which can be very uncomfortable.

>> **Your hips are rocking back and forth.** Another sign that the seat is too high is if your hips are visibly rocking up and down, from side to side, with every pedal stroke. This is your body's way of compensating and allowing your feet to get low enough to complete the pedal stroke, but it too will likely be uncomfortable — and it can cause hip and back pain over time.

The wrong saddle height not only robs you of power and feels uncomfortable but also causes knee pain and exacerbates any muscular imbalances you may have. If you just can't seem to get it right, check the section "Fine-Tuning for a Fun Ride," later in this chapter, or swing by a local bike shop and ask someone there to help you get it dialed in.

TIP

You might look at some bike saddles and think there's no way they'd be comfortable. Many are thin and lightly padded and look like racing saddles. If you're not used to them, they might seem a little firm at first, but it's worth ensuring that your saddle's height and position and angle are optimized before giving up on a particular saddle.

Adjusting the handlebars

Adjusting your handlebars' angle and the position of the items on it is important for maximizing comfort, control, and safety. Here are the things to do for both flat bars and drop bars.

For any of these adjustments, loosen the appropriate bolts enough that you can adjust the position of the bar or component, but leave them snug enough that they hold their position after you let go. This lets you make adjustments without having to constantly hold the part in place. (Check Chapter 9 for proper tool suggestions.)

Flat bars

Angle and position: First, make sure the handlebar is centered in the stem. Sounds silly, but it's worth checking and fixing if it's not.

Next, sit on the bike and rest your hands on the grips. They should feel natural, with a slight, natural bend in your wrist matching the backward sweep of the bars. Very few flat-style bars are actually flat; most have a slight *sweep*, or backward curve, to improve their ergonomics. You want this sweep to match pretty closely with your wrists' natural angle.

To adjust this (or center the handlebar), slightly loosen the stem bolts at the front of the stem so that you can rotate the bar.

Brake Levers: Once your handlebar is in a comfortable position, it's time to get your brake levers in the right spot. For flat bars, there are two or three adjustments to make – lateral, angular, and reach. Figure 10-3 shows the ideal brake lever position on flat bars.

FIGURE 10-3:
The ideal brake lever position on flat bars.

You generally want the brake levers positioned inboard from the grips so that you can easily reach the brake lever with your index (pointer) and middle fingers.

TIP

I like to brake with my index finger on the outboard side of the lever, but it's really a personal preference. Either way, it leaves your thumb and ring/pinky fingers safely gripping the bar. You shouldn't have to (and don't want to) use all four fingers to grab the brake lever!

Next, adjust the levers so that they're level with the ground, and then rotate them down about 20 degrees. Sit on the bike and reach for the levers. You should be able to quickly place your fingers on the lever to pull it without having to reach awkwardly up and over, or rotate your wrist downward, to get to it.

My recommendation of 20 degrees is just a starting point — adjust from there until it's comfortable and easy to reach. There's no right or wrong position, and a lot of it will have to do with where your handlebar height is in relation to your saddle height, and how aggressive (or not) your riding position is. I know some pro enduro racers who run them perfectly level because it's easier to reach when they're hanging off the back of the bike on steep descents!

Lastly, many brake levers have a reach adjustment that lets you move the lever in, closer to the bar. High-end models can adjust their reach without pulling the brakes. Lower-end models have a simple screw that pushes the lever close to the bar, but this will pull brake cable as they do, thereby bringing the brake pads closer to the rim or rotor. In that case, set the lever reach where you want it (closer is better for smaller hands or shorter fingers) so that you can easily reach and pull the lever, and then adjust the brake cable so that you have proper braking power (see Chapter 13).

Shifters: Next, adjust the shifter levers so that they're easy to reach and use, too. Some low-end bikes have the shifters integrated into the brake lever/mount, so you can't adjust them independently of the brake. But if you can, you can move the shifters inboard/outboard and/or rotate them until you get them where you like them. Some shifters also offer reach adjust for the shift levers themselves.

On high-end components, you may find a single clamp that holds the brake levers and shifter pod, but they still allow independent adjustment. This makes for a less cluttered cockpit, and usually allows plenty of adjustment. I've found that sometimes you can flip-flop the left and right clamps to give yourself even more options. The point is to experiment until you find the right ergonomics for you.

Adjusting drop bars

Angle and position: Some drop bars have perfectly straight top sections, others have a backsweep, and some even have a forward sweep (see Chapter 3 for more information on drop bars). With these, you don't so much angle them to get the sweep where you want it as you choose the bar that already has the amount and direction of sweep you want.

The important adjustments on these bars help you get the correct rotational angle so that you can position the brake levers in easy reach from both the hoods and the drops (see Figure 10-4) — and have both positions angled for comfortable riding.

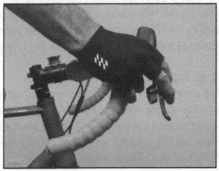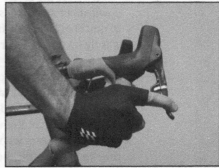

FIGURE 10-4: Brake reach examples on drop bar bikes.

Typically, this means angling the bar so that the ends of the drops (the parts pointing backward on the bottom) are either level with the ground or sloping slightly downward and then positioning the levers so that the hoods are level or sloping slightly upward toward the front. You don't want the hoods sloping to the front, because your hands will slide forward on them and you'll constantly fight to pull them back and hold your body up.

Ideally, you'll set up all of this before you wrap the handlebar tape around the bars, but if your bike is already built, prioritize getting the angle of the hoods and levers right. Then you can make more adjustments the next time you wrap your handlebars with fresh tape.

Since drop bar shifters are built into the brake levers, often you can't adjust them separately, but you can usually adjust the brake lever reach. Get them close enough that you can reach and pull them with your index and middle fingers, but not so close that they touch the bar before fully actuating the brakes and thus limiting your braking power.

Airing up the tires

Most bicycle tires have their maximum recommended pressure printed on their sidewall. Some also have a recommended minimum pressure. These are usually listed as psi, or *pounds per square inch*), which is also what most bicycle pumps show on the gauge, particularly in North America.

Some regions use *bar*, which is not precise for low pressures. One bar equals 14.5038psi, so imagine trying to get 38 psi and having to get that pump's needle to exactly 2.62 bar! Fortunately, most of the world uses psi.

What tire pressure should I run?

The short answer is if your bike has tubes, just pump up the tire pressure somewhere between its minimum and maximum psi. If you're a heavier rider, get closer to the maximum psi. Lighter riders can go lower.

Bigger, wider tires typically require lower tire pressures because there's more volume to support your weight. Smaller, skinnier tires typically require higher pressures because there's less volume to support your weight.

Seems simple, right? It can be, but here are some fun facts about high-versus-low tire pressures:

Higher tire pressures:

>> Reduce the chances of a pinch flat (described in the paragraph following these lists)

>> Support heavier loads

>> Can feel harsh

>> Are less efficient unless riding on a perfectly smooth surface like a velodrome

Lower tire pressures:

>> Increase the chances of a pinch flat

>> Feel smoother

>> Can be more efficient and improve traction

Where you end up is a matter of personal preference and your risk tolerance for *pinch flats*, which happen when you hit a curb, root, rock, or another obstacle and compress the tire all the way to the rim, thereby "pinching" it (and the tube inside it) between the hard edge and the rim. The result is usually a *snakebite* puncture, not because a black mamba has reached out from the gravel but because the impact pinches two small holes in the tube (and sometimes even the tire's sidewall), resembling a snakebite.

Tire selection also comes into play. Some tires have better sidewall support and cut/tear/puncture protection. Check Chapter 5 for more details on tire construction and how to choose the right one for your riding style.

TIP

For more information about prepping for the next ride, fine-tuning, and suspension setup, visit Dummies.com/go/bikingfd.

Before Your Next Ride

Unless you've magically grown (or shrunk) overnight, you shouldn't have to adjust your riding position after that first ride.

That said, there are a couple of reasons why you might, such as if you let a friend or family member borrow your bike. It's likely that they changed the seat height, so you'll want to check that.

Other than seat height, the main things to check before each ride are your tire pressure and that your lights are charged and on the bike.

WARNING

If the chain is squeaky, you can put a little extra lube on it, but be mindful of adding more lube on top of a dirty chain. That's a great way to make it even dirtier and actually cause it to wear faster. (See Chapter 13 for a complete guide to chain lubrication)

Chapter **11**

Riding a Bike 101

I f you're new to riding, or just trying out a new discipline, these pointers will get you up and rolling quickly and safely. I also included some of my favorite handling tips that've helped me progress as a rider, many of which I've learned from riding with top road and mountain bike pros over the years!

The Basics of Riding a Bike

Whether this is your first time, or it's been a long time, starting to ride once you're past childhood can seem intimidating. We've got farther to fall when we're not three feet tall, but there's a reason we say easy things are "like riding a bike". . . because it is, indeed, quite easy (and oh so fun!).

If this really is your first time riding a bike, just read through this section, including the part about teaching a kid to ride. There are pointers throughout for getting started that'll help you at any age.

Mounting your bike

Start by holding the handlebars while standing to the side of your bike, hips just in front of the saddle. Step one leg over the top tube, or, for taller bikes, lean the bike toward you to bring the saddle lower, then swing the leg closest to the bike over and around the rear wheel and saddle, planting it on the ground on the opposite side of the bike. You should now be straddling the top tube.

Getting in the saddle

Now, put one foot on a pedal and push off the ground with the other to create some forward motion. As you do this, step that foot onto its pedal, sit on the seat, and start pedaling.

If you're still getting comfortable balancing and steering the bike, drop the saddle really low so that you can sit on the bike with both feet flat on the ground. Use your feet to scoot along, learning to balance the bike and turn it while you're rolling along slowly, then gradually try putting your feet on the pedals, and then pedaling. There's no rush to put it all together, but I bet you'll pick it up very quickly!

Balancing the bike

The beauty of bikes is that their wheels create centrifugal force as they spin, which helps them stay upright on their own. It's why you can (in theory, maybe don't try this yet) hop off your bike while it's moving and it'll keep rolling along on its own for quite some time.

This force helps you stay upright, and helps the bike go straight, even if (when) you take your hands off the handlebars while riding. It's also why it's easier to balance the bike when you're moving along at 5mph or faster versus just wiggling along at walking pace, so don't be afraid to build up a little speed.

Balancing a bike is really just making micro adjustments to its direction as you ride, which sounds complicated, but your subconscious will mostly do this for you, so don't overthink it. Use the Force!

The other aspect of balance is balancing *your* weight on the bike. If you remember how dropper seatposts are helpful for getting your butt behind the saddle on descents (see Chapter 4), think about shifting your weight rearward on descents and forward on climbs.

In most cases, the goal is to keep your body's mass centered between the wheels so that there's equal traction. On really steep climbs, you might shift yourself onto the nose of the saddle to keep enough weight on the front wheel so you don't inadvertently do a *wheelie*. On steep descents, you want to keep your weight far enough back to avoid doing an *endo*, which is like a reverse wheelie (also known as "nose wheelie") that sends you toppling over the handlebars. See the sidebar below ("How to corner like a pro") for more tips on weighting the bike while turning.

Steering the right way

Steering a bike is really more about leaning into a corner than turning the bar. Yes, you'll turn it, but usually only a few degrees at the most.

One of the hardest things to learn is looking where you want to go, and *NOT* looking at the things you want to avoid running into. But that's the secret of steering . . . look where you want to go!

Much like your subconscious will help keep you balanced, it'll also point you directly where you look. So, if you look at the pothole or try you're afraid of hitting, you're almost certainly going to hit it.

Instead, try looking ahead of the obstacle to where you really want to go. When cornering, whether on the road or the trail, look past the corner to where you are headed and the bike will go there much more easily.

WARNING

This is hard. Our natural tendency is to look at what's right in front of us, not farther ahead to where we want to end up. When we do this, our conscious brain is trying to steer us where we want to go, but our subconscious is trying to steer us toward what we're looking at. The result is feeling like we're fighting with the bike to get it to go where we want it to rather than a smooth, flowing turn.

Even the best cyclists are always working on this, so don't get frustrated if it feels unnatural at first. It takes trust in your bike and tires to do it, especially as you start cornering faster. Just try to look a little farther ahead of each turn on each ride and you'll start to build confidence and get better and faster.

If you're struggling to point your eyes where you want to go, try pointing your body. Imagine a line sticking out of your chest, pointing straight forward. Now, when you want to turn, twist your torso slightly to point that imaginary line in the direction you want to turn. Your head and eyes will follow. You don't have to twist much, and this is easier and more helpful when you're standing on the pedals versus seated, but it's a great trick to learn to better lean into a corner, too.

HOW TO CORNER LIKE A PRO

The faster you go, the more traction you need on your front tire to handle the speed through corners. There are three tricks I've learned:

Weight the front tire – It seems counterintuitive to lean forward over the front wheel, especially if you're diving into a downhill corner, but the more weight you can get over it, the better the front tire will grab the ground, letting you turn harder and faster.

Push down on the inside grip – If you're turning left, think about pushing down on the left grip and weighting the inside of the bike. This will help push the bike into the turn and improve traction.

Weight the outside pedal – Whenever you're cornering, you usually want the outside pedal at the bottom of your pedal stroke, and the inside one at the top. This helps them clear the ground better when you're really leaning into a turn. Weighting the outside pedal (the right pedal if you're turning left) by pressing down into it with your foot puts more weight directly above the tires' contact patch with the ground, giving them more grip on the ground.

It feels a bit weird trying to weight the opposite hand and foot as you dive into a turn, so practice weighting the outside foot first, until it becomes habit and feels natural, then practice weighting the grip. It may take a few months of conscious effort, but eventually you'll be cornering like you're on rails!

Pointers on pedaling

Once you get going, pedaling should feel natural. You'll want to make sure your bike is set up with a proper fit (see Chapter 7 for bike fit tips) so that you're getting good leg extension. If it feels like you're overworking the front of your legs, hurting your knees, or you just have no power, adjusting your seat height is a great first step to fix all those issues.

Most new riders pedal with a very slow cadence, around 50-60 rpm. While comfortable, it's not very efficient. To guestimate your cadence, just count *one-one-thousand, two-one-thousand* as you pedal, and if your right leg is pedaling in sync with your counting, then you're pedaling at 60 revolutions per minute (rpm) . . . one per second. You only count the revolutions of ONE leg when determining your pedaling cadence.

ARE YOU MASHING YOUR GEARS?

You might hear the team "mashing a big gear", which simply means you're grinding it out at a slow cadence, pushing a big, or hard, gear combination. For example, if you're riding a road bike and have it in the big chainring up front and a little gear in the back, that's a tall, which also means hard, gear.

In contrast, "spinning an easy gear" means using a gear combination that is really easy. That's why, when bikes had triple chainrings, the smallest one was called the "granny gear", because it's so easy your grandma could pedal it. Most modern mountain bikes have a single 32-tooth chainring, but the cassette might have a 52-tooth large cog, which means the wheel isn't even making one full revolution per pedal stroke, so it's super easy to pedal!

There are times when you want to push a hard gear, like in a sprint, or you'll be forced to pedal slow, like on a steep hill, so it's a good idea to mix some strength training in (by mashing a big gear as hard as you can now and then, or doing squats), but most of the time, spinning a quicker cadence is your best bet.

Now watch an experienced rider, especially the pros, and they're turning their legs over at 80-100 rpm. It wasn't always that way. Prior to beleaguered pro cyclist Lance Armstrong's (in)famous multi-Tour de France streak in the early 2000s, most riders were grinding bigger gears at lower cadences. Armstrong and the USPS team brought more science to it, testing the efficiency and output at different cadences and found that ~90 rpm was much better. Now, all top cyclists are spinning faster and riding longer.

Working up to a higher cadence takes some practice, and it'll feel unnatural at first. Even when you're really good at it, pedaling above 100-110 rpm feels weird. But it's worth the effort to practice pedaling faster because it'll make you a smoother, faster, and more efficient cyclist.

TIP

Pedaling faster is also a better cardio workout, which is something you'll feel right away when you start moving your legs faster than you're used to . . . it'll get you out of breath quickly! Stick with it, shifting to an easier gear and pedaling 10 rpm faster than normal for 20-40 seconds at a time, recover for a few minutes, and then do it a few more times per ride. Eventually, you'll start spinning faster and faster without getting out of breath.

Most bikes come with normal flat pedals that work with any shoe, and you're really only able to push down on the pedal, thus creating power only on the front of the pedal stroke.

If you switch to clipless pedals, where your shoe clicks into the pedal for a more secure connection (See Chapter 6 for a detailed comparison between "Flat" pedals and "Clipless"), you're able to pull through the bottom and up the back of the pedal stroke. This gives you more power and works additional muscles, further smoothing your pedal stroke.

Braking like your life depends on it

Braking well is one of the most important skills you'll learn, and the faster you ride, the more important it is to do it well.

If you're just lollygagging along a bike path at low speeds, stopping is easy, but let's start with the obvious: If you pull the front brake lever all the way in quickly, there's a chance you could *endo* (See "Balancing the bike" above) and send you toppling (or flying!) over the handlebars.

With that in mind, here are some tips for safe, effective braking that'll help you ride more confidently and faster, too! Note that all of these techniques build on each other, too, so as you're able to combine them, you'll be braking like a pro in no time!

Slow down BEFORE you need to turn

If you're slowing down for a turn, the best time to do that is before you reach the turn. It's the same with driving a car: You want to come into the turn at the desired speed so you can carry your momentum through the turn, then accelerate out of the corner.

As you approach the corner, start slowing down so that you can let off the brakes as you start to turn and just roll through it. This tactic has three advantages over trying to brake into and through the turn:

1. It lets you focus exclusively on your line, or intended path, rather than thinking about that and how you're braking.

2. It'll let you exit the turn faster.

3. You'll have more control through the turn.

That last one is worth explaining: When you're turning, the front wheel is better able to steer the bike if it's rolling freely. The harder you're trying to brake, the less it wants to turn, so the less accurately you're able to steer. So, if you've already slowed down and can just roll through the turn, you'll have much better control. And, remember, look ahead to where you want to go!

Bias the front for more power

Your front brakes have more stopping power than your rear brakes, because as you start braking, that deceleration shifts more of your weight to the front tire, so it has more traction. It's not necessarily because the front brakes are more powerful, but because of the physics of it, and many bikes put larger disc brake rotors on the front to take advantage of that extra power.

The flip side is that as your weight shifts forward, it's easier to skid the rear tire. Which is fun if you're doing it on purpose, but unintentional skidding can cause you to lose control.

You can take advantage of that by favoring your front brake over your back brake when you need to brake hard. But, remember tip #1? Brake hard in a straight line, before the turn, not while you're corning! not while you're cornering! Once you're in a turn, you want to try to keep the front wheel turning freely and feather the brakes only as much as absolutely necessary.

Feather your brakes, don't drag them

If you're on a really long descent, it's tempting to *drag your brakes*, keeping light pressure on your brakes the whole time to maintain a safe speed. That's a great way to wear out your brake pads quickly and potentially overheat them. Instead, my preferred method is to brake a little harder where it's safe, then coast for a bit and build up speed again, hence *feathering* them on and off.

WARNING

Cook your brake pads too much and you could lose braking power (see Chapter 5 for more about how brakes work).

If the terrain is too steep for that and you need to stay on the brakes constantly, then take turns letting off the front and rear occasionally to prevent either from overheating. Modern hydraulic disc brakes cool extremely fast; they only need a 1–2 seconds to reset.

THE UK BRAKES ON THE OTHER SIDE, TOO

Brittons drive on the left in the UK, which seems backwards to some parts of the world. If you're renting or borrowing a bike in the UK, there's also a good chance the brakes will be set up opposite of what you're used to. While most of the world puts the front brake on the lefthand side of the handlebar, many UK manufacturers set it up on the right-hand side. If you're used to the front brake on the left, this can really throw you for a loop (and be unsafe!), so be sure to check the bike's setup and ask if you can flip-flop the brake's position if needed.

Practical application

I combine all of these techniques on high-speed descents down mountain passes or downhill mountain bike trails. Whenever on a straightaway, I'll use that time to manage my speed with occasional spurts of hard braking, biasing the front on straightaways and feathering the rear through turns if necessary.

Practicing these will quickly get you braking like a pro, but even the best of us are always improving, so don't get frustrated if you feel like you're not doing it right. . .no one's a pro right from the start!

Shifting gears the right way

The next skill to learn is shifting. If you've been riding your bike, you've probably figured out the mechanics of it pretty quick. Shimano, SRAM, TRP, Campagnolo, MicroSHIFT, and others all have their own system, and they're all easy to figure out, so this section isn't a guide to how each brand works.

Rather, it's about how you should think about and time your shifts for maximum comfort, safety, and performance. Basically, you have two options, downshift (shifting to an easier gear) and upshift (shifting to a harder gear). At the most basic level, you shift to keep yourself in a comfortable pedaling cadence and effort. But there are some times when you'll want to shift before you need to:

When to DOWN shift to an easier gear

WHEN APPROACHING A STOP SIGN OR RED LIGHT

Much like you would in a stick shift car, you want to downshift your bike as you come to a stop. Because just like in a car, when you stop, you want to be in an easy gear to get started again. If the light turns green, you want to be able to easily spin through the intersection. If you're still in a harder gear, you're going to have a harder time getting going, awkwardly mashing a big gear slowly across the road. Remember, with most bikes, you can't shift unless you're pedaling, so don't wait until you stop to downshift!

WHEN APPROACHING AN ABRUPT HILL OR STEEP CLIMB

When you come to a very steep hill, you'll lose momentum and speed extremely quickly, so you'll need to be able to pedal to keep going. If you're in a really hard gear (like if you were cruising downhill), you'll have a hard time cranking it up the mountain, and it's harder to shift when you're applying a lot of pressure to the pedals, so it's better to get into an easier gear as you're approaching the steep part.

For mountain bikers, early downshifting is a critical skill as many trails go up and down in rapid succession, and if you get stuck on a steep section in a too-hard gear, you could stall and topple over . . . or fall backward . . . and potentially land on rocks, roots, or worse.

When to UP shift to a harder gear

WHEN YOU'RE COASTING DOWN A LONG HILL

If you just finished a climb and now it's time to descend, start shifting into a harder gear as you're cresting the top and starting to roll down the other side. Even if you're planning on just coasting, you'll want to be ready to pedal if you need to, like if the road flattens out a bit or a headwind kills your momentum. If you're still in a too-easy gear but going much faster than you were when climbing, you'll quickly *spin out*, or exceed your maximum cadence. Best case is you just bounce on your saddle a bit before shifting, but worst case is it throws off your balance or handling. The last thing you want to do while speeding down a descent is have to take your focus off your steering to think about shifting.

This is even more important when mountain biking, especially if you're riding flat pedals (where you're not clipped in, see Chapter 6 on pedals), because if you try to spin super fast on a technical downhill section, your feet could just fly off the pedals. Additionally, good mountain bike handling is all about managing cadence and short bursts of pedaling, so you really need to be in the right gear at the right time to finesse your way up and down the trails.

Don't worry if you don't remember this right away. Just being aware of it will help you build that habit after a few times of being in the wrong gear, but even the best of us still mess up our shifting now and then.

Teaching a Kid How to Ride a Bike

The hardest part of learning to ride a bike is learning to balance it, and learning to trust yourself to steer and lean into a turn. The actual pedaling part is easy, and that's why training wheels have been replaced by balance bikes.

Unlike training wheels, which don't teach kids how to lean and turn, balance bikes don't have pedals or cranks, just a frame, wheels, handlebar, and seat. Kids sit on them and scoot along (which is why they're also "scoot bikes"), learning to balance by steering and leaning the bike into turns naturally. Which is perfect, because it's better to learn the balancing and steering *before* learning to pedal.

Trust me, if you want to get your kids riding as quickly as possible, start them on a balance bike.

But they already have a bike with training wheels . . .

No problem, just take them off, remove the pedals, and drop the saddle as low as it'll go. This should let them sit low enough to reach the ground with both feet and have enough clearance for their legs to stride beside the now pedal-free crank arms.

But kids grow so darn fast . . .

It's tempting to stick kids on a bike that's a little too big for them because they'll probably grow into it quickly. I admit, I've done it, and so have most of my cycling buddies.

As long as it's *almost* their size (as in, only *one* size too big), it can probably work. Just drop the saddle and make sure they can easily get their feet on the ground when they stop. That's the key: Make sure they can safely, quickly, and easily plant their feet so they don't fall over when they stop.

It's also tempting (for long-time cyclists, anyway) to trickle down parts from our own bikes to their bikes, which is usually an upgrade from what comes on kids bikes (and also gives us a great excuse to upgrade our own bikes!). The trick is that some items, like grips, brake levers, and saddles, might be too big for small children's tiny hands. Brake levers in particular should be adjusted so that their smaller hands can easily reach and pull the levers so they can confidently and easily come to a safe stop. And handlebars might be too wide . . . the same bike fit tips from Chapter 7 (mostly) apply to kids, too!

Be encouraging!

Kids, like adults, will rarely master a new skill the first time they try it. Give them time and encourage them with "Nice Try!" and "Good Job!".

They'll probably wreck, get a few scrapes, and fall a few times. That's fine, it's all part of the process, so don't overreact . . . they're looking to you for cues as to whether a little bump or topple is a big deal, or just part of the fun. If they wipe out (and it's not serious, of course), yell "Oooh, nice one!" or "Good save!" and clap for them to give it another go.

Let them learn at their own pace

One of the hardest things for seasoned riders to do is let novices (and especially their own kids!) learn at their own pace. We want to constantly give advice on shifting, braking, cornering, climbing, descending . . . everything!

At the beginning of the ride, ask if they'd like a few pointers. If they're receptive, start with 1-2 basics. Anything more than that is too much. Let them focus on a couple things at a time, not twenty. If they say no, just let them lead out the ride and observe how they do. If they boff a corner or tumble over a curb or roots, help dust them off and ask if they'd like some tips to do it better the next time.

Believe me, it's *really* hard to bite your tongue, but when the student is ready to learn, they will. Some kids (and adults) prefer to learn things on their own, and hard-earned lessons and figuring it out for themselves will cement those lessons for life. And you can always send them a YouTube video showing how to master a particular skill now and then, too . . . ;-)

But I want them to keep up with me!

Well, you could buy them an e-bike . . . but a better bet is to just take them on rides where you have no agenda and get them used to riding a little longer or faster than normal. Perhaps your destination includes ice cream as an incentive . . . this works well.

Eventually, they'll get faster, but riding slow with them is a great time to work on your own low-speed handling skills. Or do short sprints and circle back. Practice spinning a higher cadence.

Before you know it, they'll be teenagers and probably beating you while eating nothing but Doritos and Mountain Dew, so enjoy being the fast one while you can.

Sometimes, though, you do need to take them on a longer ride and keep them from bonking. For that, there are tow cords that you attach to both bikes so you can pull your kid along. Sounds sketchy, but TowWhee and Kids Ride Shotgun both make bungie-equipped cords that have plenty of stretch to smooth the ride so you're not yanking them along with every pedal stroke. I have several friends that swore by them when their kids were young, but this is definitely one item that I'd stick to the name-brand items for sure!

Now that you know the skills, it's time to practice them! Pick one or two things from this chapter to focus on during your next few rides, and once you're feeling good about them, come back to this chapter and pick more. Before you know it, you'll be riding like a pro!

Chapter **12**

Riding Safely: Following the Rules of the Road, Path, and Trail

After you're all set up on your bike and you know how it works, it's time to make sure you know the rules of the road and how to stay safe while you're riding, whether it's on the road, the bike path, or the trails.

Later in this chapter, I talk about some specific recommendations for safe group riding, and riding on shared bike paths and mountain bike trails — and how to interact with other riders, walkers, joggers, hikers, vehicles, and even horseback riders.

But first I want to discuss basic bike safety before covering the rules of the road and general tips to keep you safe on public streets.

Keeping Safety in Mind

Having the right bike is one thing. Knowing how to ride it safely throughout your local city streets, country roads, bike paths, and trails is another, so here are some tips to keep you (and those around you) safe.

Following the rules of the road (and bike path)

One of the biggest safety factors is how you interact with other traffic while riding, where traffic could be anything from cars to pedestrians to other cyclists. Here are the basics that will serve you well almost anywhere:

>> Yield to pedestrians.

>> Ride with traffic.

>> Use blinking lights.

REMEMBER

Virtually every town, city, state, and country requires vehicular traffic to yield to pedestrians, particularly if they're in a crosswalk, and this applies to bicycles, too.

Though the general rule of thumb for walkers and joggers is to walk facing oncoming traffic, for cyclists it's the opposite: Ride in the same direction as traffic.

Why? Because cyclists are faster than pedestrians, so if you were riding toward oncoming traffic, both parties (driver and rider) would be headed toward other very quickly — sometimes, too quickly to react. Plus, joggers can easily jump off the road if they see that a car is approaching too close. That's a bit harder (and more dangerous) to do if you're on a bike.

But if you're riding along in the same direction (and with a nice, bright blinking taillight to help them see you), drivers have more time to slow down and pass safely.

Blinky lights on the front and rear of your bike make you more visible to all other road users. Most people understand how a taillight would help, but a good flashing *front* light helps the traffic in front of you see you, too, which includes drivers pulling out from a side street or trying to cross the road.

Bright clothing helps, but lights are dramatically more effective, and most good lights have solid, nonblinking modes, too, for illuminating the path when you're riding after dark.

Reflecting their headlights

Like lights, reflectors make you more visible to drivers, particularly after dark. Actually, pretty much *only* after dark, when drivers have their headlights on. Just to state the obvious, reflectors reflect light back at the source (see Figure 12-1), so they only work when a headlight is aiming at you.

FIGURE 12-1:
Reflectors.

Credit: Depositphotos

In most places, bicycles are required by law to be sold with reflectors on them, and you typically find them on the wheels, seat posts, handlebars, and pedals so that they provide 360 degrees of visibility.

The movement of the wheel and pedal reflectors creates a highly visible "thing" in a driver's field of vision, which helps them register you as a fellow human. That way, they are more likely to use caution.

Once you own the bike, however, it's probably up to you (check local laws) if you want to keep them on there. I suggest that you do, especially if you're using the bike for general fitness or commuting or for transporting your kids.

You are free, solely at your own discretion, to make any decisions to remove, disable, or opt not to use any safety equipment. You may notice some cyclists removing the reflectors, and here's why:

Mountain bikers don't need them if they're *only* riding on the trails, where there is no vehicular traffic. And, if you're night-riding, they can be distracting for the riders behind you when their lights keep getting reflected back at them.

Road and gravel cyclists (and triathletes) don't want any non-aerodynamic equipment on their bike, and they remove anything that adds weight without also adding some performance benefit — and reflectors are usually the first to go.

But these riders often replace them with bright blinking lights, giving them all-day / all-night visibility.

If you can't stand the look of the reflectors on your bike, buy some reflective tape (it comes in colors) and get creative. Or wear reflective clothes, gloves, helmets, jackets, or bags.

Wearing your helmet the right (or wrong) way

Helmets only work if they fit well and you wear them properly. You'd be surprised to see how easy it is to do it wrong.

Your local bike shop can help you buy a helmet that fits well and has the right features, and they'll help you get it set up so that it sits in the right position on your head.

That last bit is important. You might stick a helmet on your head and think it fits, and then just strap it under your chin and hit the road, but there's more to it than that. Figure 12-2 shows the important parts of a helmet.

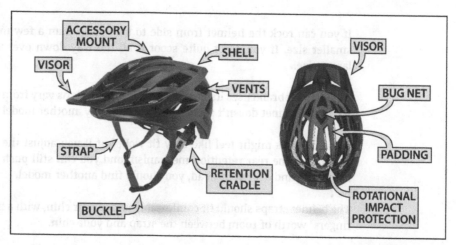

FIGURE 12-2:
The parts of
a helmet.

Those straps, buckles, and cradles have adjustments for a reason, and there's a specific way they should be positioned to ensure that a) the helmet is covering the parts of your head it's supposed to cover and b) the helmet stays in place in the event of a wreck so that it keeps covering those parts after the initial impact.

Figures 12-3, 12-4, and 12-5 show some of the most common mistakes, with some helpful advice on how to correct them:

FIGURE 12-3:
Helmet is too big
(on left) or too
small (on right).

The helmet should fit over your head comfortably, cradling your skull without squeezing it.

If you can rock the helmet from side to side more than a few millimeters, try a smaller size. If you can't quite scoot it all the way down over your head, try a larger size.

Each helmet brand uses its own head mold, and designs vary from model to model. So, if one helmet doesn't seem to fit correctly, try another model or brand.

Some helmets might feel like they fit well, but if you adjust the straps correctly and dial in the rear retention mechanism and you can still push the front of the helmet up and over your head, you should find another model.

The helmet straps should fit comfortably under your chin, with a maximum of two fingers' worth of room between the strap and your chin.

FIGURE 12-4:
Helmet straps
are too loose.

Credit: Depositphotos

Too tight and it'll be uncomfortable when you're looking up, down, and around. Too loose and it could slide out of place in an impact, leaving you exposed.

The side of the straps typically slide through a buckle before they split to meet the front and rear of the helmet. This junction should meet directly under your ear, sitting about one finger width below the ear and just a tiny bit forward of your ear lobe. You don't want the loop rubbing under your earlobe, and you don't want it dangling at the bottom of your jawbone. Getting this one set up correctly can take a little fiddling, but it's worth it to ensure a secure fit.

FIGURE 12-5:
Helmet isn't
covering
forehead.

WARNING

Lots of riders have their helmets sitting too far back on their heads, leaving their entire forehead exposed. Think of it this way: If you faceplant, you want the helmet to hit the ground before your forehead.

The front of the helmet should sit about one or two finger widths above your eyebrows. Different helmets can sit slightly lower or higher, depending on design, and if you plan to wear sunglasses with your helmet, bring those with you when you try on helmets (and bring your helmet when you're trying on new shades, too) to make sure they fit well together.

Believe it or not, I see people wearing the helmets backward, too. The retention mechanism should be on the back of your head, not the front.

Rules of the Road

The rules of the road vary by state and country, and later in this chapter, I've supplied a few links to resources. Google is your friend, however, when it comes to finding the laws that apply in your location. You can also ask your local bike shop and fellow riders, but beware that what some folks say "should" be the law isn't necessarily the actual law, even if their heart is in the right place.

Almost every locality in the world allows bicycles to use public roads just like any other vehicle does, unless otherwise posted (on most interstate highways, for example).

And, manners matter — being aware of norms and expectations will not only help you fit in but also help you ride more safely.

CARS VS BIKES? IT'S NO CONTEST!

Unfortunately, at least in the United States, drivers can hit, injure, and even kill a cyclist and still be let off with little more than a warning, despite quite literally committing vehicular homicide. Civil cases might result in compensatory damages, but criminal charges are rarely brought against the driver. Regardless of how right or wrong that situation is, the onus is on the cyclist to stay safe and do everything possible to remain visible.

As bad as all that sounds, you can take some commonsense steps to stay safe. Many car-and-cyclist accidents can easily be avoided if both parties simply pay more attention and proactively avoid dangerous situations. You can't control a driver's behavior, so the next best thing is to try to predict it and act accordingly.

This chapter is full of tips for being seen, avoiding accidents, and commanding the road.

Ride with traffic

You may hear advice that walkers and joggers should run against the flow of traffic. That's so that they can see when cars are approaching and quickly jump out of the way to avoid being struck by one. This strategy works because, compared to bikes, pedestrians are slower and cars have plenty of time to see them and give them space.

Bikes, however, move much faster than people do, so if a rider is traveling at 20 mph and a car at 30 mph, that means the two of them are closing in at 50 mph, which means neither party has much time to safely react. So cyclists should ride with traffic, moving in the same direction as cars. Using that same scenario, that means the car is approaching the cyclist at 10 mph (30 mph car minus 20 mph bike), which is slow enough to see the rider and safely slow down or move over.

Ride on the right

Generally speaking, you should stay to the right of your lane (or left, if you drive on the left side of the road). Doing so makes it easy for traffic to pass you. Give yourself at least 1 to 1½ feet (0.5 meter) between you and the edge of the road. This gives you some margin for error — and somewhere to go if a driver is approaching you too closely. The last thing you want is to be forced off the side of the road and into the grass or ditch — or worse (especially if you're going fast!). So, give yourself some room, but also give drivers room to pass.

Ride no more than two abreast

In some areas, riding more than two abreast is limited by law (or you're required to ride single-file), but in almost every instance, it's just common sense and best practice to ride no more than two cyclists side by side.

The argument for riding wider than that is that you're much more visible to drivers, which is true. If you're riding on a multilane road *and* taking up only one lane *and* there's not a lot of traffic, it's probably fine (assuming that it's legal). But you'll also take much longer to slide into single-file so that cars can pass, and you'll probably just make drivers angry.

Make passing easy

To build on the points I mention earlier in this section, you should make it easy for cars and faster riders to safely pass you. Some cyclists insist that they can take as much space as they want, because (darnit!) their taxes pay for the roads, too! But think about it this way: If you're driving and come up on a tractor or horse carriage (or a cyclist!), you want them to slide over so that you can pass, so pay it forward and be courteous by helping to maintain the flow of traffic. Intentionally blocking or slowing down traffic creates ill will toward cyclists, which is the last thing we need.

Signal your turns

Just like you learned (I hope!) in driver's ed, hand signals are used on the bike to indicate turns and stops. Figure 12-6 shows the three key signals you need to know.

FIGURE 12-6: From left to right: left turn, right turn, slowing/stopping.

Those are the official hand signals, but it's generally acceptable to point with your right hand to signal a right turn, too. And in a group ride, you can usually raise your hand high so that riders farther back can see it over the heads of riders in front of them, as shown in Figure 12-7 a little later in this chapter.

Stay off busy urban roads

This advice should be common sense, but I know several cyclists who've been hit while riding busy multilane roads with no bike lanes during busy times. Sure, cyclists legally have every right to those roads, but some battles aren't worth fighting when you can often find empty side streets and neighborhood roads (or even sidewalks) that can be used instead.

Ride predictably

Drivers, and other cyclists, are used to detecting patterns. It's how people function as a society — we get used to seeing a standard behavior and we then expect it, so we bias our behaviors around what we expect to happen. And we expect traffic, whether it's cars or bikes, to behave in a certain way.

So, if you ride with traffic, signal your turns, and use the correct lanes, cars will be able to predict where you'll be and then navigate around you. But, if you're weaving in and out of traffic, turning erratically, or hopping on and off the sidewalk or cutting across traffic, they may not be able to react in time.

Your best bet is to hold a straight line, signal, and check your surroundings before changing lanes, just like you would when driving a car.

Predict other's behaviors

Similarly to being predictable while riding, you should try to predict a driver's intentions. If someone is slowing before an intersection, they're probably turning, and if they're not signaling, you should assume that they will turn in front of you.

If a driver is approaching from a side street, they'll cross the street you're on or turn onto it — don't assume that they see you. Watch the driver, and if you don't make eye contact, you should definitely assume that they do *not* see you. I'm constantly surprised by how few drivers *do* see me in these situations, so it's best to be ready to slow, stop or take evasive maneuvers. This strategy has saved me from being hit more times than I can count!

Take your lane

In most areas, bicycles have the same rights to the roads as cars, so you have every right to hog the whole lane, if you want. But, much like that person who slides all the way over to the left lane on the highway and drives too slowly (seriously — please don't be "that guy"), that would do nothing but annoy people who want to go faster than you.

Mostly, you want to be considerate of other traffic, including cyclists who are faster than you, and stay to the right of the road so that others can safely and easily pass you. But, if the situation warrants, sometimes it's better to move to the middle of road and take the lane.

For example, if you're rolling through downtown and lots of cars are parked on the side of the street, moving to the middle of the lane ensures that no one will *door you*, or open their car door into your path as you're riding by.

Or, if traffic is slowing and you want to hold your position and not get boxed out of the lane entirely, just claim your spot and maintain it through the slowdown, and then move over after the situation returns to normal.

Know your route

It's a lot of fun to just head out, take random turns, and explore your city or a new area. But it's a good idea to have your phone, a small cycling computer or watch with GPS mapping (and know how to use it!), group ride apps, and/or local shop "intel" as a backup, too. Local shops can tell you which roads or areas are safer than others and recommend a loop based on your fitness and how long you want to ride.

Strava is a popular app for road and gravel cyclists that shows *heat maps*, or popular routes and roads. Komoot and RideWithGPS are both useful for planning a trip and linking roads and paths, offering turn-by-turn directions and syncing with popular GPS cycling computers. Trailforks and MTB Project are helpful for finding mountain bike trails and detailing their features and difficulty.

All these apps have free versions, so you can try out their mapping or routing features. Or just download various Google Maps regions for offline use so that you can route yourself home in a pinch.

Know your surroundings

Always be scanning your environment. Be aware, and look for blind corners where drivers might approach and not see you until the last second. Parking lots are particularly bad because drivers are looking for parking spots, not cyclists. (I avoid riding through parking lots as much as possible.)

TIP

I recommend not wearing headphones because they're illegal in many areas and they block out ambient sounds from traffic and other riders. You'll see just how bad they are when you're riding on a bike path and ring your bell or call out to walkers and joggers who don't hear you until you pass and then they're startled and jump. (It's because they're wearing AirPods. I promise — it's *always* AirPods!)

That said, many of us (myself included) love listening to music while we ride. So (and this is not an endorsement or a recommendation) some folks may place a single earbud in their right ear (where traffic drives on the right) to keep one ear open to hear traffic approaching from behind or, my favorite, use open-air bone conduction headsets that don't close off your ears from outside sounds.

Resources for bicycle laws

Here are a few links to help you find the local laws in various spots around the United States and the world:

https://bikeleague.org/bike-laws/traffic-laws

https://bikeleague.org/bike-laws/state-bike-laws

https://thebikeproject.co.uk/cycling-rules-for-beginner-cyclists

https://road-safety.transport.ec.europa.eu/eu-road-safety-policy/priorities/safe-road-use/cyclists_en

These links also have additional information linked within their pages. Note that some of them are about required equipment (bells or lights, for example), not just the rules of the road. If you don't see your area listed here, try searching online for the phrase *cycling laws for <your state, county, city, or country>*.

Follow Etiquette for Group Rides

When you're riding in a group, there are a few things you can do to keep yourself and others safe and keep everyone moving along safely. In addition to the points I make in the next several sections, there are local differences in how group dynamics and signaling work. And these can vary from group to group even in the same town, so when you're ready to join a group road ride, introduce yourself to the ride leader and ask if there's anything you should know about the ride.

Hold your line

It's always a good idea to hold a straight line — your ride will be smoother and more efficient. But it's especially important when riding next to someone else or when riders are directly in front of and behind you. If you can stay straight behind someone, you'll save energy by *drafting* them, letting them block the wind for you. Staying straight also helps those behind you to draft you, too, but also they'll take cues from your line — if you swerve, they'll assume that you're trying to avoid something and they may swerve, too. So try to ride straight ahead.

Be consistent

Maintain a consistent speed. You already know how frustrating it is on the highway when someone not using cruise control passes you, cuts in front of you, and then slows down so that you have to pass them — and then does it *again and again!* It's equally frustrating when the rider in front of you keeps slowing and then accelerating.

In a *paceline*, or a long line of riders in a group, the more riders you have, the more this effect becomes exaggerated. We call it a *yo-yo effect*, where the riders at the back are constantly having to slow down and speed up to stay on the back of the pack. This behavior wastes a lot of energy, so the more you can maintain your momentum and maintain the same speed, the better it is for everyone.

Avoid slamming on your brakes

Unless you have an emergency on hand, slow down predictably and slowly. In a paceline, the rider behind you is usually between six inches and three feet away, so if you brake abruptly, that person will hit you. This behavior can not only injure you both but is also likely to mess up your wheels and bike and leave you calling someone for a ride home.

Signal turns, stops, and obstacles

Just as you need to let cars know where you're going, the riders behind you need to know where you're headed, too. Figure 12-7 shows how it's helpful to raise your hands higher up to signal turns so that riders farther back can see the gesture.

When you're approaching an intersection or otherwise slowing down, pump the palm of your hand up and down, like you're trying to push something down toward the ground.

When someone is drafting you, it's hard for them to see the ground ahead of you. So, you should use hand signals to indicate obstacles that might be dangerous, like potholes or loose gravel spilling out of a driveway, so riders behind you can make the necessary course corrections.

If you see something coming up that you want to avoid, just shake your pointer finger downward on the side of the bike where the upcoming obstacle is. Sometimes I'll slap my thigh or snap my fingers as I do this to make a little noise to increase the likelihood the rider behind me noticing it.

Some bike paths have poles at entry and exit points to prevent cars from driving on them, so it's helpful to point and yell out "Pole!" if someone is following you.

You can also use audible signaling, which is important. See the later sidebar "Calling audibles" for more on that topic.

CALLING AUDIBLES

When riding in a group, in addition to hand signals, call out your intentions and other warnings to keep everyone in sync and safer. Here are the most common audibles — and when to say them:

Right turn, left turn: When you turn

Slowing: When you're slowing down

Stopping: When you're approaching a stop sign or red light

Flat! When you (or someone else) puncture a tire while riding

Clear! When the intersection is clear of cars, to let riders in the back know that it's safe to roll through with the rest of the group

Car back: When a car is approaching the group from behind

Car up: When a car is approaching the group from the opposite lane

Car right, car left: When you're trying to cross an intersection, so that riders farther back know that it isn't yet safe to cross

You don't always have to call out "Car up," by the way, but that phrase is helpful if riders have spread out and are close to (or even over) the center lane. "Car back" is helpful to let riders know to get single-file or at least shift to the right as much as they can. If you're riding in a big group, help pass the message along by repeating it loudly and clearly.

Avoid soft-pedaling

Soft-pedaling, when you're coasting and your feet are turning the pedals but you're not pedaling fast enough to create forward momentum, creates confusion behind you. To a rider drafting you, it looks like you're pedaling, so they keep pedaling, but in reality, you're coasting and slowing down, so they end up riding too close to you and having to brake or maneuver abruptly.

If you're going to coast, just coast without moving the pedals. This not only sends a clear visual signal but also lets the hub make its clickety-clickety freewheeling noise, which is a good auditory cue to other riders that the ride is slowing slightly.

Respect no-drop rides

A *no-drop* group ride is both a ride category and a way to behave. If you join one, it means that everyone on the ride will slow their pace or wait at the next stop sign for the slowest riders to catch up. It also means you won't hammer so fast that you're constantly dropping those slowest riders or forcing them to work so hard to keep up that they struggle to finish the ride.

Rules of the Bike Path

Most bike paths have any location-specific rules and speed limits posted, but common sense is the best rule. Generally speaking, you need to yield to pedestrians. Here are some other basic tips to keep you and others safe:

>> **Ride at a reasonable speed for the conditions.** If it's busy, slow down.

>> **Slow down around blind corners, and stay to the right.** If you can't see what's coming around the bend, reduce your speed and ride where people would expect oncoming traffic to be. But trust me: Sometimes, other users aren't considering this and will take the inside line no matter what, so your best bet is to call out or ring a bell as you're approaching the turn, too.

>> **When catching up to and passing other users, ring your bell or call out.** These are a few common phrases:

- *On your left:* When you're passing on the left

- *On your right:* When you're passing on the right

- *Rider back, biker back:* When a cyclist is approaching from behind

No matter what you say, how politely you say it, or how far back you are, you'll startle some folks. Or, if you say "on your left," they'll dart to their left. It happens. So slow down a little and be ready to maneuver. The earlier you can call out, the more time you both have to react.

Acknowledge that *many* people now are wearing earbuds and are oblivious to their surroundings. In this case, you should still call out and ring your bell, but if they don't hear you, that's on them, so just steer around them.

ANSWERING NATURE'S CALL

Sometimes, you just need to stop to pee. If you're deep in the woods on a mountain bike trail, just head off trail, behind a tree. Keep in mind that some trails loop back and forth, so you may think you're aiming away from the trail you're on, only to see riders coming up on an adjacent trail, so look around first.

If you're on a bike path, you can likely find trailheads and parking lots with bathrooms. Or try to duck into a nearby convenience store, which is a helpful option out on a road ride, too, though you can often find dirt roads or wooded sections off to the side that you can use.

You can have your riding buddies create a barrier if there's no natural privacy screen (like trees or bushes). I like to keep some toilet paper in a small baggie in my hydration pack or saddle bag for, um, emergencies, too, because sometimes stuff happens on its own schedule. Just bring an extra baggie to pack out the used tissue because it's *not* cool to leave it behind.

Prepare for Riding in Bad Weather

First off, I gotta say that riding in a light rain shouldn't be considered riding in bad weather. It's quite fun, especially getting surprised by a summer shower!

That said, unless you're commuting to work or school, it's unlikely that you'll intentionally head out in the rain just for fun. So if you need to do it, here are few tips to stay safe:

>> **Fenders:** Put fenders on your bike. They will help keep spray off your face and out of your eyes.

>> **Glasses:** Wear clear glasses, also to keep water spray and mud and rain-drops out of your eyes. A helmet with a visor helps keep the rain off your glasses, too.

>> **Speed:** Slow down, especially in corners in urban environments. Oil and gas that drip from cars create a slick coating that becomes extra slick whenever water causes it to lift from the road's surface.

>> **Metal grates:** Avoid these obstacles on drawbridges. They can get super-slick and act like cheese graters on your skin when you go down — and you'll almost certainly go down. It's better to dismount and walk your bike across them.

>> **Train tracks:** Cross the tracks at 90-degree angles and without pedaling. The metal rails get slick, but you can usually roll across them slowly if you're going perfectly straight across. If in doubt, walk your bike across them.

Here are a few items that'll help keep you dry:

>> Fenders

>> Brightly colored waterproof rain pants and jacket

>> Shoe covers

>> Reflective bits on your clothes, helmet, and bike

» Clear glasses

» Bright head- and taillights

If you get caught riding in the rain, I hope that you already have lights on your bike. (You do ride with lights, right?) These might be the only items that make you visible to cars if the skies darken and their windshields are streaked with rain.

Rules of the Trail

Two universal rules govern trail etiquette: Yield to other users, and yield to uphill riders.

Riders yield to pedestrians and horses

Generally speaking, you're moving faster than either pedestrians or horses, so it's up to you to slow down and pass safely (see Figure 12-8 for a common trail sign). Hikers and horseback riders will often step aside to let you pass, but they need time to find the space to do it. You don't want to ride right up to horses quickly or too closely, because you can spook them and they might buck their riders. (True, horses poop all over the trail and their riders never clean it up, but still, be nice.)

FIGURE 12-8:
This trail sign shows the right-of-way hierarchy for riders.

Credit: Aaron J Hill / Adobe Stock

So look ahead down the trail and, just like on a bike path, call out to other users to let them know you're approaching. Some hikers (and most trail runners) are wearing headphones, so you may need to call out quite loudly to grab their attention.

Common phrases are "Rider back" if you're coming up behind someone and "Rider up" if you're coming at someone who's walking or riding toward you. In the latter case, when another cyclist is coming at you, yell out loudly so that they see you and slow down, too. Some trails are tight, and you both want as much time as possible to slow down and find a safe spot for passing.

Downhill riders yield to uphill riders

When two riders are moving toward each other, terrain and timing dictate who has the right of way. If you're on flat terrain, generally it's the rider who first calls out "Rider up" who gets to keep riding while the other person pulls off, but this isn't a hard-and-fast rule. If you have a clear spot to slide over and let the other rider pass, do it and then continue on your way.

If you're descending, you should yield to the rider who's climbing up the trail. It's much harder to stop and restart when you're climbing than it is to start rolling down a hill again. The climber is working a lot harder (or maybe just a *little* harder if they're on an e-bike), so let them maintain their momentum.

Many of the best downhill trails are one-way trails, which is intended to keep riders safe because some folks can get going pretty darn fast and it's hard (and often unsafe) to make an emergency stop if you come around a corner, only to find another rider already there. So, respect any trail signage about directional use, and if you're on a two-way trail, keep your eyes up and your ears open for other riders. And always call out early and loudly!

No riding trails after it rains!

Another big no-no is riding a trail right after it rains. Some areas, like the Pacific Northwest (looking at you, Bellingham — you're amazing), have terrain that soaks up the moisture and is perfectly fine for riding when it's wet. Other areas just get muddy and full of puddles, and if you ride through them, you'll leave deep ruts and ruin the trail. Or, if you try to ride around the puddles, you'll end up widening the trail and ruining it.

Many established local trail networks have groups that will monitor and close the trails if they're too wet to ride. If you see a sign or barrier up, don't jump over it and ride anyway — that severely damages the trails, ruining it for everyone else (and also gets your bike really dirty). Other trail systems may not have someone to look over them, so if it has just rained, use your judgment or call a local bike shop and ask whether the trails are okay to ride. Every mountain biker needs to be a steward of the trails and respect the hundreds and thousands of hours that go into building them.

Look before you leap

Exploring a new mountain bike trail is an awesome feeling, but you should complete your first lap a little slower than normal — unless you're following a local who's calling out any drops, jumps, gaps, or other technical trail features.

There's no shame in stopping before a steep drop or technical section to look it over, walk the line, and plan your attack — better to finish the ride than launch yourself and break your bike (or your bones). There's also no shame in walking a section or taking the *b-line* — an alternative route around a jump or drop.

Ultimately, your safety is up to you, and you need to decide what risks you're willing to take and then take responsibility for how you ride.

IN THIS CHAPTER

» **Cleaning your bike**

» **Pumping up the tires and checking for wear**

» **Adjusting the brakes**

» **Repairing and replacing the chain**

» **Knowing what to do when a ride goes wrong**

» **Sprucing up your bike's appearance and maintaining the chain**

» **Fixing a flat and plugging a tire**

Chapter **13**

Fixing and Maintaining Your Bike

Learning the basic principles of bike maintenance and repair is empowering — and will save you money. Keeping the moving parts clean and lubricated will help them work better, obviously, but they also last longer. And knowing when to replace certain items, like brake pads and tires, will help keep you safe.

Cleaning Your Bike

A clean bike is a happy bike. We racers like to say it's a "fast bike." All you need in order to clean your bike sufficiently is a hose and some soapy water. A car wash or dish soap work fine on a budget, but a good bike wash can do a little better at removing road grime and errant chain grease from your bike. Bike wash products also typically come in a spray bottle, making it easy to apply as you're scrubbing.

You can find many brands of bike wash kits with various brush sizes and shapes. Check out the "Getting the Right Maintenance Supplies" section in Chapter 9 for product recommendations, or you can piece together your own kit with these items:

» Long-handle dish scrubber

» Thin bottle brush

» Toothbrush

» Microfiber cloth (or rag towel)

These four items let you reach into all the nooks and crannies of your bike — between the frame and the wheels, spokes, hubs, controls, and any suspension and linkages.

Follow these steps to wash your bike:

1. **Put the bike on a workstand if you have one.**

   Or, you can use a wheel stand or just lean the bike against a tree or wall. It should stand it on its own so that you have both hands free to wash it.

2. **Get the bike wet and spray off any excess mud and crud.**

   Let it soak for a bit if the grime is crusty. It's best not to spray high pressure water at any bearings on the bike.

3. **Use soap and brushes to gently clean the bike.**

   No need to scrub too hard — you don't want to scratch the finish. Washing from top to bottom prevents the crud from under the bike spreading all over its saddle and controls. A separate brush or rag for wiping greasy chainstays keeps you from smearing grease across the rest of the frame.

   Note that the suspension — particularly, the rear shocks — is intentionally a little oily on the stanchions, and that oil can also spread across the bike. I usually just wipe the shocks down with a clean paper towel rather than scrub them.

   Also note that you clean and degrease the chain separately, a topic that's covered in the later section "Cleaning the Chain."

4. **When you're done, rinse off the bike and bounce it a few times to shake off the excess water, and then wipe it dry.**

   TIP

   Look for small drain holes near the rear dropouts or bottom bracket. If your bike gets soaked (from either a good wash or a ride in the rain), hold the rear brake and lift the front wheel, holding the bike vertically and letting any water that seeped into the frame drip out.

If you want to take the bike wash to the next level, a few brands, like Muc-Off, make ceramic or silicone-based bike polishes that create an ultra-slick barrier on the frame so that water, dust, and mud can't stick to it. These polishes are useful but pricy — and they require careful application.

WARNING

Take care not to spray any degreaser product on the rims or brake pads, including overspray from cleaning the drivetrain while it's on the bike. (I explain more about specific chain cleaner and degreaser products and techniques in the later section "Cleaning the Chain.")

Cleaning the Chain

First and foremost, before you spray any sort of degreaser on your bike's chain, cassette, or crankset, remember this: You *cannot* let any of that overspray or the grease and oil it's washing off into your bike's brake rotors, pads, or the rims. They can contaminate pads with grease and chemicals, which can negatively impact braking performance.

First and foremost, before you spray any sort of degreaser on your bike's chain, cassette, or crankset, remove the rear wheel. Here's why: You cannot let any of that overspray or the grease and oil it's washing off get onto your bike's brake rotor, pads, or the rims. They can contaminate pads with grease and chemicals, which can negatively impact braking performance.

First, you need to know about various types of degreasers:

>> **Gentle degreasers:** Often bio-based, these are frequently in a spray bottle for close-up spritzing on the chain and cassette. Some come in bulk bottles for diluting and adding to a chain-cleaning device. These work okay for light cleaning duty, but require some scrubbing.

>> **Blaster degreasers:** These aerosol cans of potent degreasers (some are ecofriendly — check the label and opt for those) shoot out at high velocity in a narrow stream. They're miracle workers and magically spray all grease and crud off your bike's parts, but you do not want to use these while the parts on are on the bike, because they splatter that grease and crud everywhere.

>> **Mineral spirits:** Sometimes called white spirits, you use this product for a complete degreasing that soaks the chain and strips it of all grease and oil, even between the pins and rollers.

>> **Wax lube removers:** If you're using wax-based chain lubes, standard degreasers won't work, so you need to use a specific product (Silca and Effetto Mariposa both make some) or mineral spirits to break down the wax and remove it.

Okay, now you're ready to start. Cleaning the drivetrain can be done at three levels: good, better, and best. Depending on where you're riding and in what conditions, good enough can indeed be good enough. As the riding conditions become dustier, dirtier, or wetter, you'll want to move up the quality ladder.

You may recall my telling you how to disconnect a chain and remove it from a bike in Chapter 6. The goal of cleaning and lubing the chain is to remove any water, dust, dirt, or other contaminants from between those pins and rollers and then lubricate them to prevent new contaminants from getting in.

I discuss various types of chain lubes and their pros and cons in Chapter 9 (in the "maintainence Supplies" section), so here I focus on the three cleaning techniques.

Good chain cleaning

If your bike's chain looks more oily than dirty, you've probably just accumulated too much chain lube from periodic applications and it's time to get the old stuff off and give it a fresh coat.

For this task, the simplest method is to wrap a rag around the chain and pedal backwards (making sure not to get the rag or your fingers caught in the gears). If your chain simply has too much chain lube, sometimes this is all that is necessary.

You can also lightly spray some gentle degreaser directly on the parts and scrub them. If it's *really* dirty, spray to coat it and let it soak for a few minutes, and then respray and start scrubbing. I like to work in sections and rinse frequently, or at least keep spraying degreaser on to keep everything moist until I'm finished.

Alternatively, you can buy a chain cleaner, which is a clamshell device with brushes on rollers inside that closes around the chain, and then you backpedal the chain through it and it scrubs it for you from all angles. You pour in degreaser (check the bottle for diluted or full-strength instructions), and it does most of the work for you.

Better chain cleaning

If the chain is cruddy-looking, with dirt and dust sticking to the lube or a crunchy feeling, it's time for a better chain cleaning. You first have to take the chain off the bike and use a blaster degreaser. This task is easy to complete if the chain has a quick link; otherwise, you need to purchase a chain breaker tool and a quick link in order to reconnect the chain afterward.

Place the chain (or cassette or chainrings or whatever) over a large scrap towel or down in a shop sink and give it all a quick spray to witness the magic. Then get more strategic with your blasting strategy, by moving along in quick strokes to remove the crud from all angles. And be sure to do this in a well-ventilated area.

Best chain cleaning

If you're not rushing to get on a ride, the process I spell out in this section is the most thorough way to clean the chain. And it's the *only* way to do it if you're switching from an oil-based lube to a wax lube — for maximum performance, all oil and grease must be completely removed before you wax the chain. (Trust me — wax lubes are worth the effort. See Chapter 10 for the reasons.)

To do this, remove the chain from the bike, put the chain in a mason jar, pour in mineral spirits to cover it, close the lid, and then shake gently. I sometimes place the jar on top of an outdoor A/C compressor or my clothes dryer to gently shake and agitate it for me, letting it sit there for 30 to 60 minutes. Just be careful not to let it vibrate off and smash on the ground.

Muc-Off and other manufacturers make ultrasonic cleaners that do this, too, but a mason jar is much cheaper. I usually let the chain soak overnight, shake gently again to get all the dissolved grease and gunk out of the chain, and then pour out the liquid. (Check local laws for proper disposal procedures.) This strategy usually does the trick, but I would double-check for any remaining gunk and brush it off as needed. Your chain will now be as clean as it ever will be.

Post chain cleaning

When you're all done cleaning the chain, rinse all parts completely. The final — and vital — step is to make sure the chain is totally dry. I whip mine around to fling off excess water off, be careful: Chains hurt *bad* if they hit you or someone else.

Then, if it's a sunny day, I place the chain on my patio to dry for a couple of hours. If it isn't sunny, or if I'm in a hurry, I put the chain in my toaster oven on a sheet of tinfoil at 200 degrees Fahrenheit for about 20 minutes. Either way you choose, be careful in handling the hot chain — it can burn you.

Lubing the chain

First things first: Do *not* use standard WD-40 as a chain lube. It's a solvent meant to loosen rusty parts, and it works okay for squeaky doors, but it attracts dirt and dust, which is bad news for your chain. Also, it doesn't last long, and it makes a mess. WD-40 the brand does make a line of bike care products, but they're quite different from the standard products you find at hardware stores.

Standard oil-based lube application

Once your chain is clean, the best way to apply most lubes — the ones in the little bottles with twist-open spouts — is to drip one drop per link. And the best way to do that, according to Josh Poertner at Silca (who is a master geek at these tasks) is to follow these steps:

1. **Place the bike on a workstand.**

   Or, you can lean the non-drive (left) side of the bike against something so that the bike stands as upright as possible (and doesn't lean at much of an angle).

2. **Shift into the big ring in front (if you have more than one chainring).**

3. **Shift into the *second*-largest cog on the cassette.**

4. **Start *backpedaling*, or turning the cranks backward, slowly.**

5. **Apply the lube sparingly on top of each link about 2 to 3 inches in front of the cassette.**

6. **Continue until you've applied the lube to every link.**

This method is ideal because it puts the links at an angle, creating a small space between the pins and rollers and plates, so that the lube can slide into all the nooks and crannies. And then, as it rolls through the cassette and derailleur pulleys, the lube spreads around.

If you apply too much lube, simply wipe off the excess with a rag or paper towel. Some lubes, like DuMonde Tech, have special properties and/or require a curing period, so be sure to read the instructions for the best results.

Wax-based lube application

You can choose from three types of wax lube: dry, hot melt, and liquid/drip.

Dry wax lubes are rare, but they come in the form of a block or stick and you simply rub them on the chain. These products are easy to apply, but they aren't popular because they don't work anywhere near as well as the others.

Hot melt wax comes as a brick that's meant to be melted in a temperature-stable plastic bag in a slow cooker, and then you put the chain in the bag and let it soak in the wax while you agitate it slightly to work it deep into the chain. (Use tongs to avoid burning your hand!) Pull out the bag and reinstall the chain on your bike. Pour the leftover melted wax back in its container or keep it in the bag and let it cool and harden to save for next time. As long as the chain was clean to begin with, you can reuse the wax many times.

Liquid/drip wax lubes are quicker and easier to apply, and they also work well. Use the same application method as for oil-based lubes. You can ride immediately after application, but, ideally, give them 30 minutes or more to *set*, or harden, before riding (some require more time, so make sure to read the instructions ahead of time!).

Keep these three points in mind:

>> **Every type of wax chain lube (and especially hot melt and drip wax lubes) flakes off as you ride.** That's a good thing because any dirt or dust that's stuck to it flakes off with it, which is why wax lubes excel at keeping your chain clean.

>> **Because the wax flakes off, it makes a mess of your floor if you're using your bike indoors (on a trainer, for example).** If you have a bike that lives on the trainer, use a light, oil-based, dry lube instead — or at least don't set it up over carpet.

>> **As the wax flakes off, reapply it — but don't overdo it.** Wax lubes last a long time, especially in mild environments, but when the chain is looking bare or you start hearing it, put another coat on there. Most of the time you can apply a drip wax lube over a chain that's been dipped in hot melt to extend the time between full cleanings and re-waxing in a slow cooker.

Between chain cleanings

If your bike's chain looks mostly clean but a little dry, or if it's just a little noisy (normal-mechanical-movement noisy, not grinding or crunching or squeaking noisy.), you can simply wipe it down to remove surface dust and dirt and then reapply a light layer of the same lube you used the first time.

If you're changing the type of lube, especially going from oil-based to wax lubes (or vice versa), be sure to fully clean and degrease or de-wax the chain first.

TIP

Believe it or not, I've only scratched the surface here. If you want to geek out on chain lubes, cleaning procedures, and wax application methods, check www.zerofrictioncycling.com.au. Fair warning: It's a deep, deep rabbit hole.

REMEMBER

Many mid-motor e-bikes don't move the chain when you backpedal, so for those, you need to affix the crank arm to the chainring spider so that they move in unison. A zip tie (or cable tie) or small Velcro strap works well, but you can also just stick a hex wrench into one of the chainring bolts and let the crank arm press against it. The only downside to this method is that it can ratchet the crank arms such that the tool is wedged in there and hard to remove, so the other methods are preferable.

Pumping Up the Tires and Checking for Wear

Pumping up the tires is easy. If you have the larger Schrader valve stems (like the ones on your car tires), you just remove the cap, press on the pump, and start pumping.

The thinner Presta valve stems (see Figure 13-1) have a threaded core that must be opened before you can inflate your tire. To do that, remove the cap and twist the valve core nut counterclockwise. This lets the pressure from the pump depress it as you pump, letting air go in, but then it pops up to keep air from coming out when you remove the pump.

If the valve is open and ready to pump, you should be able to press it down and it'll let air out (assuming that your tire isn't completely flat). If you try to pump and the gauge immediately shoots to its maximum pressure, you have forgotten to open the valve core.

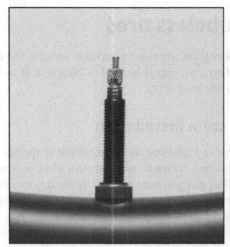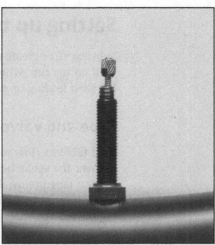

FIGURE 13-1:
Presta valve stem closed (left) and open (right).

REMEMBER

Make sure your bike pump is compatible with the type of valve stems on your bike. If you have more than one type on multiple bikes, get a pump with a dual or universal pump head.

Most pumps have a lever you pull up to lock it onto the valve stem, but some press or twist on. The twist-on type requires a threaded valve stem to thread onto, which is secure — but also a pain because it can sometimes unthread the valve stem's core (see Figure 13-2) with it and let out all the air. If you opt for a twist-on pump, make sure your valve cores are tight.

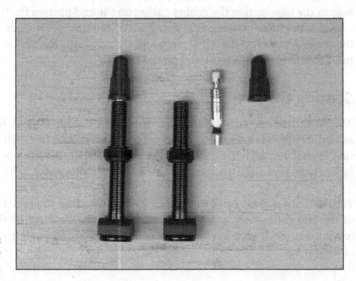

FIGURE 13-2:
A removable valve core.

Setting up tubeless tires

Tubeless tires create a seal on the rim by securely locking the tire's bead into a shelf on the rim. Whether your rim is hooked or hookless, it usually has a small, flat shelf leading up to the bead wall.

Tape and valve stem installation

Most tubeless rims require a tubeless rim tape, which is applied over the rim bed to cover the spoke holes and create an airtight rim. Most new wheels come with the rim tape preinstalled, but you may need to apply it yourself. If so, start just past the spoke hole nearest the valve stem hole (either side is fine) and start taping toward the valve stem hole. Keep working around the rim, pulling the tape snug and pressing out any bubbles as you go. The seal should be complete, and the tape should go almost all the way to the bead wall on either side of the rim. Work your way all the way around the rim and overlap the starting point so that it's just past the spoke hole on the other side of the valve hole.

Many rims come pre-taped, but not all have the valve stems preinstalled. And you have to install them if you've taped (or re-taped) your own rims. Find the valve stem hole on the inside of the rim and make a *tiny* slit. I use the tip of an Exacto blade, but a small pocket knife will do the job, too.

You only need a tiny 2-millimeter (mm) slit. (I make two cuts to create an X shape). The slit should be smaller than the valve stem's diameter. Remove the cap and washer/nut from the valve stem, and then push the valve stem through the hole in the tape so that the rubber gasket on the end presses flush against the rim tape and the valve core end is sticking out of the rim, pointing at the hub. Thread the washer/nut onto the valve stem and tighten until the gasket is lightly compressed and forming a tight seal on the tape.

Seating the tire

As you inflate the tire for the first time, you'll hear it POP! into place. That sometimes-quite-loud sound is the bead snapping onto the shelf and seating the tire. Even if you get a flat and lose all of your tire's air, the tire's bead tends to stay locked onto that shelf, making repairs and reinflation easy.

Tubeless tire sealant can be added as you're installing the tire. I install one side of the tire completely and then install the other side most of the way around, leaving a 10-inch section off the rim where I can pour sealant into the tire before closing it up.

Alternatively, you can install, inflate, and seat the tire first and then let the air out through the valve stem, remove the valve core, and squirt the sealant in through the valve stem. This is also a good way to add more sealant at any time without having to unseat the tire. This method works best with a syringe or sealant injector, or with a bottle with a narrow cap that fits into the valve stem. Otherwise, it can get quite messy. Many sealant brands offer small single-use "baby bottles" of sealant that work well for this task and can be refilled and stored in a pack or saddle bag for emergency use.

TIP

After the tires are fully seated with sealant inside, inflate them to the system's maximum pressure and let them sit overnight. This helps push sealant into any small gaps or holes and creates an airtight seal. Then check and adjust tire pressure before your first ride.

Troubleshooting tubeless setup

Modern tubeless rims and tires work together quite well, thanks to more standardization of designs and interfaces. But some combinations can still be hard to seat and form an initial seal.

If you've mounted your tubeless tire to your tubeless-ready rim and added sealant and your floor pump just can't add air fast enough to seat the tire, here are five things to try, in this order:

>> **Remove the valve cores from the valve stems.** This allows a much higher volume of air to enter the tire more quickly and easily, which might be all you need to do. Keep in mind that once you remove the pump, all the air will gush out, though the tire should remain seated. Simply reinstall the valve core, add sealant as needed, and then reinflate.

>> **Use a different inflation tool.** Air compressors can blast in a lot of air at one time, and keep blowing that air until the tire seats. Or, you can get a booster floor pump, which lets you inflate a secondary chamber to ~160 psi and then release it all at once into the tire to pop it into place.

>> **Put a tube in there.** If neither of those first two techniques works after several tries, you may just need to put a tube in there and inflate it to pop the tire onto the rim. Leave it inflated like that overnight to help mold the tire to that shape, and then deflate and remove *only one side* of the tire from the rim so that you can pull out the tube and then add your sealant and reinflate.

>> **Go for a ride.** Sometimes it takes one ride to help everything settle in. If your new tubeless tires seem to lose air each time you inflate them, try pumping them up and go for a short ride around your neighborhood. That should work the sealant into any gaps and help the tires fully settle into the rim's channels.

» **Double-check the valve stem and tubeless rim tape.** If you can't find the source of the leak but the tire keeps losing air, check to make sure the valve stem is threaded tightly onto the rim so that the gasket inside is fully sealing the valve stem hole.

If it's tight, remove one side of the tire and check the rim tape. Tire levers can sometimes push it aside or even puncture it. And, rarely, it just peels up and creates a gap. If this happens, just remove the tire, wipe away the sealant, clean the rim with rubbing alcohol, and apply fresh tubeless rim tape. Trust me — it's a waste of time to try to "fix" rim tape. Just replace it. Gorilla Tape works OK for this task, too — just make sure to buy the right width.

You're not entirely wrong in thinking tubeless tires seem like a lot of work. They do require more frequent inflation than tubes, and setup can be tricky sometimes. I definitely recommend setting them up the day before you want to ride them. But the ride quality is amazing, they're lighter overall (no tube), and they can self-seal or easily be repaired, making them totally worth the effort for performance cycling.

Buying the proper tubes

Whether you're using tubes full-time or you just want an emergency backup, you need to buy the correct stem length, width, diameter, and stem type.

Valve stem length and type

Deep aero rims require longer 60mm or 80mm valve stems, but shorter mountain bike and gravel rims might need only 36mm lengths. Check your wheel brand's recommendation, or just measure the rim depth and add about 20 millimeters. This will give you enough length to safely attach a pump to it.

REMEMBER

Tubes come with either Schrader or Presta valve stems, and you need to buy the type that fits your rim's valve stem hole. Schrader valves are too big to fit in a Presta hole, and Schrader holes are large enough to let the rubber around a Presta valve bulge out slightly, which isn't safe. Match the tube to your rim type.

Tube width and diameter

Tubes are sold by wheel size (24 inches, 26 inches, or 29 inches, for example) and width. You should match the size with your bike's wheel diameter. The width corresponds to your tire's width.

Road and gravel tubes usually list it in millimeters, with a recommended range. For example, a 25mm road bike tire uses a tube rated for 700c x 20–28mm (or something like that, where 700c is the wheel diameter and 20–28mm is the range of tire widths it will safely fit). Mountain bike tubes are likely listed in inches, such as 29 x 2.0–2.4. Check your tire's sidewall and match it to the numbers on your tube's box.

Maximum tire pressures

Most tires have a maximum tire pressure listed on the sidewall, and you shouldn't exceed it. Some high-end rims also have maximum tire pressure limits, so be sure to check any labels or decals on them, or look in their owner's manual. When in doubt, check with the brand.

Here's why: For many years, road bike tires were often inflated to 100–120 psi, so rims were made to handle that much. But modern rims are wider, and they sometimes use hookless beads designed specifically for wider tubeless tires. (Check Chapter 5 for more about rim and tire designs.) These usually have lower maximum tire pressures, so you don't want to overdo it and risk blowing the tire off the rim.

Some rims, especially Stan's NoTubes rims, also use very shallow bead walls and have lower maximum tire pressures. Whatever rim and tire you choose, the actual maximum safe tire pressure is the lower of the two products' stated maximum. For example, if the rim has a 70 psi maximum and the tire has a 90 psi maximum, your effective maximum is 70 psi.

Checking for tire wear

Kids love to skid, so checking their tires for wear is easy — just look for big bald spots. For the rest of us, there are a few things to check for. Read on.

Lower knob height

Maybe you remember what your mountain bike tires looked like when they were new. If the knob height is dramatically lower, particularly in the center compared to the side knobs, it's probably time to replace them.

Torn knobs

Some high-performance mountain bike tires have soft, grippy rubber that's intended to maximize performance, not durability, and with moderate use, you might see some side *knobs*, or tread blocks, tearing off or just wearing down very quickly. Some torn knobs can take part of the outer rubber layer with them, exposing the casing, which increases the chance of a puncture or blowout. If you see torn, ripped, cracked, or missing knobs, it's time to replace that tire.

Flattened center sections

Road and commuter tires are smoother with no tread blocks or knobs, so it's hard to gauge their wear by examining the tread. But they may have grooves or sipes that are smoothed over, or the center section may look flat, with an obvious transition to the rounded sides. If that's the case, you probably have put lots of great miles on them and deserve a new set of tires. Some of these tires also have wear indicators, which are often small circular holes molded into the tire tread. When the rubber around these wears down to the point that the indicators are no longer visible, the tire is considered worn out.

Visible threads or casing

If you've worn down your tires (or skidded a lot — looking at you, fixie riders) and the threads from the casing, or inner fabric layers, are showing, it means there's no more rubber to protect them from punctures — or you're just one skid away from disaster. Sometimes the sidewalls wear down from too-low tire pressure or repeated compressions from curbs, rocks, and roots, and they may start to look frayed. Both are signs that the tires should be replaced immediately because you're risking a blowout anytime you ride.

Dry rotting and cracking

If your bike has sat unused for a long time (usually, a couple of years), the rubber has likely dried out and is starting to crack. The tires may look discolored or pale, or tan sidewalls may have darkened and yellowed. These tires are an accident waiting to happen and could blow out at any time, so definitely replace them and the tubes inside them before riding.

Adjusting the Brakes

This section is broken down into rim brakes and disc brakes, because the methods of adjusting each one are mostly different. However, mechanical disc brakes share one adjustment with rim brakes, so I start with that and then branch off. For a refresher on the various types of brakes, refer to Chapter 5.

Adjusting pad contact with cable length

With all types of mechanical brakes (those using a cable rather than hydraulic systems to pull them), you can easily adjust the pad contact spacing by adjusting the cable length.

Wait — what is pad contact spacing?

Great question! *Pad contact spacing* is the space between the brake pad and the rim or disc brake rotor. More space means you'll pull more brake lever before the pads make contact, and less space means they'll engage more quickly.

Adjusting the pad contact space

You want a little bit of pad contact space on the brakes so that you have good leverage over them. If there's too little space, your rim or brake rotor will likely rub against the pads. Also, most brakes will feel "dead" and you'll have a hard time pulling the lever far enough to generate good braking power.

Too much space and you'll pull the lever too far toward the handlebar before the brakes start doing anything, and you'll be unable to fully engage the brakes for maximum stopping power.

You want the space somewhere in the middle so that you can have good *modulation*, or control, over how much power the brakes are providing while still getting maximum power without the brakes dragging.

Adjusting the pad contact spacing

For quick, small adjustments, most flat bar (like on a mountain bike) mechanical brake levers have a barrel adjuster where the cable enters. And all mechanical brake calipers also have a barrel adjuster, regardless of which type they are (see Figure 13-3). As you twist the barrel adjuster(s), you see the cable housing (or ferrule, if there is one on the end of the housing) move into or out of the barrel adjuster.

FIGURE 13-3: Brake lever and caliper barrel adjusters.

If it's moving outward, it's pulling the brake pads closer to the braking surface (rim or rotor). If it's moving inward, it's releasing the pads farther from the braking surface. It's an inverse relationship: If you see less housing, you have more pad space:

> More visible housing = Less pad spacing
>
> Less visible housing = More pad spacing

Some brakes will simply move the barrel adjuster itself inboard or outboard, moving the cable housing with it. If you turn the barrel adjuster and it moves further away from the lever or brake caliper, it's effectively pulling cable and decreasing pad spacing, and vice versa.

If the barrel adjuster doesn't allow enough adjustment, you need to adjust the length of the cable itself. Before you adjust the cable, adjust the barrel adjuster on the caliper and/or lever into its middle position. This lets you make minor adjustments in either direction after you've set up the brake caliper.

For rim brakes: Loosen the bolt that clamps the cable onto the brake caliper, and slide the cable in or out as needed. The easiest way to set the pad spacing is to use one hand to grab the caliper at the brake pads and squeeze it to the point where you want it. Use your other hand to pull the cable snug and retighten the bolt. It may help to have a friend tighten the bolt while you hold everything else in place (or use a third hand tool).

Ideally, you have about 2.5 to 3 millimeters between the rim and brake pad. This provides good modulation, allows dirt and water to pass through without bogging things up, and allows for a bit of wheel wobble if your rim isn't perfectly true.

For disc brakes: The pads should retract as much as possible, so you *usually* adjust the cable so that's there's no slack — but also so that it's not prematurely activating the brakes. Many mechanical disc brake calipers also have pad adjustment built in, so you can set the cable for immediate actuation and then adjust the pads in or out to achieve the desired braking feel.

Both are hard to get just right, which is why you want some adjustment range remaining at the barrel adjuster. The adjuster also allows you to take up some of the space created as your brake pads wear down, too, or add space when you replace them.

Adjusting rim brakes

Beyond pad spacing, the main adjustments for rim brakes are to center the caliper over the rim, center the brake pad contact point on the rim, and toe the brake pads to prevent squealing.

Centering road bike brakes

For road bikes, centering the caliper is usually just a matter of slightly loosening the mounting bolt — just barely loose enough to rotate the caliper, but with some friction between the caliper and the frame or fork so that you can make micro adjustments and it'll hold its new position. When you have the rim centered between the brake pads, tighten the caliper mounting bolt and check its position again. Readjust as needed. High-end caliper brakes have micro-adjustment screws that let you fine-tune the centering process.

Centering mountain bike and cyclocross brakes

Linear-pull or cantilever brakes, where each brake arm is independent of the other, use another method. Here you'll find small screws near their mounting bolt that let you adjust tension on the *return spring*, which is what keeps the brake arm pushed out away from the rim so that they open when you release the brake lever. If you add tension with those screws, the brake arm moves away from the rim, so adjust each side to reach the tension you want and to center the brake pads over the rim.

REMEMBER

Many linear pull brakes have multiple spring insertion points that let you change the tension. And many cheap bikes have plastic tension screw mounts that quickly strip and/or break and leave you with brakes that can't be adjusted or centered, usually causing one side to rub constantly — which is yet another reason to spend a bit more for a quality bike.

Adjusting the brake pad toe-in and rim contact point

Rim brake pads should be slightly *toed in* at the front, where the front of the brake pad should be slightly (0.5 to 1 millimeter) closer to the rim than the rear of the brake pad (see Figure 13-4). This improves modulation by slowly increasing the amount of pad contacting the rim, but more importantly, prevents the pads from squealing loudly and helps squeegee water and dirt off the rim.

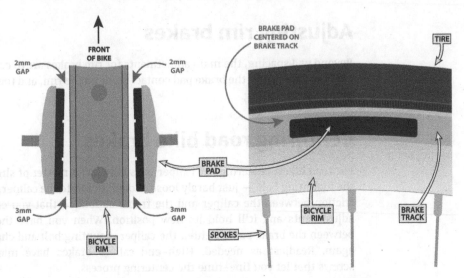

FIGURE 13-4:
Properly toed and centered rim brake pads.

Labels in figure: FRONT OF BIKE; 2mm GAP (×2); 3mm GAP (×2); BICYCLE RIM; BRAKE PAD CENTERED ON BRAKE TRACK; TIRE; BRAKE PAD; BICYCLE RIM; BRAKE TRACK; SPOKES

Most rim brakes have the same adjustment for brake pad toe, and the same bolt is used to adjust the pad height on the brake arm so that the pad is vertically centered on the rim's braking surface. This last bit is important because most rims have a braking surface that's 12 to 14 millimeters tall, and most brake pads are 9 to 10 millimeters tall. You want the pads to hit the center of the rim so that they're not too close to (or rubbing!) the tire, and not hanging off the lower part of the rim.

To adjust both toe and position, loosen the bolt that holds the pad on the caliper and slide and angle it into position. Most of these bolts have conical washers that allow angular adjustment so that you can nudge the front of the pad slightly closer to the rim. And the bolts are usually in a slot on the caliper or arm that allows vertical adjustment. Hold the pad in the desired position with one hand and retighten its mounting bolt with the other.

Don't worry if this process takes a few tries. Note the angle of the brake pad from top to bottom. Those conical washers allow every angle of adjustment, so try to get the pads to contact the rim evenly from top to bottom, and make sure they're rotated to be in alignment with the rim when viewing from the side, too. Get all of these right for maximum braking power.

REMEMBER

Some low-cost bikes have only vertical pad adjustment, but no toe adjustment.

Adjusting disc brakes

Disc brake calipers have fewer adjustments than other types (see Figure 13-5). Your main goal is to center the brake pads over the rotor, but there are definitely a few tricks to making this happen.

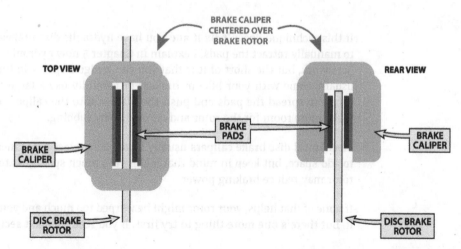

BRAKE CALIPER
CENTERED OVER
BRAKE ROTOR

TOP VIEW

REAR VIEW

BRAKE
PADS

BRAKE
CALIPER

BRAKE
CALIPER

DISC BRAKE
ROTOR

DISC BRAKE
ROTOR

FIGURE 13-5:
Caliper alignment
from every angle.

All else being perfect, you simply loosen the two mounting bolts on the brake caliper, position it so that the rotor is centered between the pads, and then tighten the bolts and go. Once you've done that, spin the wheel and listen for any rubbing between rotor and pad.

If you're having a hard time seeing a gap between the pads and the rotor, put a sheet of white paper on the ground under your bike, in your line of sight as you look through the rotor. That contrast helps you see the gap better. I like to keep the bolts lightly snugged so that I can make small adjustments and it stays where I set it. Spin the wheel to check for rubbing, and then tighten things down.

Sometimes, you hear a tiny "tsst" noise where the rotor makes the teensiest bit of contact. This is fine — ignore it and go ride. Usually, this sound goes away after you've braked a few times (or by bedding in your brakes — you did do that, right? *Right?* See Chapter 5.)

At other times, you hear a longer *chhhhhh-chhhhhhh* rubbing noise and it's obvious that the rotor is making periodic or consistent contact. Don't ignore this — it'll just drive you mad.

Here's how to fix it: First, just try to adjust it again. If that doesn't work, spin the wheel slowly and watch the rotor slide between the pads. Chances are good that the rotor isn't perfectly straight and you can bend it back in shape. As you spin the wheel, note where the rotor makes contact and move that just past the rotor. Pinch the rotor and *lightly* push or pull it to the opposite of where it's rubbing. I do mean *lightly* — it doesn't take much, and you can *lightly* increase pressure as needed. But it's easy to overdo this and make things worse.

If this technique doesn't fix it and you have hydraulic disc brakes, you may need to manually retract the pads. I explain in Chapter 5 how hydraulic disc brake calipers work, but the short of it is that you can wedge a spacer in there (these parts usually come with your bike or brakes) or carefully use a large flathead screwdriver to spread the pads and push the pistons into the caliper. This tweak may make more room for the rotor and eliminate the rubbing.

Mechanical disc brake calipers usually have pad contact adjustments you can use to add space, but keep in mind that adding too much space just to clear a wobbly rotor may reduce braking power.

If none of that helps, your rotor might be warped too much and you need to replace it. But there's one more thing to try first, if you read the next section.

Every time I tighten the caliper, it moves!

I feel your pain. Many frames and forks, especially painted ones, have disc brake mounts that aren't perfectly flat. If you notice that your caliper shifts to one side or another as you tighten its mounting bolts, you need to *face*, or flatten, the mounting area. Yes, this is annoying, and no, you shouldn't have to do it, but I've had to do it even on some very expensive bikes, and it's easier to just fix it than to complain.

WARNING

Before you attempt the solution I suggest in the next paragraph, know this: Your local bike shop has tools specifically designed to face brake mounts properly. Using the DIY tip in this chapter means you're risking doing it wrong and damaging your frame. Just because I've done it doesn't mean you should, but I wanted to explain it so you understand why some calipers are so hard to align.

If you're okay with that risk, here's how to get your calipers to line up correctly as you tighten them:

Simply take a mild file or very fine-grit sandpaper and gently remove any paint from the mounting holes on your frame or fork. This often fixes it, but if they're already bare, eyeball it and see if they look level. If you can't tell visually, then note which way the caliper slides when you tighten it. If it slides inward toward the rotor, then the mount is higher on the outside and you need to file that down *slightly* (seriously, little bits at a time — you'll ruin your frame if you get aggressive with this). And vice versa. If you're uncomfortable doing this job yourself, it's an appropriate one for your local bike shop.

Facing your brake mounts not only helps you adjust them more accurately but also ensures perfect vertical alignment so that the top and bottom of your brake pads are equidistant from the rotor, which also helps eliminate rubbing and reduces stresses for better durability and performance.

Securing the position of your bike's brake levers is vital, and I cover that topic in Chapter 11, along with lots of other fit and setup tips to help you ride safely and comfortably.

Knowing What to Do When a Ride Goes Wrong

Most things that go wrong on a ride are simple to fix as long as you have the right tools and a little know-how. My recommended on-the-bike repair kit gear list in Chapter 10 gives you everything you need, and now I'll explain how to use those tools to fix a flat tire, repair a broken chain, adjust your gears, and more.

Fixing a flat

There are three ways to fix a flat tire, depending on your setup and the severity of the puncture:

>> **With tubes:** If you're using inner tubes, you need to replace the tube.

>> **With tubeless:** Plugging the hole with a tire plug and reinflating usually fixes it and gets you rolling again.

>> **Very large punctures:** If you suffered a large puncture that tubeless sealant or a tire plug can't fix, or if it's so large that the inner tube is bulging out of it, you need to also patch the tire from the inside and, even for tubeless setups, insert a tube to finish your ride.

Replacing an inner tube

Replacing an inner tube is easy, but takes a few steps. I recommend practicing it at least once so that you're familiar with your tools and the process before you need to use them on the side of the road or trail. Here's how to do it:

1. **Remove the wheel and tire.**

    a. If you have gears, shift to one of the smallest cogs and chainring.

    b. If you have rim brakes, release the caliper or unhook the brake arms so that the tire clears the brake pads.

    c. Flip the bike over so that it's resting on the saddle and handlebars, or hang the saddle on a sign or tree branch, or have your friend hold it up.

d. Open the quick-release lever or loosen and remove the thru axle that holds the wheel inside the bike.

e. Pull the wheel out of the bike — it may help to rotate the rear derailleur backwards with your hand to help it clear the cassette as you remove the wheel. (Your helper can lay it on its side now — just don't let them get too far away).

2. **Partially remove the tire from the rim**

   a. Finish deflating the tire if there's any air left in it.

   b. You need to remove only one side of the tire from the rim, and it doesn't matter (left or right) which one you choose.

   c. Press along the side of the tire near the rim to release it from its bead seat. Once you have one section of the bead released, work your way around the tire with your hand, squeezing the remaining sections of tire bead into the center rim channel.

   d. Insert a tire lever to pry the tire off the rim, and then work the lever all the way around so that one side of the tire is completely removed. Sometimes you might have to insert one tire lever, pry the tire back, and then use a second tire lever 3-6" away from the first to do the same.

3. **Remove the tube and inspect it.**

   a. Unthread the cap and nut from the tube's valve stem (if it has them).

   b. Start pulling the tube out from the side opposite of the valve stem.

   c. Push the valve stem through the rim, and wiggle the rest of the tube out of the tire — but keep the tube next to the tire without flipping it over.

   d. Carefully inspect the tube for any holes, tears, or snakebite punctures (see Chapter 5 for a refresher on snakebite punctures). If you can't find one, pump a little bit of air into the tube until you hear and feel it coming out of the hole(s).

   e. Patch the tube if you want, or fully deflate it, roll it up, and stow it for later disposal — or recycle it at your local shop.

4. **Inspect the tire.**

   a. Once you've found the hole in the tube, line it up with the tire and inspect the tire at the same place. Look for any damage to the tire and *carefully* feel around inside for any thorns, nails, glass, or other sharp items stuck in there.

   b. Remove those sharp items so that they don't immediately puncture your new tube.

    c. Run your fingers along the inside of the rest of the tire to check for other sharp items, too. If you don't find anything sharp, inspect the rim tape — are there any spoke holes showing? Did the sharp edge of the valve hole cut the tube by the valve?

    d. Patch any big holes or tears as needed.

5. **Install the new tube.**

    a. Add just enough air to the tube to give it a loose shape.

    b. Starting at the valve stem, tuck the tube up into the tire and slide the valve stem through the rim. Loosely reattach any nut to the valve stem.

    c. Tuck the rest of the tube into the tire, working your way around the wheel. It is very important that you get the tube tucked fully into the tire cavity, and not pinched under the tire bead.

6. **Reinstall the tire.**

    a. Starting opposite of the valve stem, press the tire back onto the rim. Use both hands to work around the wheel in both directions so that they meet at the valve stem.

    b. If the tire is a tight fit, it may help to push the valve stem up slightly to create room under the tube, and then work the tire onto the rim.

    c. Using a tire lever to reinstall the tire with a tube is not advisable since it's very easy to pinch the new tube with the lever. If you're struggling to get the tire on without tools, make sure the bead is dropped into the center rim channel, and that the tube isn't overly inflated. If you absolutely can't get the tire back on the rim, you can use a tire lever to pry it on, but this should be a last resort as the tire lever can sometimes pinch a hole in the new tube or push your tubeless rim out of place, thus causing new problems.

7. **Inflate the tube.**

    a. For Presta tubes, tighten the nut on the valve stem so that it's snug before inflating.

    b. Inflate to the desired pressure. Go by feel if your pump doesn't have a gauge.

    c. Close the valve core and replace the cap.

8. **Reinstall your wheel.**

    a. Reverse the process for removing the wheel.

    b. You may need to pull the rear derailleur back slightly to rest the chain properly on the cassette, making sure to line it up with the same cog it was in when you removed the wheel.

    c. Carefully slide it up so that the rotor or rim slots between the brake pads.

    d. If you have quick release skewers, rest the bike on the wheels and put a little weight on the saddle or handlebar to ensure that the wheel is fully, evenly seated in the dropouts, and then close the skewer.

    e. If you have thru axles, slide them through and bolt them tight.

You should be all set, but give the wheel a quick spin and make sure everything's rolling right. You may want to shift the gear into an easier cog before you hop on and start pedaling, too. This is also a good time to look at the tire as it's spinning. Notice any bulges? If so, quickly deflate the tire before the tube works its way out and pops!

Plugging a tubeless tire

If you're running tubeless tires and the puncture is small, you do *not* need to remove the wheel from the bike or the tire from the rim to repair it — as long as you have a tire plug kit. Figure 13-6 shows a tire repair kit.

FIGURE 13-6:
A tire repair kit,
plugging a tire.

To plug a tire, place the plug through the prongs in the setter (the gizmo that looks like a small pitchfork or slotted tip), and then push that into the hole in the tire. The plug is tacky and will stick in the tire as you pull the setter back out.

Tire plugs, sometimes affectionately called "bacon strips" because of the way they're packaged in strips, come in different diameters to fix holes of different sizes. Usually, the smaller ones are for road, medium for gravel, and big for mountain bike tires, but it's a good idea to have some of each. You can double up or mix and match to plug larger holes.

Some brands (Dynaplug, Blackburn Design, Clever Standard) use a setter with a tube or "bullet" tip rather than a prong, but the process is the same — insert plug, press it into the hole, remove the tool.

Some tools also include a small blade that lets you cut off the excess plug. This tool is handy because, if there's too much plug dangling out of the tire, it can feel bumpy (on a road or gravel bike) or get yanked out of the tire during a skid. Trim the plugs close to the surface, but leave a little bit exposed so that it doesn't get mashed all the way into the tire.

Tire plugs are generally a semi-permanent fix. There's no need to remove them and perform additional repairs later.

What if I don't have a tire plug tool?

If you don't have a plug, locate the puncture by listening for where the air is coming out and/or looking for tire sealant bubbling (or spraying!) out of your tire.

If the sealant is just barely bubbling out, rotate the tire so that the hole is on the bottom of the wheel. This lets the sealant pool above the hole and (hopefully) seal it. You can hold your finger over the hole to prevent too much air from escaping, but if the sealant is going to plug it for you, it usually does so within ten seconds.

If the hole is too big and sealant is spraying out, you can try rubbing some dirt in there to help it congeal, but most likely the hole is too big and you'll need to patch the tire from the inside or put a tube in there. This is a lot more work, and it's why I *highly* recommend having a tire plug kit if you're running tubeless tires.

Can I plug a tire with a tube in it?

No. If you're using inner tubes, it's the tube, not the tire, that's holding the air, so a tire plug won't work. But you can *patch* a tube — refer to the previous section.

Patching a tire

Sometimes a hole in the tire is too big, or the sidewall gets a long tear in it and also needs to be repaired before you can reinflate the tube. As you're inspecting the tire for any sharp, pokey items, look for the hole. If it's bigger than 5 millimeters (~0.2-inch), you're better off patching the tire before reinflating it.

If you have a patch kit (which I highly recommend keeping in your on-the-bike kit), you can simply stick it on the *inside* of the tire to cover the hole. Always put the patch on the inside of the tire, not on the outside.

If you don't have a patch kit, you can improvise with a folded dollar bill, an energy bar wrapper, or any tough-but-flexible material you can find on the side of the road. Plastic grocery bags and standard paper aren't tough enough, you need something that won't stretch. Fold the patch material so that it's at least 5 times bigger than the puncture or tear, and then place it between the tire and the tube and reinflate. The larger the hole, the stronger the material needs to be, and, ide-ally, the more layers you can fold it into.

Patching a tubeless tire

If you're patching a tubeless tire, wipe away all the sealant and dry the inside of the tire so that the patch will stick. If you're adding a tube, which you probably should, remember that you also need to remove the tubeless valve stem from your rim so that you can insert the tube's valve stem through that hole.

Standard tube patches won't work well as a permanent fix for a tubeless tire, but Lezyne's Tubeless Pro Plugs are purpose-built for this job. They're not a trailside fix — you need to install them at home — but they're a helpful way to save your tire from an early re-tire-ment. (Sorry!)

Using a CO_2 cartridge or a pump

Once your tube is installed and your tire is repaired, it's time to reinflate it. If you're in a hurry, a CO_2 cartridge will fully inflate it in seconds. Just be careful when handling the cartridge, because it freezes as it discharges its compressed gas and can cause frostbite. (I'm not kidding.) Hold the cartridge with a glove or rag — *not* with your bare fingers! Each CO_2 chuck/tool is a little different, so read the instructions and learn how to use it *before* you need it.

Mini pumps attach directly to the valve stem, or with a short hose. Read about the pros and cons of each style and other options in Chapter 10. Once it's attached, pump to the desired pressure and then remove it — and then you're on your way.

Adjusting Gears and Shifting: Mechanical Derailleurs

You can make four main adjustments to improve shifting: cable tension, derailleur alignment, limit screws, and B-screw adjustments. All but the latter apply to both front and rear derailleurs, and those also mainly apply to mechanical shifting groups. I cover wireless and electronic shifting adjustments at the end of this main section, and you'll find additional images and tips for tuning mechanical derailleurs and shifting in Chapter 11.

Front derailleurs

Truth be told, most front derailleurs rarely come out of adjustment, which is good because they have few on-the-fly adjustments.

Some bikes have inline barrel adjusters in the cable housing between the shifter and derailleur. These let you fine-tune the derailleur's position over the chain to center it. Much like brakes, the main setup is done during installation, and then this adjuster is used for micro-adjustments later. Unlike rear derailleurs, front derailleurs have no built-in barrel adjusters, but you (or your shop) can easily add an inline one at any time.

Front derailleurs also have upper- and lower-limit screws to set their limits. This prevents it from moving too far inboard or outboard and throwing the chain off the chainrings. Each brand is different, and some use reverse-threaded bolts that move the derailleur in the opposite direction than you'd think, so it's best to read the instructions for whichever brand you have.

When a front derailleur is first set up, it also has to be angled properly and set at the right height. Many have set up guides that help simplify the process. Unless your derailleur mounting bolt comes loose during a ride (or you changed chainrings), you shouldn't have to worry about this adjustment after the initial alignment.

Rear derailleurs

You may hear the phrase *cable stretch*, which is when a steel shift or brake cable elongates over time. Snarky Internet trolls will remind you that braided metal cables doesn't stretch. Which is true. What *does* happen is the ferrules (the end caps on the housing) can settle in and the end of the housing's sheath can compress a bit over the first 20 or so hours of use. This means your derailleur's position will move slightly, which reduces shifting accuracy. It also causes more drivetrain noise.

Sometimes things get knocked out of place or your derailleur hanger gets a little bent or gremlins fiddle with your setup. Regardless of why it happens, you should adjust your derailleurs.

Most mechanical rear derailleurs have a small barrel adjuster where the cable enters the derailleur. This is one of the easiest adjustments on the entire bike, and one of the best ways to impress your new cycling friends with your skills.

Whichever way you turn the top of the barrel adjuster, that's the direction the derailleur will move:

>> Turn it counterclockwise (top goes to the left), and the derailleur moves the chain to the left.

>> Turn it clockwise (top goes to the right), and the derailleur moves the chain to the right.

All you need to do is squat behind the bike, eyeball the derailleur's upper pulley wheel, and then tighten the barrel adjuster until it's aligned under the desired cog.

Where shifting gets tricky

There are times when you think you've adjusted the shifter into the correct gear, but in fact it was so close to being in a different gear that you adjust it into that incorrect gear. For example, if the shifter says it's in sixth gear but everything is so out of adjustment that it's trying to get into seventh gear, it may appear as though you need to adjust it toward seventh gear. It's fine — this situation happens to the best of us.

You will then notice that your shifting has improved, but you're now unable to move into the top or bottom gear. In that case, shift all the way to the smallest cog and then check it. One of two things will happen:

>> You'll be unable to get into the smallest cog, in which case you turn the barrel adjuster clockwise until it drops into that gear.

>> You'll shift into that smallest cog and still have a click left in the shifter that creates slack in the cable. In this case, you turn the barrel adjuster counterclockwise until you take up all that slack.

Once you've made these adjustments, shift up and down the first few gears a couple of times and recheck your work. Sometimes when you use the barrel adjuster to make major adjustments, you need to go back and fine-tune after shifting a couple of times.

The bike is shifting, but it's not happy about it

This problem is common and usually just takes a small twist of the barrel adjuster to resolve it. You can usually look at the cassette and derailleur and see that it's misaligned, causing shifting in one direction to be slow and feeling like it's hesitant to complete the shift. If it's bad, you can hear it making a clicking sound as you pedal, in which case you should stop and take a look at it at the next stop sign.

TIP

All these adjustments are easier if you have a friend help hold up the bike and turn the cranks while you shift and adjust. Or, hang the bike's saddle on an object so that you can spin the cranks and shift.

Checking derailleur hanger alignment

The *derailleur hanger* is the small, replaceable part that your rear derailleur mounts to. The hanger is designed to fail first because it's relatively cheap and easy to replace — unlike your derailleur or your frame. That's good, but it also means it's easy to bend if your bike falls over on the drive side or a stick gets jammed up in the derailleur, for example.

Once the rear derailleur is bent or twisted, it will be misaligned and shifting will be less than optimal. It may also create a lot of noise. Sometimes, it's pretty obvious just by looking at it and you can grab the derailleur and bend it back into a better position. At other times, it's subtle, leaving you scratching your head about why your bike won't shift well. If you've tried everything else, take it to your local shop and ask them to check it because (yep) there's a tool specifically for that purpose, too.

Adjusting electronic drivetrains

One of the biggest selling points of electronic shifters is that they shift perfectly every time and there are no cables to fall out of adjustment. That said, hangers bend and other mishaps happen, so they all still have some adjustments. Most have high/low limit screws to set their boundaries, but the chain alignment adjustments are done with either a smartphone app or small buttons on the shifters. Shimano's first-generation Di2 group had a button on their wire junction boxes that you held down and then used the shifters to make micro adjustments.

With new groups and apps and designs always on the horizon, your best bet is to check your brand's manual (or search online for the phrase How to adjust <your drivetrain>) for up-to-date adjustment instructions.

Repairing and Replacing a Chain

Most modern chains use quick links to connect and disconnect them. This item is helpful for removing your chain to clean it (a process covered earlier in this chapter), but if you break a chain at any other link, you need a way to remove the broken links to use a quick link to fix it.

That's where a chain breaker tool comes in. This item uses a threaded press to push the pin out of a chain link, thus "breaking" the chain open. Lots of mini tools have them, and it's a good tool to have in your kit. Without it, you could be stranded.

I also carry with me quick links for 10-, 11-, and 12-speed chains. Most of my bikes are 12-speeds, but you never know when someone in your group may need a different one — and you get to be the hero. Make sure you have — at minimum — one quick link that matches your type of chain.

TIP

Release any derailleur clutch or cage, and/or pull the chain off the chainring(s) before working on the chain. This relieves tension and makes it much easier to work with.

Once you break the chain to remove any busted links, loop the chain back through the derailleur(s), and be sure to get the pattern right as it loops through the rear derailleur's pulleys. Then use the quick link to connect them.

Here are some tips for using quick links:

1. A quick link replaces only the outer plates, so if your chain fails at an inner link, you may need to remove both outer links on either side of it and then use the quick link to reconnect it. This shortens your chain, so shifting may be affected on the largest cogs, and you'll probably want to replace your chain — or at least ask your local shop for some spare links and buy another quick link to add those in.

2. Opening a quick link is best done with a tool, and not a lot of mini tools have a quick link tool. Some tire levers (Clever Standard is a good one) do, but, fortunately, you rarely need to *open* one out in the field. However, in a pinch, you can angle it 90 degrees from the inner links on either side of it and use two tire levers to "pinch" it open.

3. If you need to *close*, or connect, a quick link without a tool, simply install it on the chain, turn the cranks until it's on the top side of the drivetrain between the cassette and cranks, hold the rear brake, and then step on the crank arm to pull it tight. You don't need to step hard (just a little body weight will do), and you'll feel the link snap closed. Just make sure it's slotted together properly before you do this or else you could ruin it.

Less expensive chains often don't have quick link options (KMC does make a quick link for 6, 7, and 8 speed chains), but you may be able to find replacement pins. You need to carry a chain breaker tool (which is also used to press the new pin into the chain to reconnect it). Some single speed chains also use quick links, though many use what's commonly called a master link. This is a three-piece chain link that functions similarly to a quick link.

If you can't fix your chain, or if it's time for a new one (or an upgrade), you need to replace it. New chains come with either a quick link or a pin, but you need a chain breaker tool to "cut" it to the proper length. Each drivetrain brand has its own guidelines for the proper length, but if you're replacing one, the easiest thing to do is measure your old one and cut the new one to the same length. Note that if you let your drivetrain go too long without replacing the chain, putting a new chain on very-worn gears can sometimes cause the new chain to skip.

What to Do If You Wreck

Think of wrecking as a rite of passage. Every cyclist does it eventually, so it's a good idea to know what to expect and what do to after the wreck.

Minor tumbles

Maybe you didn't get clipped out in time and toppled over. Or you bumped into a curb and ended up sitting (rather uncomfortably) on the top tube. Most of the time, you can just take a breath, dust yourself off, and start riding again.

But just to be safe, give yourself a second to make sure. Look over your bike for any obvious issues. Spin the wheels, turn the cranks, check your cockpit position, and put your helmet on straight. Make sure nothing fell out of your pockets (or bike basket) and that your shoes are still tied.

Major tumbles

If you're ripping through the trails and smack a tree or fly off a jump you didn't see until it was too late or otherwise end up arse-over-elbows, stop and chill for a minute. The same advice applies if you're speeding along the road and you end up in the brush because a squirrel (or worse) jumped out in front of you.

If you take a tumble at high speed on any terrain, take a moment before you hop up. Then make sure you can feel everything (fingers and toes, especially). Make sure you can move all your joints normally. Check for blood. Check your helmet: If it's smashed, you may want to take an extra few minutes.

Don't rush to get right back on the bike. If you're in a spot where you're not in danger of getting hit, bit, or run over, take your time getting up. Check over your bike and make sure it brakes and shifts and rolls like it should. Check the frame and cockpit for dents, cracks, and breaks. There's no shame in calling someone to come pick you up, and 9-1-1 exists for a reason if you're seriously injured. Let your rescuer be the hero, not you.

If you hit someone

If you run into another cyclist and you're okay, make sure they are, too. If you're hurt, follow the advice in the previous section, and then make sure the other person is okay. If everyone's okay and the location is safe, it's time to assess the situation. If it's obviously your fault, be apologetic. Nothing is gained by trying to point out what *they* could have done differently to avoid *your* mistake. Offer your ID and phone number and to pay for any damage to their bike.

If it's the other person's fault (maybe they pulled out in front of you), calmly take some pictures of the scene and ask how they want to handle it. If it was a minor tumble, there's no damage, and everyone's okay, it's probably fine to just roll on about your day. If not, ask for the phone number and ID and how they want to handle the damage to your bike and gear.

Regardless of who's at fault, if the damage is considerable or someone is seriously hurt, call 9-1-1 and file a police report so that the insurance company can handle it.

If someone hits you

If someone hits you, call 9-1-1 and file a police report — no matter what.

Read that again. No. Matter. What. Always get a police report.

Even if you feel fine and don't want to cause a scene, file a police report. It doesn't matter whether it's a bike or a car or a horse that hit you.

Health issues can turn up later. Or, maybe your $1,000 smartphone and $400 prescription glasses got smashed but you didn't notice until you got home. And maybe your back and neck start hurting a week later.

Without a police report, your insurance company has no documentation to work from or third party to make a claim against, so you're stuck paying any medical bills and replacing your bike or gear out of your own pocket.

If you notice the smell of alcohol or drugs, mention that to the police.

Taking photos for documentation

While you're waiting for the police, take pictures and make notes (a voice memo is good, too) of what happened. Take pictures of their vehicle, any damage to it, the intersection or scene, and damage to you and your bike. Take a picture of the person responsible and ask to see their ID. If it looks like they're going to flee, snap a photo of their license plate and car.

Watch the driver. Are they hiding anything in their car? Ditching empty bottles behind some bushes? (Yes, I've seen this happen.) Take photos if you can, and at least mention it to the police.

If you're too injured to take stock of the situation

Hopefully, the person who hit you stopped, too. If you can, ask them to call 9-1-1 — or ask any passersby to call. Then ask any third party to take photos of the scene, the car, the people, or any other necessary aspect.

With all that said, if you're too hurt to move, don't try unless it's critical to your survival. Use your voice assistant ("hey, Siri!") to try calling for help so that you don't have to move your head, neck, or spine. Some apps like Strava offer free features that automatically alert your emergency contact and show them your location on the ride — this can provide peace of mind to your loved ones while you're out riding, and also provide your whereabouts if you don't return home.

Help others, too

If you see anyone get hit or have an accident, stop to check whether they're okay. Hold their bike up for them, make sure they're coherent, and call 9-1-1 if necessary. Take pictures for them or get info from witnesses.

Get back in the saddle

Assuming that you can, and that you want to, get right back in the saddle after a wreck.

Especially after small tumbles, or a wipeout because you made a technical mistake, immediately trying that section or trick again is the best way to avoid having it become a major mental block later. Process what happened, and then correct it and try again right away.

For bigger accidents, you should obviously give yourself time to heal. *Then get right back on the bike.* It's helpful for physical therapy, and you can join group rides or stick to back roads and easier trails while you regain your confidence.

Repairing, Replacing, and Retiring Old Bikes and Parts

Every bike and part has a finite lifespan. Some parts are higher-wear than others (chains, tires, grips). Others can last for many thousands (or tens of thousands) of miles. Here's a quick guide to when to repair, replace, or retire them.

When to repair or replace a part

Assuming that you still love your bike, this section describes the main items to replace on it. Of course, replacements offer a useful opportunity to upgrade parts, so you don't *need* to wait for something to wear out before replacing it.

Drivetrains

Your drivetrain sees a lot of wear and tear. If it's properly maintained, you can get more than 10,000 miles from a drivetrain, maybe only replacing your chain once or twice during that time. If it's poorly maintained, you may not even get 1,000 miles out of it. If you see excessive rust or the chain doesn't move freely, it's time to replace it. If the chainring teeth are worn down and keep dropping or snagging the chain, replace them. If the chain skips over the cassette, replace the cassette (and likely the chain).

Derailleurs move and bounce a lot, and lower-tier models have looser tolerances and lower-end materials. If the joints in them feel sloppy and shifting is no longer precise despite your best efforts at adjusting them, it's time to replace them. Similarly for shifters, many use plastic ratchet rings inside that wear down after thousands of shifts. Some third-party companies make replacement parts, but if you're unwilling to tear them apart and fiddle with small parts, replace your shifters when they start feeling loose or shift inconsistently.

The crankset is likely the longest-lasting part of the drivetrain, but if it starts to feel loose and the bottom bracket is in good shape, you may have worn down the spindle and you need to replace the crankset. Some brands use bonded-metal clamshell designs that may separate, so check those periodically and stop riding them immediately if you see any gaps or they feel loose. The crankset is usually under warranty, so check with the manufacturer.

Wheels and tires

I explained tire wear and when to replace tires earlier in this chapter, so I focus on wheels here. Anytime you see a crack in a rim, it's time to replace it. If it's dinged or dented to the point where it won't completely seat a tire, or if it won't stay true even after being straightened, replace it.

Inside the hub, bearings can wear out or become contaminated and ruined. High-end wheels and bearings have better seals and last longer, but if things start feeling loose or crunchy and don't improve after cleaning and regreasing them, it's time to replace the bearings.

Most good shops can replace any or every part of your wheel and rebuild or true it. But if all the parts have seen better days, it may be time to upgrade your entire wheelset rather than repair it.

Cockpit

If any part of your cockpit (handlebar, saddle, seatpost, stem) is broken or damaged, replace it immediately. If your saddle's cover gets torn, it'll likely tear more and degrade quickly, potentially exposing sharper parts of the frame that could hurt you, so just replace it.

Grips and handlebar tape wear out. Grips can get worn smooth so that they're no longer grippy enough to keep your hands on board, or they wear down so much that they can tear and cause you to lose all grip. Handlebar tape may stretch, or eventually shifts, and it definitely gets dirty and discolored from sweat, mud, and rain. Fresh grips or bar tape is a helpful way to refresh your entire bike for very little money.

Other items

Headsets, pedals, forks, and shocks all have a lot of moving parts. From bearings to bushings to seals, these items wear out and can be replaced or serviced to extend their lifespan. Some suspension forks have kept the same chassis for a decade or more, which means you can upgrade the internals without having to buy an entirely new fork. If any of those parts starts to feel loose, crunchy, or sticky and cleaning or relubing them doesn't help, it may be time to replace some internal parts or just replace them altogether.

When to replace your bike

Assuming that you love your bike, the only time you'd need to replace it is if you break it or outgrow it or it no longer meets your needs.

Any cracks or breaks in the frame, or even significant dents, mean you should replace your frame. Many carbon and metal frames can be repaired, too, but if you're not going to fix it (which can sometimes cost almost as much as a new frame), definitely replace it.

If you have outgrown your frame, it's better to move up to one that fits. It's also possible that your bike has outgrown you. Maybe you're not as flexible as before or you've shrunk with age. Or maybe your bike is made for more aggressive riding than you're willing to do now. These are all good reasons to replace your bike with one that fits you better, in both size and body position.

Another good reason to replace your bike is when your skills have outgrown your current bike or your riding style has changed. Maybe you've switched from XC to enduro or from gravel racing to bikepacking. Or, you used to race crits, but now you enjoy gran fondos instead. Your current bike will work for a while as your riding skills progress, but at some point, you need a bike suited for where you're going, to help you progress faster and better.

What to do with your old bike and parts

I'm constantly surprised by how many perfectly good bikes I see sitting by the side of the road for trash pickup — sometimes, even perfectly new-looking kids' bikes. It's sad because lots of people would love to have them.

The following four sections describe things you can do with your old bikes and parts to keep them out of a landfill and help others.

Donate them

Even if you think an old bike is junk, *someone* can probably use it, so please donate it. A recycled bike is life-changing for folks who can't afford a car and aren't served by public transportation, and you can help them by donating your unused or unwanted bikes and parts.

Almost every town has some person or group that fixes and rebuilds bikes for those who need them, and they always need parts — any part and every part, and they can often scavenge those off unwanted bikes if the bike itself can't be saved. Just ask your local bike shop where to take them, or ask whether you can drop off parts at their shop for them to use — every bike shop should know who to get them to.

Can't find a local bike co-op? Take it to a nearby thrift shop. Ask your local police or social services or shelter personnel if they can pass along the bike to someone who can use it. Or put up a flyer in your church or civic group.

Share them

My family had three balance bikes that we shared with ten other families as they had kids. Two of them I found in the trash and cleaned up, and they worked well, so we probably helped 15 or more kids learn to ride. Every time someone would return a bike, we'd pass it along again to another family.

Kids' bikes are useful for sharing because they outgrow them so quickly, and many are lightly used. But adult bikes are, too. Ask around — I'd bet someone you know knows someone who would love to have a bike.

Trade them in

Some bike shops take trade-ins, giving you a bit of a discount on a new bike. You probably won't get much for it, but something is better than nothing, and some shops can help get those bikes to people who can't afford a new bike.

Sell the bike

You can always list your bikes on craigslist, Next Door, OfferUp, Facebook Marketplace, eBay, or whatever other new service pops up. If you were going to trash the bike, list it for free if someone comes to pick it up. If it's still in good shape, make it a deal that's too good to refuse so that you can make room for your new bike.

Regardless of what you do with your old bikes and parts, just know that they're helping do some good and making others happier and healthier.

IN THIS CHAPTER

» **Scrolling through the best ride apps**

» **Finding the best places to ride**

» **Riding with your family members**

» **Vacationing with (or on!) your bike**

» **Carting your bike around**

Chapter **14**

Finding Good Places to Ride

We humans are living in a golden age of technology, and that means you can find lots of apps to scope out places to bike, no matter how, when, or where you want to ride. But some of us still enjoy the good old-fashioned method of just rolling out of the driveway and exploring. In between those two strategies are advice from local shops, charity rides, and events to check into. Even if you don't take part in them, most will publish their routes so that you can ride them outside of the organized gathering.

In this chapter, I share some of the best apps and other ways to find fun, interesting, and safe places to ride!

There's an App for That

I mention these apps throughout this chapter, so let's kick things off with a brief description of the most popular apps used to find and guide your rides.

REMEMBER

Let me spell out two important points: First, these apps are updated all the time, so features may change or improve since this book was published. Second, though some features are available only with paid subscription plans, all of them have a free version to get you started.

Check out these apps:

>> **Strava:** Strava tracks your rides, runs, and tons of other activities, saving your performance for later analysis. It also gamified cycling by adding leaderboards for popular *segments,* or stretches of road or trail, showing who's ridden them the fastest! The app also shows you heat maps of popular areas, which makes it easy to see where most people ride in a given area — and it can use that data to automatically create routes for you.

>> **Ride with GPS:** This app is popular among cyclists for planning rides, with desktop and mobile versions making it easy to create and save routes on a map and then use them for navigation with your phone. You can also export the route as a GPX file and share it with others so that everyone in your group follows the same route and everyone (including you) can load it onto their GPS cycling computer for easy turn-by-turn directions and prompts while riding.

>> **Komoot:** Komoot tracks your rides, showing them on the map with speed, time, elevation, and other data afterward. It lets you upload photos and tag them to certain spots on the ride as points of interest. Many people make these tours public, which makes it a helpful app for finding other riders' routes and seeing whether you want to try them on your own. You can also use Komoot to create your own routes and navigate with it.

>> **Sherpa Map:** This upstart app combines artificial intelligence with weather data, surface data, your fitness level, and your bike setup to provide some truly geeky info, like which tire setup will work best for you, how many calories you'll need, and whether you'll have headwinds or tailwinds throughout the ride. Upload your past ride data along with your friends' (or competitors') data and the app will show you where each person is faster — which is useful "intel" before a race!

>> **Trailforks:** When you're looking for trails anywhere in the world, this top mountain bike app shows you their difficulty, distance, recommended riding direction, and elevation change. It tells you whether e-bikes are allowed and can even guide you along them while you're riding. Its huge, active user base means local trail conditions are frequently updated based on weather and tree falls, for example, making it the best way to find new mountain bike (MTB) trails to ride. You can view a single state or region for free, but you have to pay to access all regions on the mobile app. When you open the app's website in your browser, however, all the info is free — you just won't have offline access or the best user experience out on the trail.

>> **MTB Project, by onX Backcountry:** MTB Project is similar to Trailforks, but totally free. Trail maps and info are crowdsourced, and they're extensive. You can save trail maps for offline use, too, though the background (terrain or satellite imagery) will disappear, leaving only the trail outlines and a dot to indicate your position. MTB Project is owned by onX, a leading outdoor GPS mapping service, and you can see MTB Project trail maps and ratings inside onX Backcountry, which is more fully featured for mapping and terrain (and requires a paid subscription).

>> **Chasing Watts, Link My Ride:** These two apps can help you find group rides. Add your zip code or city, whether local or anywhere you're traveling, and they'll show you a list of nearby group rides.

Locating Local Hotspots

My first bit of advice is to simply ask your local bike shop for recommendations for good routes, bike paths, and other loops popular with area cyclists. Tell them what type of bike you have and how long or far you want to go, and they'll likely give you several good options to get started.

My next suggestion, once you're comfortable riding out on the road or bike paths, is to just start exploring. I like to take random turns (or intentionally missed turns) just to see where I end up. On a smartphone, you're never really lost, so don't be afraid to explore new areas of your neighborhood and then your city and then your county and beyond!

One of my favorite aspects of riding bikes is that I can cover much more ground than just walking. I often look for new roads and paths in my hometown but also use bikes to get around in new cities (domestic and abroad) so that I can see more of the city.

Scouting out safe roads and routes

Using Strava's Heatmaps app makes it easy to see where other people ride, which is some indication of a road's safety level. But keep in mind that if you have a big cycling scene in your area, that data will be influenced by experienced cyclists who are more comfortable on busier roads.

If you're just cruising around for exercise, then neighborhoods, parks, and bike paths are perfect for you. If you want to ride to a specific destination, look for roads with bike lanes or ride on side streets and back roads.

I also look at where the general path of development is. For example, in my hometown, most of the suburbs and sprawl are on the north side of town. South of us, it's mostly country folks with farms and horse pastures, which is much less densely populated. That means less parents in oversized SUVs racing between activities, appointments, and PTA meetings while being distracted by their kids in the back seat. (I'm not making this up — this is how quite a few cyclists have been hit!)

TIP

If you're riding at dawn and dusk, look at which way the sun is rising or setting. Avoid riding directly into the sun, because drivers are less able to see you. Even the brightest blinky light can't outshine the sun.

TIP

Here's a fun fact for you: The Bike Lane Uprising website (bikelaneuprising. com) lets you report bike lane obstructions, and then it uses this crowdsourced data to identify problem spots and repeat offenders and to provide that data to the appropriate municipal parties.

Lastly, use common sense. Stay off busy roads, and keep an eye out for traffic — glance behind you as you near intersections to make sure no one will race past you into a right turn, potentially hitting you or cutting you off. And always follow the rules of the road and other tips from Chapter 12.

Hitting the trails

Looking for the mountain bike trails? Your local bike shops will have all the "intel" on where to find singletrack, and someone there can guide you to the best trails for your skill level.

If you're using Trailforks or MTB Project, the trails are usually rated for difficulty and often use the same color-coding as ski slopes — green for beginner, blue for intermediate, and black for advanced.

Riding with the Family

Riding bikes with "the fam" is a fun-filled way to explore your town, get to school, enjoy some fresh air, and instill healthy exercise habits. Whether it's with your parents (or grandparents!), significant other, or kids, here are some tips to keep the ride fun and safe.

Setting a compatible pace and distance

Though no one likes being seen as the weakest link, there's one in every group, including families, and most family rides are beholden to the slowest rider. That's fine — if you want a fast ride, ride with your fast friends. If you want quality time with your family, or to share your newfound passion for cycling and get them hooked, the key is to make it fun on their level — meet them where they are.

REMEMBER

If your family members are just getting started (or joining you on this journey), share the plan in advance. Let everyone know your route and the anticipated distance. If there are ice cream (or beer) stops along the way, definitely mention them, too — they're powerful motivators!

Select a route that's easy enough for everyone, and use roads that keep everyone in their comfort zone with regard to traffic. Some riders, especially inexperienced ones, become nervous when lots of cars are passing them, so look for low-traffic areas, bike lanes, and bike paths. Parks with paved or hard gravel loops are perfect spots for keeping everyone together and safe.

Once you're riding, monitor everyone's pace and ensure that no one is struggling to keep up. Stop at intersections and make sure everyone is ready to continue, and always signal your turns and provide words of encouragement. If someone's struggling with a hill or headwind, ride next to them (if it's safe to do so, of course) and strike up a conversation about what flavor of ice cream or other treat or distraction you'll be stopping for after the ride.

Family rides are a time to have fun together, not to stress about being able to keep up or be nervous about traffic.

Riding with kids on the bike

If you're adding a kid seat or trailer or sticking your kids on a cargo bike, here are a few things to remember:

>> **The extra weight will change the way your bike handles.** Especially with kids' seats, where the weight sits up high, make sure you can easily plant your feet solidly on the ground when you stop.

>> **The extra weight will make it harder to travel uphill, so choose your routes wisely.** You'll also need more time to slow down and stop, so brake sooner and pay close attention to traffic lights (and crosswalk signals) to predict when you'll need to stop.

>> **Your kid *must* have a helmet that fits well.** And, if they're sitting in front of you or in an open-faced trailer, get them some sunglasses to protect their eyes, too.

If you're towing a trailer, take corners more slowly. I know several people who have flipped one, and I've even done it when mine was empty. Fortunately, trailers are built like little roll cages, but still, they tip over when you rip around a corner. Strap your kids in with the five-point harness to keep them in place. This strategy not only keeps them from climbing around in there, it also keeps them protected inside the trailer's frame if you do manage to tip over.

Riding alongside your kids

Once your kids know how to ride a bike, it's time to explain the rules of the road, how to ride safely, and what to pay attention to in traffic.

When they're first learning, stick to sidewalks and bike paths before graduating to bike lanes and then the open streets. Make sure their braking and handling skills are up to the task.

Then, at some point, after your kids grow tired of being coached, throttled, and reeled in, they'll want to just take off and ride. My advice is to ride behind them and monitor their skills, but do your best to trust them. Unless they're weaving in and out of traffic or blowing through intersections without looking, save your comments for the major problems — and then have a post-ride recap to applaud what they did well and address the issues where they can improve.

Joining a Cycling Club

A local cycling club is a fun way to meet new riders and improve your skills and fitness. As with many other bike-related matters, the best place to start is your local bike shop. Depending on the size of your city, you might find anywhere from one club to dozens of clubs.

Some clubs might not be well structured — they're more of a weekly meet-up than an official club. And some bike shops have their own clubs, possibly even offering in-store discounts if you join.

Some brands have ambassador programs, which may offer discounts and occasional meet-ups or other perks at major events. (I usually find links to these types of opportunities in the *footer*, or bottom, of brands' websites.)

National organizations, like International Mountain Bike Association (IMBA), provide partner discounts (including on new Subaru cars!) and other benefits. These larger organizations aren't usually hosting local rides like a club would, but your membership typically funds advocacy, trail building, legal support, and other things that benefit cyclists and cycling in general.

On the local level, some charity rides (the MS Society hosts many rides in many cities – events.nationalMSsociety.org) let you create or join a team to raise money for a good cause. Bigger rides often host training rides and meet-ups for weeks or months before the event, too, like a short-term club!

Taking a Biking-Focused Vacation

Whether I'm signing up for a guided tour — or planning my own — a cycling vacation is one of my favorite ways to really, truly, see a new area.

Most guided tours provide all the food and logistical support you need, and sometimes even provide (or rent) bikes. All you need to do is get yourself there and bring your helmet, shoes, cycling kits, and any other personal items you want to have on the ride.

If you're planning your own cycling vacation, it's more work, but it can also be a lot more affordable. You'll be your own logistics team, so here are some questions to think about:

>> Where will you stay each night?

>> How will you secure the bikes when you're not riding?

>> Can you make your own repairs if something happens on the ride?

>> What resources are available in that area if you can't fix something?

Once you have the location and type of riding nailed down, it's time to pack. If you'll have your car with you, go nuts. Bring anything you can think of: workstand, floor pump, toolkit, spare tires, tubeless sealant, drink mix, bottles, and hydration packs, for example.

But, if you're flying or otherwise limited in what you can bring, focus on the essentials, and make sure that the mini tool and pump you'll be riding with has all the bits you need in order to adjust all the parts on your bike, fix a flat, and keep you rolling.

SHOULD I GO BIKEPACKING OR BICYCLE TOURING?

Trick question! They're the same, really, but most people think of touring when they're only riding on the road, and they think of bikepacking when they're headed off-road. But both are typically fully (or mostly) self-supported, with all the food, cooking gear, camping gear, clothes, tools, and supplies on board the bike.

Or, you could go credit-card-bikepacking, which is my favorite style: Pack a few clothes and your flip-flops, basic tools, and snacks, but stay in hotels and eat at restaurants. This is a useful way to both see places and taste local cuisine, because food and drink are often one highlight of travel.

Either way, start planning as early as you can, and consider carefully which items you need. (You probably should skip items that are nice to have rather than essential.) Get your frame bags, racks, and other gear mounted to your bike, load it up, and go for a test ride. Even better, head out for an overnighter somewhere close and test your setup. Chances are good that you've packed too many items, and if you didn't think about using it on your test trip, you can probably save the weight and leave it home for the big trip. Just don't forget charging cables for your phone, bike computer, and lights!

TIP

Regardless of your mode of transportation, take at least a basic first aid kit with you, a small flashlight, and the appropriate clothing for the weather. (A light windbreaker or rain shell is always a good idea, and some are small enough to fit in a jersey pocket.) And, as silly as this sounds, if you need reading glasses to read your phone, you'll want to have a pair in your riding kit for making small repairs or finding tiny tire punctures. Trust me — and thank me later.

Transporting Your Bike

Traveling with your bike means you need a way to transport it, and the method and equipment change based on your mode of transportation.

On the car

Whether you're heading to the local trails or out for a road trip, you want a good bike rack. The best ones are *hitch-mounted* — they slide into a trailer hitch on your car. These are the most stable, most secure, and safest, but they do require that you have a hitch installed on your car.

If you're adding a hitch, I recommend going for the larger 2-inch hitch over the smaller 1.25-inch hitch. This gives you more flexibility in which racks you can use, and the larger racks for three, four, or more bikes all but require the 2-inch standard. In Europe and certain other parts of the world, racks are made to clamp onto the standard ball hitch and use an entirely different design.

Hitch mounts come in two styles:

>> **A hanging-style bike rack** has prongs over which you slide your bike's top tube and then strap the frame down over small rubber cushions (see Figure 14-1). This style is fine for bikes with traditional double-triangle designs (the basic safety bike, described in Chapter 1), but don't work well for step-through frames, many full-suspension mountain bikes, or other oddly shaped or small bikes. Also, because the rack is strapping around the frame, it may scratch your paint.

>> **A tray-style rack** uses wheel trays that your bike's tires sit on, and it's the better choice (see Figure 14-2). Most tray racks have hooks or gates that loop up and over the tires so that they never even touch the frame or rims. This is the most stable style, and it's better especially if you're transporting more than two bikes or heavier e-bikes. Some even have ramps to help you roll heavy e-bikes on board.

FIGURE 14-1:
Hanging-style hitch mount rack.

image credit: Thule

FIGURE 14-2:
Tray-style hitch
mount rack.

image credit: Thule

If you can't (or won't) add a hitch to your car, you need to use a strap-on rack (see Figure 14-3). These usually employ rubber-coated hooks around your trunk or tailgate and under your bumper. Then you tighten the straps to secure it, with foam or rubber bumpers resting between the rack and your car.

Strap mount racks are usually much less expensive, but they're all hanging-style racks, and depending on your vehicle's design, their prongs may angle upward so much that your bikes are awkwardly positioned. The strap mount takes more work to install and remove — and might scratch your car's paint. But, most of them fold down small enough to fit in a trunk and can even travel with you to use on a rental car.

Another option is suction-cup-mounted racks (see Figure 14-4), which is exactly what it sounds like. Wheel trays and fork mounts use suction to adhere to your vehicle's roof, trunk, or rear window, and you mount your bike to it. These are tiny and easy to travel with, and as odd as they might seem, the SeaSucker brand has been making them with lots of happy customers for many years.

Truck tailgate pads (see Figure 14-5) let you rest your bike over the tailgate, with the fork and front wheel behind it. Good-quality pads have thick, durable padding, a waterproof exterior material, and Velcro straps to secure the frame to it so that your bike(s) can't slide around. Many have ports for your tailgate's handle and backup camera, too.

image credit: Thule

FIGURE 14-3:
A strap-mounted
bike rack.

image credit: Jayson O'Mahoney / GravelCyclist.com

FIGURE 14-4:
Suction-cup-
mounted
bike rack.

FIGURE 14-5:
Tailgate pad
with bikes.

image credit: Kuat Racks

One last type of rack, the upright hanging rack, is most often used when you have lots of bikes (some hold as many as six) or you frequently take them on and off your vehicle. Shuttle companies like them because they can quickly load a lot of bikes, drive customers to the top of the mountain, and quickly pull the bikes off.

WARNING

The upright hanging rack, shown in Figure 14-6, is also hitch-mounted, but double-check the design because most are made specifically for mountain bikes with suspension forks and may not work well (or at all) with road bikes, kids' bikes, or other designs.

On a plane

The good news is that most major airlines no longer charge to transport bikes — fees used to be $200 or more each way! But now it's more affordable to take your bike, as long as its total weight when packed is less than the airline's weight limit (usually 50 to 70 lbs., but double-check with your airline).

To fly with a bike, you need either a hard case, a soft case, or a sturdy cardboard box. For the last option, ask your local bike shop if they have any extras you can take off their hands. (Bike shops get lots of these boxes — one for every bike on the floor — and they usually just recycle them, so they're often happy for you to come take one.) Make sure the box is in good shape and has thick cardboard with no holes or tears. Most likely, the shop also has plenty of foam tubes, bubble wrap, and other packing materials that came supplied on the new bikes, so you'll definitely want to grab some.

image credit: Yakima

If you have no idea how to pack your bike, most shops will do it for you for a small fee, but usually you just need to remove the front wheel, block the front brake (slide some thick cardboard between the disc brake pads if you don't have an actual spacer), and remove the handlebars from the stem so that they can dangle next to the fork. Wrap everything up with whatever protective material you have, slide the front wheel into the box, and you're mostly good to go. You can find plenty of videos online showing how to do this. Pay careful attention to make sure that the front brake rotor, shifter and brake levers, and other metal or pokey bits aren't rubbing against the frame.

It's also a good idea to let 50% of the air out of the tires and shift the rear derailleur all the way inboard (closer to the spokes). If you don't do this, unbolt it from the frame and wrap it (with the chain still looping through it) in bubble wrap, too.

TIP

If you're going to use the box to get your bike back home, too, bring a roll of packing tape in your luggage so that you can repack your bike.

If you start flying with your bike more frequently, invest in a good bike case. I like the Thule Round Trip Transition hard-sided case because it provides complete protection for your bike and has an integrated workstand to make its reassembly easier. The downside is that some larger long-travel MTBs may not fit, and, like all hard cases, it's heavy — often putting me close to the weight limit by the time I put my bike in it. Scicon is another popular brand of hard-shell bike case for travel, and you can find more.

Soft-shell bike cases are much lighter and less expensive and can be compressed for storage when not in use. Look for one with thickly padded sides and walls and some corner structure and reinforcements. The good ones have separate wheel compartments inside and loops and straps to keep things in place during transit. The EVOC Pro Bike Travel Bag is extremely popular and well featured, but you can find lots more good options. Check the reviews to find something in your budget.

Shipping it

If you're heading to a big event and don't want to fly or drive with your bike, you can ship it in advance. The upside is that you don't have to worry about checking it on a plane or pulling it off your car and into a hotel at night while traveling. The downside is that you'll be without your bike for two to ten days before and after the trip, depending on how far away you're going.

You need a *solid* box or bike case to put it in (see the earlier section "On a plane"), and you should use BikeFlights.com to ship it. Go ahead — check the retail rates for UPS or FedEx or a similar freight company, and then go check BikeFlights. I'll wait here until you return.

Told ya. The company's rates are not only 30 to 50% less than you and I can get, but they also provide excellent tracking info and can help find and return a lost bike if the worst-case scenario happens. They also insure the shipment, and their customer service is much easier to work with than at the shipping companies.

BikeFlights even offers its own collapsible-yet-sturdy shipping box that makes a useful container for flights, too. It comes with packing materials and flattens for easy storage under a bed or in a closet or attic at home, but it's rigid and durable enough for several trips worth of use, even with the abuse your package takes from freight companies.

Though a cardboard box may not seem like the toughest idea, keep in mind that bike brands ship brand-new $10,000 bikes in cardboard boxes all the time. And they're lighter than a bike case, which saves on shipping costs.

Regardless of how or where you go with your bike, enjoy the freedom it offers and the people you'll meet out on the ride.

4

The Part of Tens

Ten exercises to help you ride faster.

Ten awesome bike events.

Chapter **15**

Ten Training Tips

W hether you're just trying to get in shape or training for your next (for first!) bike race, here are ten exercises to boost strength, stamina, and speed. I've grouped them into five to do on the bike, and five for off the bike, making it easy to spread them out between ride days.

Before you get started, it's a good idea to know your basic heart rate zones. This gives you a good metric you can do without technology, or by pairing a simple heart chest rate strap (Polar and Wahoo make good ones) to your cycling computer. Most sports smartwatches have heart rate monitors built in, too.

Calculate your estimated max heart rate by subtracting your age from 220. There are more sophisticated ways to do it, but this provides a good ballpark to start with. Here's a simplified guide to training zones based on a percentage of your max:

| ZONE 1 | 50-60% | Recovery, good for moving fresh blood through the muscles to reduce soreness. Very important to keep your HR below 60% of max or this switches from Recovery to Training. |
| ZONE 2 | 60-70% | Foundational endurance building, where your muscles build more capillaries for better oxygen delivery during harder efforts. This is also where you burn more fat, and you should be able to carry on a conversation like normal. |

ZONE 3	70-80%	Tempo riding to build aerobic capacity. It should feel like you're working, but you should be able to keep it up for at least 30-60 minutes.
ZONE 4	80-90%	Lactate / Anaerobic Threshold training improves your muscles' ability to buffer lactic acid and use oxygen more efficiently. Both let you push harder for longer.
ZONE 5	90-100%	These VO_2 max efforts are at the limit of what your body can do and train it to maximize oxygen utilization. Raising your VO_2 max means you can do more work at a given breathing rate, making you a more efficient cyclist.

On-the-Bike Workouts

You'll notice that most of the on-bike workouts are intervals, which are short, specific workouts designed to improve a certain aspect of your performance. These can be worked into most rides, or done on a trainer in your home or a stationary bike at the gym.

Base miles

Base miles are what cyclists call our long, easy rides. They're a mix of Zone 1 and Zone 2, depending on whether it's a recovery day or training day. Long, slow rides may not seem like they're doing much, but they're helping your body make more oxygen pathways by growing more micro capillaries and teaching your mitochondria to make more energy.

These rides should make up 90 percent of your training, and it's really important to keep your heart rate within the correct zone to make it count. Most cyclists make the mistake of thinking they need to go harder and "feel the burn" for it to count, but that's what intervals are for.

Intervals – long, intermediate efforts

Now we're working our way up the zones. These "intervals" are really more like regular rides where you push yourself a bit harder. They could be 20-30 minutes of Zone 3, with 10-minute recovery times between. If you're not focused on a pure recovery ride, you could mix a couple of these into a two-hour base mile ride. If you're just getting started and all of that sounds way too long, think about mixing 3- to 5-minute efforts into a 30-minute ride and build up as you go.

Intervals – medium, hard efforts

These intervals are shorter, from 3-10 minutes, but harder. Aim for Zone 4 and keep it there for the duration of the interval. Keep in mind that it takes 20-30 seconds for your heart rate to catch up to your effort, so pay attention to your exertion level on the first interval and then use that to gauge effort on subsequent intervals. Once you're warmed up, do 3-5 of these per ride, then cool down.

Intervals – short, explosive efforts

These are the hardest efforts you'll do, and they're not fun. There are two ways to do them . . . near VO_2 max, and beyond it, but make sure you're fully warmed up before going this hard. Basically, your VO_2 max is the maximum effort you can maintain before you go into oxygen debt and have to back off and recover. It's the fastest and hardest you can go.

For "near VO_2 max" efforts, try to hold that pace for 1-5 minutes, then fully recover for 5-10 minutes, and do it again. Three sets of this will crush you, so cool down and ride home.

Your "beyond VO_2 max" intervals will be 10-30 seconds and are best done at the tail end of a Zone 4 interval. Imagine you're building speed toward the finish line and pushing hard (Zone 4) and then you jump into a final sprint to win the race (Zone 5+). That's what these "finishers" are and they're great extra credit!

Intervals – high-cadence efforts

This last one is equal parts skill and fitness. Most new riders cruise along with a pedaling cadence around 60 rpm, which is fine on beach cruisers but not for performance riding. You're most efficient between 80 and 95 rpm, but it takes deliberate practice to raise your cadence by 30 percent or more.

To start, determine what your current cadence is. If you don't have a cycling computer that measures this, watch a clock and count how many pedal revolutions your right leg (you only count for one leg, not both) does in 30 seconds, then multiply by two. (30 revolutions in 30 seconds) x 2 = 60 rpm.

Now, increase your cadence 5-10 rpm and hold that pace for 60 seconds, then recover for 60 seconds at your normal pace, then repeat. Aim for 10 intervals per ride (that's 20 minutes of riding, plus a short warmup and cool down). At first, your heart rate is likely to go up when pedaling faster and you'll breathe harder, but gradually (over several months) you'll notice that you're spinning faster and easier without getting out of breath or working harder. This is a great indication of improved fitness, and it'll make you a much more efficient cyclist, too!

TIP

While base miles and cadence are crucial to becoming a good cyclist, if you're mainly just trying to get in shape, intervals are your Fast Pass to fitness. They'll build more muscle and power, burn more calories more quickly, and don't take very long. A 7-minute warmup followed by 5-10 minutes of intervals, then a 5-minute cool down is a killer workout as long as you're really, *really* pushing yourself during the intervals.

Off-the-Bike Workouts

The workouts below are designed to build leg strength and power, because more strength and power means you can go faster! Also, the stronger you are, the easier any effort will be, relatively speaking, because you're using a smaller percentage of your total power to maintain a given speed.

I also included "core" as a general category, and I suggest you add some upper body (chest, shoulders, back, arms) workouts on your own to maintain a balanced physique. This is a very superficial description of each exercise; you'll want to search online for more details. I also strongly recommend the Athlean-X (https://www.youtube.com/@athleanx) YouTube channel for tips on proper form and technique to avoid injury.

Deadlifts

Deadlifts are considered the best total-body workout because they work almost everything, but particularly your *posterior chain*, the series of muscles that run from your Achilles tendon all the way up your back to your neck. This exercise provides total body and leg strength, and it's great for building general resiliency to life's demands, too. It's one of my absolute favorites.

My preference is using a hex bar (also known as "trap bar"), but you can also use a barbell or dumbbells. Stand with feet shoulder width, brace your core, and bend your knees and hips to squat down and grab the weight, then stand straight up to lift. Repeat for 5-10 reps, and do that for 3-5 sets.

Single-leg step-ups

Set a Plyo Box (the variable height boxes used in Crossfit gyms) on its lowest side, grab two dumbbells and place your right foot on top of the box. As slowly as you can, use your right leg to step your body up onto the box, then return your left foot to the ground. If you can't step up without a little bounce, you can use your left foot to spring upward. It's perfectly fine to start without any weights, then add hand weights or dumbbells as you progress.

The key is to lower yourself under control and slowly. That *negative*, or eccentric, movement will build more strength, and the act of moving slowly and under control will also help with nervous system development and motor control. Do 5 reps per leg for 3-5 total sets.

Single-leg deadlifts

Stand with feet together, then lightly lift your left foot off the ground. Imagine your left leg and torso are a rigid "stick," then hinge forward at the hips so that your left leg sticks out straight behind you and your torso is bent forward 90 degrees, such that your "stick" body is parallel to the ground. The trick is to hinge as though your hips were on a horizontal bar, so that you're not opening them up to the side . . . your left toes should be pointing straight down when you're bent over.

This exercise works your glutes (butt muscles) and hamstrings (back of thighs), which helps balance out all the exercise your quadriceps (front of thighs) get from cycling. Do 5-10 reps per leg, then switch to the other leg. Do 3-5 sets total. If you have trouble keeping your balance, try focusing on a spot on the ground about 6 feet in front of you throughout the entire range of motion. Once you're able, try holding dumbbells or kettlebells in one or both hands. This exercise also helps with balance and proprioception, especially if you only have a weight in one hand!

Core

Developing a strong core is key to improving cycling performance. Your core is what stabilizes your hips through to your arms, which are stabilizing you on your bike. If your core is weak, your body will be like a noodle and your legs won't be able to drive all of their power straight down into the pedals!

There are a million core exercises, and Athlean-X and Boho Beautiful's YouTube channels both have numerous safe, excellent options. Three good basics are planks with hip dips, side planks with hip dips, and crunches with feet flat together and knees splayed out. I also like bicycle crunches, where you're tapping opposite elbows and knees in an alternating pattern.

Hip flexor exercises

Cycling, like running, exclusively moves your legs in a fore-aft plane, ignoring your support muscles called hip flexors. These are critical for proper hip function, support, balance, and posture, yet they're severely underdeveloped in most modern humans (*thanks, sitting!*). A simple set of $15 workout bands let you remedy this by adding resistance to lateral leg movements.

Just loop them around both feet and lift one leg out to the side 10 times, then switch legs. Then kick your leg across your body to the opposite side 10x each. Next, kneel on hands and knees and raise one leg out to the side (*this one's called Rover's Revenge . . . get it?*). Finish off with lateral walking, 10 steps in either direction, back and forth a few times. You'll be surprised (and humbled) by how weak your hip flexors probably are. But do this 3x per week and you'll be equally impressed with how much stronger you feel after just a few weeks!

You should do this entire workout routine at least once per week, plus upper body. Two times per week is fine, too, when you're not riding as much.

WARNING You should check with your doctor before starting any physical fitness program to make sure you're healthy enough to handle the strain. The workouts mentioned here are modified versions of what the pros do, so if you're not a professional cyclist, ease into them. Start on the short side of the recommended ranges and build from there.

It's all about overload

Getting started exercising is one thing, but progression is the key to, well, progressing! If you want to get faster, stronger, or just be able to ride longer and farther, then you need to go faster, lift heavier, and ride longer and farther. Basically, you need to overload your system and push yourself beyond your current fitness level to improve. If you just keep doing the same thing repeatedly, you'll get really good at doing that same thing, but you won't improve.

Don't forget to recover!

Recovery is when your body adapts to the strain and grows, so build rest days in between major workouts. Once you've consistently ridden and exercised for a year or more, you can build in multi-day, multi-session workouts, to overload your body and force adaption. For instance, you could do a leg workout in the gym, then hop on the bike for a few intervals.

Or do two really long, hard rides on back-to-back days. You'll feel tired starting day two, but once your legs are spinning you'll be surprised at how good it feels. This is great training for a multi-day cycling tour or stage race (see Chapter 16 for some great events to do!).

Eating right is also key to recovery. If you're training two or more days in a row, be sure to take in plenty of carbs during and immediately after your ride. That's called your glycogen window, when your body will divert excess sugar directly into the muscles to be used for fuel (as opposed to storing excess as fat). Combine it with protein (whey protein isolate is best, but milk is good too, or pea protein for vegans) to give your muscles the amino acids they need to rebuild, too! During hard training, aim for 0.5g to 1g of protein per pound of body weight.

Chapter **16**
Ten Bucket List Events

S ome of these events I've done, others are on my own bucket list, but all of them offer a truly next-level experience. I've included a mix of casual "party" events plus some bigger, faster options for road, gravel, and mountain biking.

Most of these events sell out every year and are massively popular, so mark your calendars for the day registration opens and get on their mailing lists. All of these events are best enjoyed with friends and family, too. Enjoy!

RAGBRAI

Known as a rolling 8-day party on a bike, RAGBRAI (Register's Annual Great Bicycle Ride Across Iowa) is the longest-running multi-day bicycle touring event in the world. Started in 1973, it now sees 8,500 riders roll across the state from West to East, stopping at bars, restaurants, and even farms and residents' homes for local treats and drinks.

In other words, it's not a race, it's just a really, *really* fun ride covering about 67 miles per day at a casual pace. Support trucks carry your luggage and camping gear between stops (or have your own support team driving an RV), and you can register for a day pass if you can only spare a day or two. RAGBRAI is held in the last full week of July every year. (ragbrai.com)

Five Boro Bike Tour

If you've dreamt of cruising through Manhattan and the Bronx on a bike, with no cars, this is the event for you. Once per year, in May, NYC closes a 42-mile route to cars and sees 32,000 people ride their bikes through Central Park, across the Queensboro and Verrazzano-Narrows Bridges, down the Brooklyn-Queens Expressway, and finishing at Fort Wadsworth before catching the ferry past the Statue of Liberty back to Lower Manhattan.

This one's best done with friends, and you can even rent a bike there to travel light. People dress up, decorate their bikes, and stop for food, drinks, and snacks along the way. Just be sure to register early and do your best to get into one of the earlier waves if you plan on taking it easy . . . if the "broom wagon" catches you, you'll have to peel off the course. (https://www.bike.nyc/events/td-five-boro-bike-tour)

Levi's GranFondo

A Gran Fondo is like an amateur road race that you don't actually have to race, and Levi's Gran Fondo is one of America's largest and most scenic. Created by former pro cyclist Levi Leipheimer, it follows some of the toughest stages and climbs of the former Tour of California, rolling through Sonoma County's wine region.

If you choose to "race," there are awards for top finishers, but the real reward is the food and wine at the finish, with enough for everyone no matter how fast or slow you go. It's not an easy ride, but if you're looking for an event to train for, this one is epic. (https://www.levisgranfondo.com)

Multi-Day Bicycle Tours

The great thing about cycling tours is there are options all over the world, all through the year, and they're fully supported. Plus, the tour company handles all of the logistics for you, and sometimes even provides bikes, so all you need to do is get in shape and show up!

My suggestion is to pick the region of the world you'd like to explore, then search for tours there. Some allow or cater to e-bikes, too, making it easier for anyone to join in the fun. Cycling tours can seem pricy, but remember that they include all meals, snacks, and lodging, but typically don't include airfare. Four of my favorite tour providers are:

Thomson Bike Tours (https://www.thomsonbiketours.com)

REI (https://www.rei.com/adventures/a/cycling)

Ride & Seek (https://rideandseek.com)

Trek Travel (https://trektravel.com)

For mountain biking, check out Chasing Epic, Sacred Rides, and Western Spirit. These are the ones I have some experience with, but there are lots more great trip organizers out there. Check reviews and photos online, even searching their social media handles to see what others have posted from the trips.

Belgian Waffle Ride

When you're ready to check out gravel, the Belgian Waffle Ride has events from coast to coast, plus one in Mexico City! They offer multiple route lengths, ranging from ~30 miles to ~130 miles, with a mix of road and gravel segments (and occasionally even a bit of mountain bike trail!) to keep it interesting.

They're challenging, but your day kicks off with waffles and ends with a beer garden and more waffles and a sponsor expo where you can check out new bikes, components, and kits. (https://www.belgianwaffleride.bike)

Grinduro

Grinduro is a global series of gravel bike events that focus on fun over grinding long miles. They only time the funnest segments, just like a mountain bike enduro race, letting you regroup with friends and enjoy the ride between them.

Past events have been in Scotland, Canada, Germany, France, Italy, Japan, and the United States, with new locations introduced annually to keep it fresh. The race is sandwiched in a weekend-long party with live music, art, food, drink, and camping in an amazing location. As they say, it's the perfect "party to race ratio." (https://grinduro.com)

24 Hours of Old Pueblo

One of the longest-running (and only remaining) 24-hour mountain bike races in the world, the 24 Hours of Old Pueblo is a true MTB party in the beautiful Sonoran Desert. You could race it solo, but it's better as a relay team with up to ten people so there's plenty of time for everyone to enjoy the expo and hang out by the campfire.

It's held every February, when the weather is perfectly cool. Don't plan on sleeping much during the race, and definitely don't sleep on registration — the event sells out in two hours every year! And watch out for those Teddy Bear Cholla Cactus . . . they look cute, but you don't want to punch one by taking a corner too sharp! (https://epicrides.com/events/24-hours-in-the-old-pueblo)

Sea Otter Classic

Part race, part expo, all fun, the Sea Otter Classic in Monterey, California, is the world's largest consumer cycling expo and it's one of my favorite events every April. More than 1,000 brands show off their latest bikes, components, and gear, and they host races for nearly every possible cycling discipline. Plus kids and women's fun rides, pros hanging out for pics, and (usually) great weather! (https://www.seaotterclassic.com)

Breck Epic

When you're ready for something truly epic, the Breck Epic mountain bike stage race is it. Featuring six loops ranging from 35-50 miles, some capping out over 13,000 feet of elevation, all starting and finishing in downtown Breckenridge, Colorado, it's a big week of racing.

Or just ride it and have fun, enjoy the pre- and post-ride meals each day, full sag support (they bring your drop bags to all three aid stations, every day!), and full camp setup with hot showers (there's also nearby lodging if you don't like tents). Plus, race organizer Mike McCormack's emails will keep you entertained before, during, and after the event! (https://breckepic.com)

Great Divide Mountain Bike Route

With a fixed 2,696 mile (4,339km) course from Banff, Alberta (Canada) all the way south to the U.S.-Mexico border in Antelope Wells, New Mexico, the Great Divide route is the world's longest off-pavement cycling route. Some people race it (the official record is 13 days, 22 hours, 51 minutes), but many more people set out simply to conquer it with an estimated time around 35-40 days.

It's mostly self-supported, with spans up to 100 miles (or more) between amenities, so you'll need a proper bikepacking setup with sleeping, cooking, and repair gear, plus a good gravel or mountain bike with tough, fat tires. Go for it all at once, or break it into segments and bite off a little at a time. Check out *Ride the Divide* for a documentary about doing it, and get the full route with intel here: https://bikepacking.com/routes/great-divide-mountain-bike-route-gdmbr/

But what about . . .

There are a *LOT* more great events out there, too many to list here. For gravel, there's Unbound, The Rift, SBT GRVL, The Oregon Trail, and so on . . . and that's just for the United States! The more you get into it, the more you'll hear about, and there's bound to be something near you.

If you're just getting started, ask your favorite bike shop for any local charity rides. These are typically smaller, more chill, and a great way to try out an organized event while also helping out a worthy cause. Just like running has 5k races to ease you into it, most cycling events have shorter route options for beginners and kids.

Index

A

accessories, common, 176–179

accidents, 256–258

adaptive bikes, 136–137

adventure gravel bikes, 122–123

aero bars, 36–37

aero bikes, 119

aero fairings, 136

air springs, 51

airing up tires, 190–192

Alchemy Bicycles, 149

all mountain (AM) bikes, 129–130

alloy
   crank arms, 95
   handlebars, 37–38
   rims, 80
   seatposts, 54

all-road endurance, road bikes for, 118

all-terrain bikes (ATBs), 125

alternative brakes, 70–71

alternative diameters, 52–55

aluminum frames, 138, 140

angles
   about, 15–29
   bracing, 79
   saddle, 57

angular contact bearing (ACB), 108

apex, for tires, 88

apps, 263–265

Ari, 149

ART label rating, 167

Asia, 150

Athlean-X, 282, 283

Attia, Peter (author), 13

audibles, calling, 218–219

axles, 76

B

backsweep, of handlebars, 35, 37

bakfiets cargo bikes, 134–135

balance bikes, 137–138

balancing weight, 194–195

bar clamp, 48

bar clamp diameters, 49–50

base bar, 36

base miles, 280–282

bead, for tires, 88

beanie, 177

bearings
   about, 75, 108–109
   cup-and-cone, 75
   quality, 108
   size of, 108–109

bedding in, 69–70

Belgian Waffle Ride, 289

bells, 168–169

benefits, of riding bikes, 12–14

Berd, 77

bibshorts, 170

Bicycle Blue Book, used bikes from, 156

bicycle touring, 270

bicycles
   about, 7
   benefits of, 12–14
   buying, 146–150
   cleaning, 225–227
   cost of, 150–154
   finding, 115–143
   law resources, 216
   origin of, 8–10
   parts of, 10–11
   purpose of, 12
   replacing, 260–261
   selecting, 145–156

bicycles *(continued)*
  shipping, 276
  transporting, 270–276
  types of, 12
big-box stores, for buying bikes, 147–148
Bike Exchange, used bikes from, 156
bike park riders, handlebar width for, 35
bike paths, rules of the, 220–221
bike shops
  benefits of, 151–152
  for buying bikes, 147
  online, 149
  used bikes from, 155–156
bike shorts, 170–171
bikepacking bikes, 123–124, 270
bikes. *See* bicycles
The Bike Lane Uprising, 266
Blackburn, 41, 170, 249
blaster degreasers, 228
blinking lights, 207
BMX
  about, 96
  wheel size for, 83
Boho Beautiful, 283
bolt circle diameter (BCD), 101
bolt-on axles, 76
the Boneshaker, 8
Bontrager, 164
booster pump, 172
bottle cages, 170
bottom bracket (BB), 97–100
bottom bracket (BB) drop, 21
bracing angle, 79
brake levers, adjusting, 188–189
brake pads
  adjusting, 238–245
  materials for, 69–70
  rim, 63
brake pump, 61
brake rotors, 67–69
brakes
  about, 59–604
  adjusting, 238–245
  alternative, 70–71

avoiding slamming on, 217
braking process, 198–200
calipers, 60, 244–245
disc, 64–70
hydraulic brake lever, 60–61
mechanical brake lever, 60
rim, 61–63, 68
brands, high-quality, 153. *See also specific brands*
breakers, for tires, 87
Breck Epic, 290
Breeze, Joe (cyclist), 125
brifter, 95
brushes, 175–176
buckles, on helmets, 160
bullhorns, 36–37
butted spokes, 78
butting, 139

C

cables, for locks, 166
calipers, 60, 244–245
calling audibles, 218–219
Camelbak, 169
cameras, 272
Campagnolo, 95, 200
Cane Creek Thudbuster, 51
cantilever brakes, 62–63
Canyon, 149
carbon fiber
  crank arms, 95
  frames, 141–143
  handlebars, 38
  rims, 80
  seatposts, 54
  spokes, 77–79
cargo bikes
  about, 12, 133
  bakfiets, 134–135
  hub width for, 77
  pedals for, 111
  standard, 133–134
cars, transporting bikes on, 270–274
casing, for tires, 87, 238

cassette, 104–106
cassette brush, 175
Center Lock, 72–73
centering brakes, 241
ceramic bearings, 108
chainrings
  about, 100–102
  narrow-wide, 102–103
chains
  about, 103–104
  cleaning, 175, 227–232
  for locks, 166
  lubing, 174–175, 230–231
  repairing, 254–255
  replacing, 254–255
chainstay length, 20–21
chamois, 171
Chasing Watts, Link My Ride app, 265
Cheat Sheet (website), 4
chin bars, 159
chuck, 172
cleaning
  bikes, 225–227
  chains, 227–232
  kit for, 175–176
  pressure washer, 227
climbing, road bikes for, 119
clipless pedals, 28, 111–112, 198
CO_2 cartridges/pumps, 174, 251
coaster brakes, 71
cockpits, repairing/replacing, 260
commuter bikes
  about, 12, 132
  flat bars and, 35
  helmets for, 159
  pedals for, 111
  wheel size for, 83
  width of tires for, 91
components, systems compared with, 94–95
composite handlebars, 38
cone brush, 175
consistency, for speed, 217
Consumer Product Safety Commission (CPSC), 158

core exercises, 283
cork, for grips, 40
cornering, 196
costs
  of bikes, 150–154
  of bottle cages, 170
counterfeit bikes, 154
cracking, in tires, 238
cranksets
  about, 95
  crank arm length, 96–97
  crank arm material, 95–96
  spindle, 96
crit bikes, 119–120
cross-country (XC) bikes
  about, 127–128
  all mountain/freeride (AM/FR), 129–130
  dirt jump/slopestyle, 131
  downcountry, 128
  downhill (DH), 130
  Enduro (EN), 129
  fat bikes, 130–131
  flat bars and, 34
  geometry of, 126
  handlebar width for, 35
  light trail, 128–129
  trail, 128–129
  trials, 131
cruiser bikes
  about, 133
  bottle cages for, 170
  wheel size for, 83
cup-and-cone bearings, 75
cycling cap, 177
cycling clubs, 268–269
cycling gloves, 171
cyclocross bikes
  about, 124
  centering brakes, 241

D
deadlifts, 282
Decathlon, 148

degreasers, 228

degrees of engagement, 75

department stores, buying bikes from, 147

depth, of rims, 80–82

derailleur
  about, 106–107
  front, 251–252
  rear, 252

derailleur hanger, 253–254

designs, stems, 50

diameter
  alternative, 52–55
  bar clamp, 49–50
  of seatposts, 52
  of tubes, 236–237

direct mount (DM) chainrings, 101, 102

direct-to-consumer (DTC) brands, 149–150

dirt jump bikes, 131

disc brake rotor mounts, 72–73

disc brakes
  about, 64
  adjusting, 242–244
  adjusting pad contact spacing for, 240
  brake bed-in procedure, 69–70
  brake pad materials, 69–70
  brake rotors, 67–69
  hybrid disc brakes, 66–67
  hydraulic disc brakes, 64–65
  mechanical disc brakes, 65–66
  rim brakes compared with, 68

disposing of bikes/parts, 261–262

distance, for family rides, 267

donating bikes/parts, 261

downcountry bikes, 128

downhill (DH) bikes
  about, 130
  geometry of, 126
  handlebar width for, 35
  yielding to uphill bikes, 223

downshifting, 200–201

downsweep, for handlebars, 35–36

drafting, 217

Drais, Karl von (Baron), 8

drip wax, 231

drive ring, 74

drivetrains
  about, 10, 93–94
  adjusting, 254
  bearings, 108–109
  bottom bracket, 97–100
  cassette, 104–106
  chain, 103–104
  chainring, 100–103
  crankset, 95–97
  derailleur, 106–107
  1X, 126–127
  pedals, 109–112
  repairing, 259
  replacing, 259
  shifter, 107
  systems *versus* components, 94–95

drop, of handlebars, 33

drop bars
  about, 32–33
  adjusting, 189–190

dropper seatposts, 50

dry lubes, 174–175

dry rotting, in tires, 238

dry wax lubes, 231

dual slalom (DS), 131

durometer, 86

E

e-bikes
  about, 12, 135–136
  rotor sizes for, 67–68

effective top tube (ETT), 16, 23, 24–25

eMTB bikes, width of tires for, 91

Endura, 177

endurance bikes, 118

Enduro, 108, 129

engagement, degrees of, 75

equipment. *See* gear and equipment

Ergon brand, 40

etiquette, for group rides, 216–219

European Committee for Standardization (EN)
    safety, 158

events, recommended, 287–291

EVOC Pro Bike Travel Bag, 276

expanded polystyrene (EPS), 160

experience, at bike shops, 152

eye protection, 162–163

F

faceplate, 48

family rides, 266–268

fat bikes

  about, 130–131

  hub width for, 77

  width of tires for, 91

feathering brakes, 199

features, of helmets, 160–161

fenders, 123, 221

file tread tires, 89

finger tight, 110

Fisher, Gary (cyclist), 125

fitness bikes, 12, 132

fitting your bike, 26–29

Five Boro Bike Tour, 288

fixing flats, 245

flanges, 72

flared bars, 32

flat bars

  about, 34–36

  adjusting, 188–189

flat pedals, 111

flats, fixing, 245

floor pump, 172

foam, on helmets, 160

foam grips, 40

folding locks, 166

fork offset, 17, 18

forward-sweep, 35

frame pump, 173

frames, material for, 138–143

freehub (FH) body, 74

freeride (FM) bikes, 129–130

freewheel, 104–106

front center, 22

front derailleur, 251–252

fully integrated routing, 117

G

gauge

  for pumps, 173

  for spokes, 78

gear and equipment

  about, 157–158

  basic repair kit, 172–174

  bells, 168–169

  bike shorts, 170–171

  bottle cages, 170

  for cargo bikes, 179

  chain lube, 174–175

  chamois, 171

  cleaning kit, 175–176

  common accessories, 176–179

  for commuter bikers, 176–177

  cycling gloves, 171

  eye protection, 162–163

  floor pump, 172

  for gravel bikers, 177–178

  helmets, 158–160

  horns, 168–169

  lights, 163–165

  locks, 165–168

  maintenance supplies, 172–176

  for mountain bikes, 178

  reflectors, 163

  for road bikers, 177

  for safety, 158–165

  sunglasses, 162–163

  water bottles, 169

gear steps, 105

gears

  adjusting, 251–254

  mashing, 197

  shifting, 200–201

geometry, for mountain bikes, 126

geometry chart, 15–29

glasses, for bad weather, 221

gloves, 171
grades, in bearings, 108
gran fondo bikes, 118
gravel bikes
  about, 12, 121
  adventure, 122–123
  basic, 122
  bikepacking, 123–124
  bottle cages for, 170
  cassettes for, 106
  racing, 122
  rim width and depth for, 81
  seatpost diameter for, 52
  stem length for, 49
  tire sizing for, 90
  of tires, 91
  touring, 123–124
  wheel size for, 83
  width of tires for, 91, 92
grease, in bearings, 108
Great Divide Mountain Bike Trail, 123, 291
Grinduro, 289
grips
  about, 31, 39
  cork, 40
  features of, 39–40–55
  rubber, 39
  silicone, 40
group rides, etiquette for, 216–219

H

handlebar tape, 40–41
handlebars
  about, 31–32
  adjusting, 187–190
  aero bars, 36–37
  bullhorns, 36–37
  drop bars, 32–33, 189–190
  features, 40–41
  flared, 32
  flat bars, 34–36, 188–189
  grips, 39–40
  height of, 26, 27
  materials for, 37–38
  riser bars, 34–36
  tape, 40–41
  width of, 33
hanging-style bike rack, 271
hardtail, 125
head angle
  about, 17
  geometry of, 126
  stem angle and, 49
head tube length, 16–17
headlights, 164–165, 207–208
headsets
  about, 31, 41
  loose, 44
  stealth routing, 44–45
  threaded, 41–42
  threadless, 42–44
health benefits, of riding bikes, 12–14
Heatmaps app, 265
helmets
  about, 158
  brain safety and, 161
  care of, 161
  features of, 160–161
  ratings of, 162
  types of, 158–160
  wearing, 208–211
Hexlox, 168
high-quality brands, 153
high-quality online bike stores, 154
high-wheeled bicycle, 8
hip flexor exercises, 284
hitch mounts, 271–272
hobby horse, 8
holding straight lines, 217
horns, 168–169
horses, yielding to, 222–223
hot melt wax, 231
hotspots, 265–266
hub shell, 72
hubs
  about, 72
  axle, 76

bearings, 75
flanges, 72
freehub body, 74
hub shell, 72
racheting mechanism, 74–75
thru axle, 76
widths of, 77
hybrid bikes, 12, 132
hybrid disc brakes, 66–67
hydraulic brake lever, 60–61
hydraulic disc brakes, 64–65
hydroforming, 139

I

Ice spray certified rating, 167
icons, explained, 3–4
inner tubes
about, 173
replacing, 245–248
installing pedals, 109–110
integrated cockpit, 116–117
internal routing, 116
International Mountain Bike Association (BA), 269
International Standards Organization (ISO), 91
intervals, 280–282
ISIS standard, 98, 108–109

J

j-bend spokes, 78
jumps, 224

K

K-Edge, 165
kids' bikes
about, 137–138
family rides, 267–268
helmets for, 159
pedals for, 111
teaching kids to ride, 202–204
wheel size for, 83
kinematics, 19–20

knobby tire, 89
Komoot app, 264

L

Lauf, 38, 149
LEDs, 164
length
of crank arm, 96–97
of seatposts, 53
of valve stems, 236
Levi's GranFondo, 288
light trail bikes, 128–129
lights
about, 163–165
blinking, 207
headlights, 164–165, 207–208
taillights, 165
linear pull brakes, 63
liquid wax, 231
Lizard Skins, 41
local bike shops, 147
local knowledge, at bike shops, 152
locks
about, 165
cables, 166
chains, 166
folding locks, 166
how to use, 168
positioning, 167
security ratings for, 167
strength of, 168
U-locks, 166
long travel, 126
lubing chains, 230–231
lumen, 164

M

maintenance
about, 225
accidents, 256–258
adjusting
brakes, 238–245
gears, 251–254

maintenance *(continued)*

  buying tubes, 236–237

  checking tires for wear, 232–238

  cleaning

    bikes, 225–227

    chains, 227–232

  disposing of bikes/parts, 261–262

  fixing flats, 245

  of helmets, 161

  maximum tire pressures, 237

  mechanical derailleurs, 251–254

  patching

    tires, 250–251

    tubeless tires, 250–251

  plugging tubeless tires, 248–250

  pumping up tires, 232–238

  quick-release wheel skewers, 248

  repairing

    chains, 254–255

    parts, 259–260

  replacing

    bikes, 260–261

    chains, 254–255

    inner tubes, 245–248

    parts, 259–260

  setting up tubeless tires, 234–236

  shifting, 251–254

  supplies for, 172–176

  using CO_2 cartridges/pumps, 251

mashing gears, 197

materials

  for brake pads, 69–70

  for crank arm, 95

  for frames, 138–143

  for handlebars, 37–38

  for seatposts, 54

  for tires, 86

maximum tire pressures, 237

mechanical brake lever, 60

mechanical disc brakes, 65–66

mental health benefits, of riding bikes, 13

metal grates, for bad weather, 221

MicroSHIFT, 95, 200

mineral spirits, 228

mini pump, 173

mini tool, 173

minimum-insertion line, 53

money-saving, as a benefit of riding bikes, 13–14

Mongoose, 148

mountain bikes (MTB)

  about, 12, 125

  backsweep for, 35

  cassettes for, 106

  centering brakes, 241

  chainrings for, 102

  dropper seatposts for, 50

  geometry, 126

  handlebar width for, 34, 35

  helmets for, 159

  hub width for, 77

  1X drivetrain, 126–127

  pedals for, 111

  rim width and depth for, 81

  seatpost diameter for, 52

  spindles for, 96

  stem length for, 49

  suspension, 125–126

  tire sizing for, 90

  of tires, 91

  wheel size for, 83

  wheels, 125

  width of tires for, 91, 92

Mountainflow, 175

mounting

  bikes, 193–194

  headlights, 164–165

MS Society, 269

MTB Project app, 265

Muc-Off, 175, 229

mud spikes, 89

multi-day bicycle tours, 288–289

Multidirectional Impact Protection (MIPS), 160–161

mustache handlebars, 37

N

narrow-wide chainring, 102–103

nature's call, 220–221

nipples, 77–79

Nishiki, 148
no-drop rides, 219

O

Oakley, 162
obstacles, signaling, 217–218
Octalink, 98
offset, of seatposts, 53–54
off-the-bike workouts, 282–285
1X drivetrain, 126–127
OneUp, 38
online bike stores
    about, 149
    buying from, 153–154
    high-quality, 154
online marketplaces, used bikes from, 156
on-the-bike workouts, 280–282
origin, of bicycles, 8–10
outboard bearings, 99
Outlive (Attia), 13
overload, 284

P

pace, for family rides, 267
Pactimo, 177
pad contact spacing, 238–240
padding, on helmets, 160
pannier bag, 176–177
Park Tool, 175
passing safety, 213
patching
    tires, 250–251
    tubeless tires, 250–251
pawl-and-ratchet system, 74
pedal assist, 131
pedaling
    about, 196–198
    soft-pedaling, 219
pedals
    about, 109, 120
    feet placement on, 186
    installing, 109–110
    types of, 111–112

pedestrians, yielding to, 222–223
penny-farthing, 8
performance bikes
    saddle width for, 56–57
    valve types for, 84–86
physical health benefits, of riding bikes, 12–13
pinch flat, 80, 191
Pinhead, 168
Pirelli, 178
pistons, 64–65
planes, transporting bikes on, 274–276
plugging tubeless tires, 248–250
Polar, 169
polarized lenses, 162
positioning locks, 167
predictable riding, 214
preparation
    about, 183–184, 192
    adjusting
        handlebars, 187–190
        saddle height, 184–187
    airing up tires, 190–192
    pedals, 186
    troubleshooting, 184
PressFit, 98, 99
PressFit bottom brackets (PFBBs), 99
pressure, tire, 191–192
pressure washer, 227
Presta, 172
Presta valves, 84–86, 232, 233
PRO Bike Gear, 170
pump head, 172
pumping up tires, 232–238
pumps, 172

Q

quick release (QR) axles, 76
quick-release skewers, 248
quill stems, 50

R

Race Face, 38, 96
races, in bearings, 108

racheting mechanism, 74–75
racing
    gravel bikes for, 122
    road bikes for, 117–118
rack bags, 176–177
rad, 66
radial compliance, 82
rain, riding trails after, 223–224
ratings
    for helmets, 162
    for locks, 167
reach, 17, 33
rear derailleur, 252
rear rack, 176
recovery, 284–285
recumbent bikes, 136
Redshift Shockstop, 51
reflecting headlights,
    207–208
reflectors, 163
Register's Annual Great Bicycle Ride Across Iowa
    (RAGBRAI), 287
REI, 147, 289
Remember icon, 3
repair kit, 172–174
repairing
    chains, 254–255
    cockpit, 260
    drivetrains, 259
    tires, 259–260
    wheels, 259–260
replacing
    bikes, 260–261
    chains, 254–255
    cockpit, 260
    drivetrains, 259
    inner tubes, 245–248
    tires, 259–260
    wheels, 259–260
resources, for bicycle law, 216
retainer, in bearings, 108
retention mechanism, on helmets, 161
Ride & Seek, 289
Ride with GPS app, 264

riding
    about, 193
    balancing weight, 194–195
    braking, 198–200
    cornering, 196
    finding rides, 263–276
    mashing gears, 197
    mounting, 193–194
    pedaling, 196–198
    saddle, 194
    shifting, 200–201
    steering, 195–196
    teaching kids to ride, 202–204
    types of, 145–146
rim brakes
    about, 61
    adjusting
        about, 241
        pad contact spacing for, 240
        rim contact point, 241–242
    brake pads, 63
    cantilever brakes, 62–63
    disc brakes compared with, 68
    linear pull brakes (V-Brakes), 63
    traditional brakes, 61–62
rims
    about, 80
    depth of, 80–82
    width, 80–82
riser bars, 34–36
Ritchey, Tom (cyclist), 125
road bikes
    about, 12, 116
    aero, 119
    all-road endurance, 118
    bottle cages for, 170
    cassettes for, 105
    centering brakes, 241
    climbing, 119
    crit, 119–120
    helmets for, 159
    hub width for, 77
    integrated cockpit, 116–117
    racing, 117–118

rim width and depth for, 81
spindles for, 96
tire sizing for, 90
of tires, 91
track, 120
triathlon, 120–121
wheel size for, 83
width of tires for, 91
road buzz, 38
roads, safe, 265–266
Rockrider, 148
Rolf Prima, 79
rotational impact layer, on helmets, 160–161
Rotor, 96
routes, safe, 265–266
rubber
  for grips, 39
  for tires, 86
rules of the road, 206, 211–216
running machine, 8

S

saddle angle, 57
saddle clamp, 54–55
saddle height
  about, 24, 26, 27
  adjusting, 184–187
saddle position, 27–28
saddles
  about, 55–56
  width of, 56–57
safety
  bicycle law resources, 216
  cars *vs.* bikes, 212
  gear and equipment for, 158–165
  helmets, 208–211
  knowing your route, 215
  knowing your surroundings, 215–216
  passing, 213
  predictable riding, 214
  predicting other's behaviors, 214
  for riding, 205–224
  riding no more than two abreast, 213
  riding on the right, 212
  riding with traffic, 212
  signaling turns, 213–214, 217–218
  staying off urban roads, 214
  taking your lane, 215
Salsa Warbird, 121
Schrader, 172
Schrader valves, 84
Schwinn, 148
Sea Otter Classic, 290
sealant, tubeless tire, 85
sealed cartridge bearing (SCB), 108
seals, in bearings, 108
seat angle, 19
seat height, 25
seating tires, 234–235
seatposts
  about, 50
  diameter, 52
  dropper, 50
  length, 53
  material for, 54
  saddle clamp, 54–55
  setback, 53–54
  suspension, 51–52
security ratings, for locks, 167
selling bikes/parts, 262
semi-integrated routing, 117
semi-knob tires, 89
service, after purchase, 151–152
setback, of seatposts, 53–54
shapes, of handlebars, 34
sharing bikes/parts, 261–262
shells, for helmets, 160
Sherpa Map app, 264
shifters
  about, 107
  adjusting, 189
shifting
  adjusting, 251–254
  gears, 200–201
Shimano, 95, 200
Shimano's ICEtech rotors, 67

shipping bikes, 276

short travel, 126

Showers Pass, 177

signaling turns, 213–214, 217–218

Silca, 170

silicone, for grips, 40

single-bolt saddle clamps, 54

single-leg deadlifts, 283

single-leg step-ups, 282–283

sipes, for tires, 88–89

6-bolt brake mount, 73

size

  of angles, 15–29

  of bearings, 108–109

  choosing correct, 23–25

  fitting yourself to your bike, 26–29

  special considerations, 22–23

  of tires, 91

  of wheels, 83, 125

skewer, 76, 77

slammed stem, 29

slopestyle bikes, 131

Smith, 162–163

snakebite puncture, 191

soft-pedaling, 219

soft-shell bike cases, 276

Sold Secure rating, 167

spacers, 48

Spandex, 170

special considerations, 22–23

Specialized, 149, 169

specialty materials, for handlebars, 38

speeds

  for bad weather, 221

  consistency for, 217

spindle, 96

Spinergy, 77

spoke count, 78

spokes, 77–79

Spur Cycle, 169

square taper BB, 98, 108

SRAM, 95, 200

stack, 17

standard cargo bikes, 133–134

standard oil-based lube application, 230–231

standover, 22, 25

stealth routing, 44–45

steel frames, 138–139

steerer tube, 43

steering, 195–196

stem angle, 48–49

stem clamp, 48

stem length, 27, 29, 49

stems

  about, 47–50

  bar clamp diameters, 49–50

  designs, 50

  quill stems, 50

  stem angle, 48–49

  stem length, 49

stops, signaling, 217–218

straight drops, 32

straight gauge spokes, 78

strap mount racks, 272, 273

straps, on helmets, 160

Strava app, 264, 265

strength, of locks, 168

suction-cup-mounted racks, 272, 273

sunglasses, 162–163

SunTour, 95

Supacaz, 41

suspension, for mountain bikes, 125–126

suspension seatposts, 51–52

systems, components compared with, 94–95

T

taillights, 165

Taiwan, 150

tape

  about, 234

  handlebar, 40–41

Technical Stuff icon, 4

The Pro's Closet (TPC), used bikes from, 156

31.6mm, for bar clamp diameter, 49–50

35mm, for bar clamp diameter, 50

Thomson Bike Tours, 289

threaded headsets, 41–42

threadless headsets, 42–44

threads, in tires, 238

threads per inch (TPI), 87

thru axle, 76

Thule Round Trip Transition, 275

Tip icon, 4

tire levers, 173

tire plugger, 174

tires

  about, 59, 84

  airing up, 190–192

  apex, 88

  bead, 88

  breaker, 87

  casing, 87

  checking for wear, 237–238

  materials for, 86

  maximum pressures, 237

  patch kit for, 174

  patching, 250–251

  pressure of, 191–192

  pumping up, 232–238

  repairing, 259–260

  replacing, 259–260

  rubber, 86–87

  sealant, 85

  seating, 234–235

  siping, 88–89

  sizes of, 91

  terminology for, 86

  tread cap, 87

  treads, 88–89

  tubeless, 90, 234–236

  valve types, 84–86

  widths of, 89–92

titanium frames, 140–141

titanium handlebars, 38

toe overlap, 23

toe-in, adjusting, 241–242

top cap, 48

top tube length, 25

touring bikes, 123–124

TPU tubes, 178

track bikes, 120

trading bikes/parts, 262

traditional brakes, 61–62

trail bikes, 128–129

trail chatter, 38

Trailforks app, 264

trails

  about, 17, 18–19

  finding, 266

  rules of the, 222–224

train tracks, for bad weather, 221

training, tips for, 279–285

transporting bikes, 270–276

tray-style rack, 271, 272

tread cap, for tires, 86

treads, for tires, 88–89

Trek, 149

Trek Travel, 289

trial bikes, 131

triathlon bikes

  about, 120–121

  helmets for, 160

TRP, 95, 200

TRP HyRD, 67

truck tailgate pads, 272, 274

tubeless tire sealant, 85

tubeless tires

  patching, 250–251

  plugging, 248–250

  setting up, 90, 234–236

tubeless-ready tires, 84

tubes

  buying, 236–237

  diameter, 236–237

  width, 236–237

tube-type tires, 83

Tubolito, 178

tubular tires, 84

22.2mm, for bar clamp diameter, 49

24 Hours of Old Pueblo, 290

25.4mm, for bar clamp diameter, 49

two-bolt saddle clamps, 55

U

U-Lock, 166, 168
Union Cycliste Internationale (UCI), 118
uphill bikes, yielding to downhill bikes, 223
upright hanging rack, 274
upshifting, 201
upsweep, for handlebars, 35–36
urban roads, safety on, 214
used bikes, buying, 155–156
utility bikes, 133

V

vacations, biking-focused, 269–270
valve core, 172
valve stems, 234, 236
valve types, 84–86
Van Rysel, 148
V-brakes, 63
Velocipede, 8

W

Warning icon, 4
water bottles, 169
wax, 174–175
wax lube removers, 228
wax-based lube application, 231
WD-40, 174, 230
wear, of tires, 237–238
weather, 221–222
wet lubes, 174–175
wheelbase, 21
wheelbuilder, 78
wheels
  about, 59, 71–72
  bracing angle, 79
  degrees of engagement, 75
  hub widths, 77

hubs, 72–77
  for mountain bikes, 125
  nipples, 77–79
  repairing, 259–260
  replacing, 259–260
  rims, 80–82
  size of, 83
  spokes, 77–79
wheel/toe overlap issues, 83
width
  of handlebars, 33, 34–35
  of hubs, 77
  of rims, 80–82
  of saddles, 56–57
  of tires, 89–92
  of tubes, 236–237
Wolf Tooth Components, 41, 170
wood handlebars, 38
working, 140
workouts
  off-the-bike, 282–285
  on-the-bike, 280–282

X

XC. See cross-country (XC) bikes

Y

yielding
  to pedestrians and horses,
    222–223
  to uphill riders, 223
Yokozuna Ultimo, 67
yo-yo effect, 217
YT Industries, 149

Z

Zero Friction Cycling, 175

About the Author

Tyler Benedict has been riding a bike his whole life — to friends' houses, the beach, school, and the local 7-11. He discovered mountain biking while at the University of Florida, where he graduated with a journalism degree he thought he'd never use! Between classes, he'd sneak out to ride the trails, at which point he became a "cyclist" and hasn't looked back since.

His passion for cycling extends equally to the bikes, components, and tech, not just the riding. Tinkering and upgrading is as much a part of his cycling experience as rolling out for hours on the road or trail.

A serial entrepreneur, he worked his way into the cycling industry by first creating a sports drink brand before launching into the media space with Bikerumor. com in 2008 and growing it into the world's largest cycling tech blog. His constant fascination with "shiny new things" makes his job easy covering the latest road, gravel, and mountain bikes, as well as their components and trends.

When he's not riding or writing, Tyler loves to explore the world on two wheels or four. He's travelled all through North America, Europe, Taiwan, Japan, and has touched down a few times in South America, South Africa, and other places, always looking for off-the-beaten-path local spots and getting out into nature.

Dedication

This book is dedicated to all of the cyclists out there working hard in their communities to improve access to trails, create new bike lanes, promote safe routes to school, and teaching others how to ride. Thank you for all of your time, energy, and enthusiasm; your efforts do not go unnoticed, even if we don't always have the chance to show our appreciation in person.

Author's Acknowledgments

First off, I would like to thank all of the bike brands who humored me when I was just starting Bikerumor, wandering Interbike's halls and asking "What's new?" And to all of the people at those brands who've taken the time to answer all of my numerous technical questions and teaching me the inner workings of everything from suspension to brakes, drivetrains to carbon fiber manufacturing, and so much more. Thank you for inviting me to your headquarters, your factories, and your launch events. I wouldn't have been able to write this book without all of you so generously sharing your knowledge and expertise. There are too many of you to list, but you know who you are. And thank you for trusting me to tell your story.

I'd also like to thank my team at Bikerumor, starting with Zach Overholt, who's been a great technical guide and sounding board over the years. He's also the technical editor for this edition and fixed or added more than a few points that made this book better. Thanks to Cory, Saris, Ron, Jessie-May, Steve, Jayson, Nick, Colin, Michael, and all the others who've contributed to Bikerumor and, perhaps unknowingly, to me by introducing new ideas about how people ride and what bikes mean to different people.

I also have to thank Watts Dixon at Revolution Cycles NC for letting me use his shop, bikes, tools, and parts as props for some of the photos in this book — and the beers afterward!

Thanks to Jennifer Yee, Thomas Hill, Becky Whitney, and the rest of the Dummies team for checking my work and ensuring this highly technical subject matter remained approachable — and for giving me the opportunity to bring a fresh version of this popular title to your bookshelf!

Finally, thank you to my wife, Kristi, for always supporting my wild ideas and allowing me the freedom to pursue passion projects like this, and my kids, Harrison and Cameron, for helping with the photos! And thank you for reading. I hope you enjoy reading *Biking for Dummies* as much as I enjoyed writing it!

Publisher's Acknowledgments

Senior Acquisitions Editor: Jennifer Yee

Editor: Thomas Hill

Copyeditor: Becky Whitney

Technical Editor: Zach Overholt

Production Editor: Saikarthick Kumarasamy

Cover Photo: © Thomas Barwick/Getty Images